AN

ESSAY

CONCERNING

Human Underftanding;

WITH

houghts on the Conduct of the Underftanding.

BY JOHN LOCKE, ESQ.

COLLATED WITH DESMAIZEAUX'S EDITION.

To which is prefixed,

THE LIFE OF THE AUTHOR.

IN THREE VOLUMES.

VOL. II.

EDINBURGH:

TED BY AND FOR MUNDELL & SON, ROYAL BANK CLOSE.

1801.

CONTENTS.

CHAP. XXII.

Of mixed Modes.

CHAP. XXIII.

Of the complex Ideas of Subftances.

CHAP. XXIV.

Of collective Ideas of Subſtances.

SECT.

CHAP. XXV.

Of Relation.

CHAP. XXVI.

Of Caufe, of Effect, and other Relations.

CHAP. XXVII.

Of Identity and Diverfity.

CHAP. XXVIII.

Of other Relations.

CHAP. XXIX.

Of Clear and Distinct, Obscure and Confused Ideas.

CHAP. XXX.

Of Real and Fantastical Ideas.

CHAP. XXXI.

Of Adequate and Inadequate Ideas.

CHAP. XXXII.

Of true and falſe Ideas.

CHAP. XXXIII.

Of the Aſſociation of Ideas.

Sect.

BOOK III.—CHAP. I.

OF WORDS.

Of Words, or Language in general.

Sect.

CHAP. II.

Of the Signification of Words.

SECT.

CHAP. III.

Of general Terms.

SECT.

CHAP. IV.

Of the Names of Simple Ideas.

CHAP. V.

Of the Names of mixed Modes and Relations.

CHAP. VI.

Of the Names of Substances.

CHAP. VII.

Of Particles.

CHAP. VIII.

Of Abstract and Concrete Terms.

CHAP. IX.

Of the Imperfection of Words.

CHAP. X.

Of the Abuse of Words.

CHAP. XI.

Of the Remedies of the foregoing Imperfections and Abuses.

OF HUMAN UNDERSTANDING.

BOOK II.—CHAP. XXII.

OF MIXED MODES.

§ 1. *Mixed Modes, what.*

HAVING treated of *simple modes* in the foregoing chapters, and given several instances of some of the most considerable of them, to show what they are, and how we come by them, we are now, in the next place, to consider those we call *mixed modes*; such are the complex *ideas* we mark by the names *obligation*, *drunkenness*, a *lie*, &c., which consisting of several combinations of simple *ideas* of different kinds, I have called *mixed modes*, to distinguish them from the more simple modes, which consist only of simple *ideas* of the same kind. These mixed modes, being also such combinations of simple *ideas*, as are not looked upon to be characteristical marks of any real beings that have a steady existence, but scattered and independent *ideas* put together by the mind, are thereby distinguished from the complex *ideas* of substances.

§ 2. *Made by the Mind.*

THAT the mind, in respect of its simple *ideas*, is wholly passive, and receives them all from the existence and operations of things, such as sensation or reflection offers them, without being able to make any one *idea*, experience shows us; but, if we attentively consider these *ideas* I call *mixed modes*, we are now speaking of, we shall find their original quite different. *The mind often exercises an active power in making these* several *combinations*; for, it being once furniſhed with ſimple *ideas*, it can put them together in ſeveral compoſitions, and ſo make variety of complex *ideas*, without examining whether they exiſt ſo together in nature. And hence I think it is that theſe *ideas* are called *notions*, as if they had their original and conſtant exiſtence more in the thoughts of men than in the reality of things; and, to ſuch *ideas*, it ſufficed that the mind puts the parts of them together, and that they were conſiſtent in the underſtanding, without conſidering whether they had any real being; though I do not deny but ſeveral of them might be taken from obſervation, and the exiſtence of ſeveral ſimple *ideas* ſo combined, as they are put together in the underſtanding. For the man who firſt framed the *idea of hypocriſy* might have either taken it at firſt from the obſervation of one who made ſhow of good qualities which he had not, or elſe have framed that *idea* in his mind, without having any ſuch pattern to faſhion it by; for it is evident, that in the beginning of languages and ſocieties of men, ſeveral of thoſe complex *ideas*, which were conſequent to the conſtitutions eſtabliſhed amongſt them, muſt needs have been in the minds of men before they exiſted any where elſe; and that many names that ſtood for ſuch complex *ideas* were in uſe, and ſo thoſe *ideas* framed, before the combination they ſtood for ever exiſted.

§ 3. *Sometimes got by the Explication of their Names.* INDEED, now that languages are made, and abound with words ſtanding for ſuch combinations, *an uſual way of getting thoſe complex ideas, is by the explication of thoſe terms that ſtand for them.* For, conſiſting of a company of ſimple *ideas* combined, they may, by words ſtanding for thoſe ſimple *ideas*, be repreſented to the mind of one who underſtands thoſe words, though that complex combination of ſimple *ideas* were never offered to his mind by the real exiſtence of things. Thus a man may come to have the *idea* of *ſacrilege* or *murder*, by enumerating to him the ſimple *ideas* which theſe words ſtand for, without ever ſeeing either of them committed.

§ 4. *The Name ties the parts of mixed Modes into one* Idea.

EVERY *mixed mode* confifting of many diftinct fimple *ideas*, it feems reafonable to inquire *whence it has its unity*, and how fuch a precife multitude comes to make but one *idea*, fince that combination does not always exift together in nature To which I anfwer, It is plain it has its unity from an act of the mind combining thofe feveral fimple *ideas* together, and confidering them as one complex one, confifting of thofe parts; and the mark of this union, or that which is looked on generally to complete it, is one name given to that combination. For it is by their names that men commonly regulate their account of their diftinct fpecies of mixed modes, feldom allowing or confidering any number of fimple *ideas* to make one complex one, but fuch collections as there be names for. Thus, though the killing of an old man be as fit in nature to be united into one complex *idea* as the killing a man's father, yet, there being no name ftanding precifely for the one, as there is the name of *parricide* to mark the other, it is not taken for a particular complex *idea*, nor a diftinct fpecies of actions, from that of killing a young man, or any other man.

§ 5. *The Caufe of making mixed Modes.*

IF we fhould inquire a little farther, to fee *what* it is that *occafions men to make feveral combinations of fimple* ideas into diftinct, and, as it were, fettled *modes*, and neglect others, which, in the nature of things themfelves, have as much an aptnefs to be combined, and make diftinct *ideas*, we fhall find the reafon of it to be the end of language, which being to mark or communicate mens thoughts to one another with all the difpatch that may be, they ufually make fuch collections of *ideas* into complex modes, and affix names to them, as they have frequent ufe of in their way of living and converfation, leaving others, which they have but feldom an occafion to mention, loofe, and without names that tie them together; they rather choofing to enumerate (when they have need) fuch *ideas* as make them up, by the particular names that ſtand for them, than to trouble their memories by multiplying of complex *ideas* with names to them, which they ſhall ſeldom or never have any occaſion to make uſe of.

§ 6. *Why Words in one Language have none anſwering in another.*

THIS ſhows us *how it comes to paſs that there are in every language many particular words, which cannot be rendered by any one ſingle word of another.* For the ſeveral faſhions, cuſtoms, and manners of one nation, making ſeveral combinations of *ideas* ſimilar and neceſſary in one, which another people have never had any occaſion to make, or perhaps ſo much as take notice of; names come of courſe to be annexed to them, to avoid long periphraſes in things of daily converſation, and ſo they become ſo many diſtinct complex *ideas* in their minds. Thus ὀστρακισμὸς amongſt the Greeks, and *proſcriptio* amongſt the Romans, were words which other languages had no names that exactly anſwered, becauſe they ſtood for complex *ideas*, which were not in the minds of the men of other nations. Where there was no ſuch cuſtom, there was no notion of any ſuch actions; no uſe of ſuch combinations of *ideas* as were united, and, as it were, tied together by thoſe terms; and therefore in other countries there were no names for them.

§ 7. *Why Languages change.*

HENCE alſo we may ſee the reaſons *why languages conſtantly change*, take up new, and lay by old terms; becauſe change of cuſtoms and opinions bringing with it new combinations of *ideas*, which it is neceſſary frequently to think on, and talk about, new names, to avoid long deſcriptions, are annexed to them, and ſo they become new ſpecies of complex modes. What a number of different *ideas* are by this means wrapped up in one ſhort ſound, and how much of our time and breath is thereby ſaved, any one will ſee, who will but take the pains to enumerate all the *ideas* that either *reprive* or *appeal* ſtand for; and, inſtead of either of thoſe names, uſe a periphraſis, to make any underſtand their meaning.

§ 8. *Mixed Modes, where they exiſt.*

THOUGH I ſhall have occaſion to conſider this more at large when I come to treat of words and their uſe, yet I could not avoid to take thus much notice here of the names of *mixed modes*, which, being fleeting and tranſient combinations of ſimple *ideas*, which have but a ſhort exiſtence any where but in the minds of men, and there too have no longer any exiſtence than whilſt they are thought on, *have not ſo much any where the appearance of a conſtant and laſting exiſtence, as in their names;* which are therefore, in theſe ſort of *ideas*, very apt to be taken for the *ideas* themſelves. For if we ſhould inquire where the *idea* of a *triumph* or *apotheoſis* exiſts, it is evident they could neither of them exiſt altogether any where in the things themſelves, being actions that required time to their performance, and ſo could never exiſt altogether; and as to the minds of men, where the *ideas* of theſe actions are ſuppoſed to be lodged, they have there too a very uncertain exiſtence; and therefore we are apt to annex them to the names that excite them in us.

§ 9. *How we get the* Ideas *of mixed Modes.*

THERE are therefore *three ways whereby we get the complex* ideas *of mixed modes.* 1. By experience and *obſervation* of things themſelves. Thus, by ſeeing two men wreſtle or fence, we get the *idea* of wreſtling or fencing. 2. By *invention*, or voluntary putting together of ſeveral ſimple *ideas* in our own minds; ſo he that firſt invented printing or etching had an *idea* of it in his mind before it ever exiſted. 3. Which is the moſt uſual way, by *explaining the names* of actions we never ſaw, or notions we cannot ſee; and, by enumerating, and thereby, as it were, ſetting before our imaginations all thoſe *ideas* which go to the making them up, and are the conſtituent parts of them. For having, by *ſenſation* or *reflection*, ſtored our minds with ſimple *ideas*, and, by uſe, got the names that ſtand for them, we can, by thoſe names, repreſent to another any complex *idea* we would have him conceive; ſo that it has in it no ſimple *ideas* but what he knows, and has with us the ſame name for. For all our complex *ideas* are ultimately reſolvable into ſimple *ideas*, of which they are compounded and originally made up, though perhaps their immediate ingredients, as I may ſo ſay, are alſo complex *ideas*. Thus the *mixed mode*, which the word *lie* ſtands for, is made of theſe ſimple *ideas*: 1. Articulate ſounds. 2. Certain *ideas* in the mind of the ſpeaker. 3. Thoſe words the ſigns of thoſe *ideas*. 4. Thoſe ſigns put together by affirmation or negation, otherwiſe than the *ideas* they ſtand for are in the mind of the ſpeaker. I think I need not go any farther in the analyſis of that complex *idea* we call a *lie*. What I have ſaid is enough to ſhow that it is made up of ſimple *ideas*; and it could not be but an offenſive tedioufneſs to my reader, to trouble him with a more minute enumeration of every particular ſimple *idea* that goes to this complex one; which, from what has been ſaid, he cannot but be able to make out to himſelf. The ſame may be done in all our complex *ideas* whatſoever, which, however compounded and decompounded, may at laſt be reſolved into ſimple *ideas*, which are all the materials of knowledge or thought we have, or can have. Nor ſhall we have reaſon to fear that the mind is hereby ſtinted to too ſcanty a number of *ideas*, if we conſider what an inexhauſtible ſtock of ſimple modes number and figure alone affords us. How far then *mixed modes*, which admit of various combinations of different ſimple *ideas*, and their infinite modes, are from being few and ſcanty, we may eaſily imagine. So that before we have done, we ſhall ſee that nobody need be afraid he ſhall not have ſcope and compaſs enough for his thoughts to range in, though they be, as I pretend, confined only to ſimple *ideas* received from ſenſation or reflection, and their ſeveral combinations.

§ 10. *Motion, Thinking, and Power, have been moſt modified.*

It is worth our obſerving, *which of all our ſimple* ideas *have been moſt modified, and had moſt mixed modes made out of them, with names given to them;* and thoſe have been theſe three: Thinking and motion (which are the two *ideas* which comprehend in them all action) and power, from whence theſe actions are conceived to flow. Theſe ſimple *ideas,* I ſay, of thinking, motion, and power, have been thoſe which have been moſt modified, and out of whoſe modification have been made moſt complex modes, with names to them. For action being the great buſineſs of mankind, and the whole matter about which all laws are converſant, it is no wonder that the ſeveral modes of thinking and motion ſhould be taken notice of, the *ideas* of them obſerved, and laid up in the memory, and have names aſſigned to them, without which laws could be but ill made, or vice and diſorder repreſſed. Nor could any communication be well had amongſt men, without ſuch complex *ideas,* with names to them; and therefore men have ſettled names, and ſuppoſed ſettled *ideas,* in their minds, of modes of actions diſtinguiſhed by their cauſes, means, objects, ends, inſtruments, time, place, and other circumſtances; and alſo of their powers fitted for thoſe actions, *v. g.* boldneſs is the power to ſpeak or do what we intend before others, without fear or diſorder; and the Greeks call the confidence of ſpeaking by a peculiar name, παῤῥησία, which power or ability in man, of doing any thing, when it has been acquired by frequent doing the ſame thing, is that *idea* we name *habit;* when it is forward, and ready upon every occaſion to break into action, we *call* it *diſpoſition.* Thus *teſtineſs* is a diſpoſition or aptneſs to be angry.

To conclude, let us examine any *mode of action, v. g. conſideration* and *aſſent,* which are actions of the mind; *running* and *ſpeaking,* which are actions of the body; *revenge* and *murder,* which are actions of both together; and we ſhall find them but ſo many *collections of ſimple ideas,* which together make up the complex ones ſignified by thoſe names.

§ 11. *Several Words ſeeming to ſignify action, ſignify but the Effect.*

POWER being the ſource from whence all action proceeds, the ſubſtances wherein theſe powers are, when they exert this power into act, are called *causes;* and the substances which thereupon are produced, or the simple *ideas* which are introduced into any subject by the exerting of that power, are called *effects.* The *efficacy* whereby the new substance or *idea* is produced, is called, in the subject exerting that power, *action;* but in the subject wherein any simple *idea* is changed or produced, it is called *passion;* which efficacy, however various, and the effects almost infinite, yet we can, I think, conceive it, in intellectual agents, to be nothing else but modes of thinking and willing; in corporeal agents, nothing else but modifications of motion. I say, I think we cannot conceive it to be any other but these two: For whatever sort of action, besides these, produces any effects, I confess myself to have no notion nor *idea* of, and so it is quite remote from my thoughts, apprehensions, and knowledge, and as much in the dark to me as five other senses, or as the *ideas* of colours to a blind man; and therefore *many words, which seem to express some action,* signify nothing of the action or *modus operandi* at all, *but* barely *the effect,* with some circumstances of the subject wrought on, or cause operating; *v. g.* creation, annihilation, contain in them no *idea* of the action or manner whereby they are produced, but barely of the cause, and the thing done. And, when a country man says the cold freezes water, though the word freezing seems to import some *action,* yet truly it signifies nothing but the effect, viz. that water that was before fluid, is become hard and consistent, without containing any *idea* of the action whereby it is done.

§ 12. *Mixed Modes made also of other* Ideas.

I THINK I shall not need to remark here, that though power and action make the greatest part of mixed modes, marked by names, and familiar in the minds and mouths of men; yet other simple *ideas,* and their several combinations, are *not* excluded; much less, I think, will it be *necessary* for me *to enumerate all the mixed modes* which have been settled, with names to them. That would be to make a dictionary of the greateſt part of the words made uſe of in divinity, ethics, law, and politics, and ſeveral other ſciences. All that is requiſite to my preſent deſign, is to ſhow what ſort of *ideas* thoſe are which I call *mixed modes*, how the mind comes by them, and that they are compoſitions made up of ſimple *ideas* got from ſenſation and reflection, which, I ſuppoſe, I have done.

CHAP. XXIII.

OF OUR COMPLEX *IDEAS* OF SUBSTANCES.

§ 1. Ideas *of Subſtances, how made.*

THE mind being, as I have declared, furniſhed with a great number of the ſimple *ideas*, conveyed in by the *ſenſes*, as they are found in exterior things, or by *reflection* on its own operations, takes notice alſo, that a certain number of theſe ſimple *ideas* go conſtantly together; which being preſumed to belong to one thing, and words being ſuited to common apprehenſions, and made uſe of for quick diſpatch, are called, ſo united in one ſubject, by one name; which, by inadvertency, we are apt afterwards to talk of, and conſider, as one ſimple *idea*, which indeed is a complication of many *ideas* together: Becauſe, as I have ſaid, not imagining how theſe ſimple *ideas* can ſubſiſt by themſelves, we accuſtom ourſelves to ſuppoſe ſome *ſubſtratum* wherein they do ſubſiſt, and from which they do reſult; which therefore we call *ſubſtance.*

§ 2. *Our* Idea *of Subſtance in general.*

So that if any one will examine himſelf concerning his *notion of pure ſubſtance in general*, he will find he has no other *idea* of it at all, but only a ſuppoſition of he knows not what ſupport of ſuch qualities, which are capable of producing ſimple *ideas* in us; which qualities are commonly called accidents. If any one ſhould be aſked, What is the ſubject wherein colour or weight inheres? he would have nothing to ſay, but the ſolid extended parts: And if he were demanded, What is it that ſolidity and extenſion inhere in? he would not be in a much better caſe than the *Indian* before mentioned, who, ſaying that the world was ſupported by a great elephant, was aſked what the elephant reſted on; to which his anſwer was, A great tortoiſe. But being again preſſed to know what gave ſupport to the broad-backed tortoiſe, replied, Something, he knew not what. And thus here, as in all other caſes where we uſe words without having clear and diſtinct *ideas*, we talk like children, who being queſtioned what ſuch a thing is, which they know not, readily give this ſatisfactory anſwer, That it is *ſomething:* which, in truth, ſignifies no more, when ſo uſed either by children or men, but that they know not what; and that the thing they pretend to know and talk of, is what they have no diſtinct *idea* of at all, and ſo are perfectly ignorant of it, and in the dark. The *idea*, then, we have, to which we give the general name Subſtance, being nothing but the ſuppoſed, but unknown, ſupport of thoſe qualities we find exiſting, which we imagine cannot ſubſiſt *ſine re ſubſtante*, without ſomething to ſupport them, we call that ſupport *ſubſtantia*, which, according to the true import of the word, is, in plain Engliſh, *ſtanding under*, or *upholding*.

§ 3. *Of the ſorts of Subſtances.*

An obſcure and relative *idea* of ſubſtance in general being thus made, we come to have the *ideas of particular ſorts of ſubſtances*, by collecting ſuch combinations of ſimple *ideas*, as are, by experience and obſervation of mens ſenſes, taken notice of to exiſt together, and are therefore ſuppoſed to flow from the particular internal conſtitution, or unknown eſſence of that ſubſtance. Thus we come to have the *ideas* of a man, horſe, gold, water, &c. of which ſubſtances, whether any one has any other clear *idea*, farther than of certain ſimple *ideas* co-exiſting together, I appeal to every one's own experience. It is the ordinary qualities obſervable in iron, or a diamond, put together, that make the true complex *idea* of thoſe ſubſtances, which a ſmith or a jeweller commonly knows better than a philoſopher; who, whatever ſubſtantial forms he may talk of, has no other *idea* of thoſe ſubſtances than what is framed by a collection of those simple *ideas* which are to be found in them: only we must take notice, that our complex *ideas* of substances, besides all those simple *ideas* they are made up of, have always the confused *idea* of *something* to which they belong, and in which they subsist. And therefore, when we speak of any sort of substance, we say, it is a *thing* having such or such qualities; as body is a *thing* that is extended, figured, and capable of motion; spirit, a *thing* capable of thinking; and so hardness, friability, and power to draw iron, we say, are qualities to be found in a loadstone. These, and the like fashions of speaking, intimate, that the substance is supposed always *something* besides the extension, figure, solidity, motion, thinking, or other observable *ideas*, though we know not what it is.

§ 4. *No clear* Idea *of Substance in general.*

Hence, when we talk or think of any particular sort of corporeal substances, as *horse*, *stone*, &c. though the *idea* we have of either of them be but the complication or collection of those several simple *ideas* of sensible qualities, which we use to find united in the thing called horse or stone; yet because we cannot conceive how they should subsist alone, nor one in another, we suppose them existing in and supported by some common subject; *which support we denote by the name Substance*, though it be certain we have no clear or distinct *idea* of that thing we suppose a support.

§ 5. *As clear an* Idea *of Spirit as Body.*

The same happens concerning the operations of the mind, *viz.* thinking, reasoning, fearing, &c. which we concluding not to subsist of themselves, nor apprehending how they can belong to body, or be produced by it, we are apt to think these the actions of some other substance, which we call *spirit*: whereby yet it is evident, that having no other *idea* or notion of matter, but *something* wherein those many sensible qualities which affect our senses, do subsist; by supposing a substance, wherein *thinking*, *knowing*, *doubting*, and a power of moving, &c. do subsist, *we have as clear a notion of the substance of spirit, as we have of body*, the one being supposed to be (without knowing what it is) the *ſubſtratum* to thoſe ſimple *ideas* we have from without; and the other, ſuppoſed (with a like ignorance of what it is) to be the *ſubſtratum* to thoſe operations we experiment in ourſelves within. It is plain, then, that the *idea* of corporeal *ſubſtance* in matter, is as remote from our conceptions and apprehenſions, as that of ſpiritual *ſubſtance* or *ſpirit:* and therefore, from our not having any notion of the *ſubſtance* of ſpirit, we can no more conclude its non-exiſtence, than we can, for the ſame reaſon, deny the exiſtence of body; it being as rational to affirm there is no body, becauſe we have no clear and diſtinct *idea* of the *ſubſtance* of matter, as to ſay there is no ſpirit, becauſe we have no clear and diſtinct *idea* of the *ſubſtance* of a ſpirit.

§ 6. *Of the ſorts of Subſtances.*

Whatever, therefore, be the ſecret abſtract nature of *ſubſtance* in general, all *the* ideas *we have of particular diſtinct ſorts of ſubſtances* are nothing but ſeveral combinations of ſimple *ideas*, co-exiſting in ſuch, though unknown, cauſe of their union, as makes the whole ſubſiſt of itſelf. It is by ſuch combinations of ſimple *ideas*, and nothing elſe, that we repreſent particular ſorts of *ſubſtances* to ourſelves; ſuch are the *ideas* we have of their ſeveral ſpecies in our minds; and ſuch only do we, by their ſpecific name, ſignify to others, *v. g. man, horſe, ſun, water, iron:* upon hearing which words, every one who underſtands the language, frames in his mind a combination of thoſe ſeveral ſimple *ideas* which he has uſually obſerved, or fancied to exiſt together under that denomination; all which he ſuppoſes to reſt in, and be, as it were, adherent to that unknown common ſubject, which inheres not in any thing elſe. Though, in the mean time, it be manifeſt, and every one upon inquiry into his own thoughts will find that he has no other *idea* of any *ſubſtance*, *v. g.* let it be *gold, horſe, iron, man, vitriol, bread*, but what he has barely of thoſe ſenſible qualities which he ſuppoſes to inhere, with a ſuppoſition of ſuch a *ſubſtratum*, as gives, as it were, a ſupport to thoſe qualities or ſimple *ideas* which he has obſerved to exiſt united together. Thus, the *idea* of the *ſun*, what is it but an aggregate of thoſe ſeveral ſimple *ideas*, bright, hot, roundiſh, having a conſtant regular motion, at a certain diſtance from us, and perhaps ſome other? as he who thinks and diſcourſes of the *ſun*, has been more or leſs accurate in obſerving thoſe ſenſible qualities, *ideas*, or properties, which are in that thing which he calls the *ſun*.

§ 7. *Power, a great part of our complex* Ideas *of Subſtances.*

For he has the perfecteſt *idea* of any of the particular ſorts of *ſubſtances*, who has gathered and put together moſt of thoſe ſimple ideas which do exiſt in it, among which are to be reckoned its active powers and paſſive capacities; which, though not ſimple *ideas*, yet in this reſpect, for brevity ſake, may conveniently enough be reckoned amongſt them. Thus, the power of drawing iron is one of the *ideas* of the complex one of that ſubſtance we call a *loadſtone;* and a power to be ſo drawn, is a part of the complex one we call *iron:* which powers paſs for inherent qualities in thoſe ſubjects. Becauſe every *ſubſtance*, being as apt, by the powers we obſerve in it, to change ſome ſenſible qualities in other ſubjects, as it is to produce in us thoſe ſimple *ideas* which we receive immediately from it, does, by thoſe new ſenſible qualities introduced into other ſubjects, diſcover to us thoſe powers which do thereby mediately affect our ſenſes, as regularly as its ſenſible qualities do it immediately: *v. g.* we immediately, by our ſenſes, perceive in *fire* its heat and colour, which are, if rightly conſidered, nothing but powers in it to produce thoſe *ideas* in us: We alſo, by our ſenſes, perceive the colour and brittleneſs of *charcoal*, whereby we come by the knowledge of another power in fire, which it has to change the colour and conſiſtency of wood. By the former fire immediately, by the latter it mediately diſcovers to us theſe ſeveral powers, which therefore we look upon to be a part of the qualities of fire, and ſo make them a part of the complex *ideas* of it. For all thoſe powers that we take cogniſance of, terminating only in the alteration of ſome ſenſible qualities in thoſe ſubjects on which they operate, and ſo making them exhibit to us new ſenſible *ideas;* therefore it is that I have reckoned theſe powers amongſt the ſimple *ideas*, which make the complex ones of the ſorts of *ſubſtances;* though theſe powers, conſidered in themſelves, are truly complex *ideas.* And in this looſer ſenſe I crave leave to be underſtood, when I name any of theſe *potentialities amongſt the ſimple ideas*, which we recollect in our minds, when we think of *particular ſubſtances.* For the powers that are ſeverally in them, are neceſſary to be conſidered, if we will have true diſtinct notions of the ſeveral ſorts of ſubſtances.

§ 8. *And why.*

NOR are we to wonder, that *powers make a great part of our complex* ideas *of ſubſtances*, ſince their ſecondary qualities are thoſe, which in moſt of them ſerve principally to diſtinguiſh ſubſtances one from another, and commonly make a conſiderable part of the complex *idea* of the ſeveral ſorts of them. For our ſenſes failing us in the diſcovery of the bulk, texture, and figure of the minute parts of bodies, on which their real conſtitutions and differences depend, we are fain to make uſe of their ſecondary qualities as the characteriſtical notes and marks, whereby to frame *ideas* of them in our minds, and diſtinguiſh them one from another; all which ſecondary qualities, as has been ſhown, are nothing but bare powers: For the colour and taſte of *opium* are, as well as its ſoporific or anodyne virtues, mere powers depending on its primary qualities, whereby it is fitted to produce different operations on different parts of our bodies.

§ 9. *Three ſorts of* Ideas *make our complex ones of Subſtances.*

THE Ideas *that make our complex ones of corporeal ſubſtances*, are of theſe three ſorts. *Firſt*, The *ideas* of the primary qualities of things, which are diſcovered by our ſenſes, and are in them even when we perceive them not; ſuch are the bulk, figure, number, ſituation, and motion of the parts of bodies, which are really in them, whether we take notice of them or no. *Secondly*, The ſenſible ſecondary qualities, which, depending on theſe, are nothing but the powers thoſe ſubſtances have to produce ſeveral *ideas* in us by our ſenſes; which *ideas* are not in the things themſelves, otherwiſe than as any thing is in its cauſe. *Thirdly*, The aptneſs we conſider in any ſubſtance to give or receive ſuch alterations of primary qualities, as that the ſubſtance ſo altered ſhould produce in us different *ideas* from what it did before; theſe are called active and paſſive powers: All which powers, as far as we have any notice or notion of them, terminate only in ſenſible ſimple *ideas*. For whatever alteration a *loadſtone* has the power to make in the minute particles of iron, we ſhould have no notion of any power it had at all to operate on iron, did not its ſenſible motion diſcover it: and I doubt not, but there are a thouſand changes, that bodies we daily handle have a power to cauſe in one another, which we never ſuſpect, becauſe they never appear in ſenſible effects.

§ 10. *Powers make a great part of our complex* Ideas *of Subſtances.*

POWERS therefore juſtly *make a great part of our complex* ideas *of ſubſtances.* He that will examine his complex *idea* of gold, will find ſeveral of its *ideas* that make it up, to be only powers: as the power of being melted, but of not ſpending itſelf in the fire; of being diſſolved in *aq. regia*; are *ideas* as neceſſary to make up our complex *idea* of gold, as its colour and weight: which, if duly conſidered, are alſo nothing but different powers. For to ſpeak truly, yellowneſs is not actually in gold, but is a power in gold to produce that *idea* in us by our eyes, when placed in a due light: And the heat, which we cannot leave out of our *idea* of the ſun, is no more really in the ſun, than the white colour it introduces into wax. Theſe are both equally powers in the ſun, operating, by the motion and figure of its inſenſible parts, ſo on a man, as to make him have the *idea* of heat; and ſo on wax, as to make it capable to produce in a man the *idea* of white.

§ 11. *The now ſecondary Qualities of Bodies would diſappear, if we could diſcover the primary ones of their minute parts.*

HAD we ſenſes acute enough to diſcern the minute particles of bodies, and the real conſtitution on which their ſenſible qualities depend, I doubt not but they would produce quite different *ideas* in us; and that which is now the yellow colour of gold would then diſappear, and inſtead of it we ſhould ſee an admirable texture of parts of a certain ſize and figure. This microſcopes plainly diſcover to us: For what to our naked eyes produces a certain colour, is, by thus augmenting the acuteneſs of our ſenſes, diſcovered to be quite a different thing; and the thus altering, as it were, the proportion of the bulk of the minute parts of a coloured object to our uſual ſight, produces different *ideas* from what it did before. Thus ſand or pounded glaſs, which is opaque, and white to the naked eye, is pellucid in a microſcope; and a hair ſeen this way loſes its former colour, and is in a great meaſure pellucid, with a mixture of ſome bright ſparkling colours, ſuch as appear from the refraction of diamonds, and other pellucid bodies. Blood, to the naked eye, appears all red; but by a good microſcope, wherein its leſſer parts appear, ſhows only ſome few globules of red, ſwimming in a pellucid liquor; and how theſe red globules would appear, if glaſſes could be found that yet could magnify them 1000, or 10,000 times more, is uncertain.

§ 12. *Our Faculties of Diſcovery ſuited to our State.*

THE infinite wiſe Contriver of us, and all things about us, hath fitted our ſenſes, faculties, and organs, to the conveniencies of life, and the buſineſs we have to do here. We are able, by our ſenſes, to know and diſtinguiſh things, and to examine them ſo far, as to apply them to our uſes, and ſeveral ways to accommodate the exigencies of this life. We have inſight enough into their admirable contrivances and wonderful effects, to admire and magnify the wiſdom, power, and goodneſs of their Author. Such a knowledge as this, which is ſuited to our preſent condition, we want not faculties to attain. But it appears not that God intended we ſhould have a perfect, clear, and adequate knowledge of them: That perhaps is not in the comprehenſion of any finite being. We are furniſhed with faculties (dull and weak as they are) to diſcover enough in the creatures to lead us to the knowledge of the Creator, and the knowledge of our duty; and we are fitted well enough with abilities to provide for the conveniencies of living: Theſe are our buſineſs in this world. But were our ſenſes altered and made much quicker and acuter, the appearance and outward ſcheme of things would have quite another face to us, and, I am apt to think, would be inconſiſtent with our being, or at leaſt well-being, in this part of the univerſe which we inhabit. He that conſiders how little our conſtitution is able to bear a remove into parts of this air, not much higher than that we commonly breathe in, will have reaſon to be ſatisfied, that in this globe of earth allotted for our manſion, the allwiſe Architect has ſuited our organs, and the bodies that are to affect them, one to another. If our ſenſe of hearing were but 1000 times quicker than it is, how would a perpetual noiſe diſtract us? and we ſhould, in the quieteſt retirement, be leſs able to ſleep or meditate, than in the middle of a ſea-fight. Nay, if that moſt inſtructive of our ſenſes, ſeeing, were in any man 1000 or 100,000 times more acute than it is now by the beſt microſcope, things ſeveral millions of times leſs than the ſmalleſt object of his ſight now, would then be viſible to his naked eyes, and ſo he would come nearer the diſcovery of the texture and motion of the minute parts of corporeal things, and in many of them, probably get *ideas* of their internal conſtitutions: But then he would be in a quite different world from other people: Nothing would appear the ſame to him and others; the viſible *ideas* of every thing would be different: So that I doubt, whether he and the reſt of men could diſcourſe concerning the objects of ſight, or have any communication about colours, their appearances being ſo wholly different. And perhaps ſuch a quickneſs and tenderneſs of ſight could not endure bright ſunſhine, or ſo much as open day-light; nor take in but a very ſmall part of any object at once, and that too only at a very near diſtance. And if, by the help of ſuch microſcopical eyes (if I may ſo call them), a man could penetrate farther than ordinary into the ſecret compoſition and radical texture of bodies, he would not make any great advantage by the change, if ſuch an acute ſight would not ſerve to conduct him to the market and exchange; if he could not ſee things he was to avoid, at a convenient diſtance, nor diſtinguiſh things he had to do with, by thoſe ſenſible qualities others do. He that was ſharp-ſighted enough to ſee the configuration of the minute particles of the ſpring of a clock, and obſerve upon what peculiar ſtructure and impulſe its elaſtic motion depends, would no doubt diſcover ſomething very admirable: But if eyes ſo framed could not view, at once, the hand and the characters of the hour-plate, and thereby, at a diſtance, ſee what o'clock it was, their owner could not be much benefited by that acuteneſs, which, whilſt it diſcovered the ſecret contrivance of the parts of the machine, made him loſe its uſe.

§ 13. *Conjecture about Spirits.*

AND here give me leave to propoſe an extravagant conjecture of mine, viz. that ſince we have ſome reaſon (if there be any credit to be given to the report of things that our philoſophy cannot account for) to imagine, that ſpirits can aſſume to themſelves bodies of different bulk, figure, and conformation of parts; whether one great advantage ſome of them have over us, may not lie in this, that they can ſo frame and ſhape to themſelves organs of ſenſation or perception, as to ſuit them to their preſent deſign, and the circumſtances of the object they would conſider. For how much would that man exceed all others in knowledge, who had but the faculty ſo to alter the ſtructure of his eyes, that one ſenſe, as to make it capable of all the ſeveral degrees of viſion which the aſſiſtance of glaſſes (caſually at firſt lit on) has taught us to conceive? What wonders would he diſcover, who could ſo fit his eyes to all ſorts of objects, as to ſee, when he pleaſed, the figure and motion of the minute particles in the blood, and other juices of animals, as diſtinctly as he does, at other times, the ſhape and motion of the animals themſelves? But to us, in our preſent ſtate, unalterable organs, ſo contrived as to diſcover the figure and motion of the minute parts of bodies, whereon depend thoſe ſenſible qualities we now obſerve in them, would perhaps be of no advantage. God has, no doubt, made them ſo as is beſt for us in our preſent condition: He hath fitted us for the neighbourhood of the bodies that ſurround us, and we have to do with: And though we cannot, by the faculties we have, attain to a perfect knowledge of things, yet they will ſerve us well enough for thoſe ends above mentioned, which are our great concernment. I beg my reader's pardon, for laying before him ſo wild a fancy, concerning the ways of perception in beings above us: But how extravagant ſoever it be, I doubt whether we can imagine any thing about the knowledge of angels, but after this manner, ſome way or other in proportion to what we find and obſerve in ourſelves. And though we cannot but allow, that the infinite power and wiſdom of God may frame creatures with a thouſand other faculties and ways of perceiving things without them, than what we have, yet our thoughts can go no further than our own; ſo impoſſible it is for us to enlarge our very gueſſes beyond the *ideas* received from our own ſenſation and reflection. The ſuppoſition, at leaſt, that angels do ſometimes aſſume bodies, needs not ſtartle us; ſince ſome of the moſt ancient and moſt learned Fathers of the Church ſeemed to believe that they had bodies; and this is certain, that their ſtate and way of exiſtence is unknown to us.

§ 14. *Complex* Ideas *of Subſtances.*

BUT to return to the matter in hand; the *ideas* we have of ſubſtances, and the ways we come by them: I ſay, *our ſpecific* ideas *of ſubſtances* are nothing elſe but *a collection of a certain number of ſimple* ideas, *conſidered as united in one thing.* Theſe *ideas* of ſubſtances, though they are commonly called ſimple apprehenſions, and the names of them ſimple terms, yet in effect are complex and compounded. Thus, the *idea* which an Engliſhman ſignifies by the name *ſwan*, is white colour, long neck, red beak, black legs, and whole feet, and all theſe of a certain ſize, with a power of ſwimming in the water, and making a certain kind of noiſe; and perhaps, to a man who has long obſerved thoſe kind of birds, ſome other properties which all terminate in ſenſible ſimple *ideas*, all united in one common ſubject.

§ 15. Idea *of Spiritual Subſtances as clear as of Bodily Subſtances.*

Besides the complex *ideas* we have of material ſenſible ſubſtances, of which I have laſt ſpoken, by the ſimple *ideas* we have taken from thoſe operations of our own minds, which we experiment daily in ourſelves, as thinking, underſtanding, willing, knowing, and power of beginning, motion, &c. co-exiſting in ſome ſubſtance; we are able to frame *the complex* idea *of an immaterial ſpirit.* And thus, by putting together the *ideas* of thinking, perceiving, liberty and power of moving themſelves and other things, we have as clear a perception and notion of immaterial ſubſtances, as we have of material: For, putting together the *ideas* of thinking and willing, or the power of moving or quieting corporeal motion, joined to ſubſtance, of which we have no diſtinct *idea*, we have the *idea* of an immaterial ſpirit; and, by putting together the *ideas* of coherent ſolid parts, and a power of being moved, joined with ſubſtance, of which likewiſe we have no poſitive *idea*, we have the *idea* of matter. The one is as clear and diſtinct an *idea* as the other; the *idea* of thinking, and moving a body, being as clear and diſtinct *ideas*, as the *ideas* of extenſion, ſolidity, and being moved. For our *idea* of ſubſtance is equally obſcure, or none at all in both; it is but a ſuppoſed I know not what, to ſupport thoſe *ideas* we call accidents. It is for want of reflection that we are apt to think that our ſenſes ſhow us nothing but material things. Every act of ſenſation, when duly conſidered, gives us an equal view of both parts of nature, the corporeal and ſpiritual: For whilſt

I know, by seeing or hearing, &c. that there is some corporeal being without me, the object of that sensation, I do more certainly know, that there is some spiritual being within me that sees and hears. This, I must be convinced, cannot be the action of bare insensible matter, nor ever could be, without an immaterial thinking being.

§ 16. *No* Idea *of abstract Substance.*

By the complex *idea* of extended, figured, coloured, and all other sensible qualities, which is all that we know of it, we are as far from the *idea* of the substance of body, as if we knew nothing at all: *Nor*, after all the acquaintance and familiarity which we imagine we *have* with matter, and the many qualities *men* assure themselves they perceive and know in bodies, will it perhaps, upon examination, be found that they have any *more or clearer primary* ideas *belonging to body, than they have belonging to immaterial spirit.*

§ 17. *The Cohesion of Solid Parts and Impulse, the primary* Ideas *of Body.*

The primary ideas *we have peculiar to body*, as contradistinguished to spirit, *are the cohesion of solid*, and consequently separable *parts, and a power of communicating motion by impulse.* These, I think, are the original *ideas* proper and peculiar to body; for figure is but the consequence of finite extension.

§ 18. *Thinking and Motivity the primary* Ideas *of Spirit.*

The ideas *we have* belonging and *peculiar to spirit, are thinking and will*, or a power of putting body into motion by thought, and, which is consequent to it, liberty. For as body cannot but communicate its motion by impulse to another body which it meets with at rest, so the mind can put bodies into motion, or forbear to do so, as it pleases. The *ideas* of existence, duration, and mobility, are common to them both.

§ 19. *Spirits capable of motion.*

There is no reason why it should be thought strange, that I make *mobility belong to spirit*: For, having no other *idea* of motion but change of distance with other beings that are conſidered as at reſt, and, finding that ſpirits, as well as bodies, cannot operate but where they are, and that ſpirits do operate at ſeveral times in ſeveral places, I cannot but attribute change of place to all finite ſpirits; (for of the infinite ſpirit I ſpeak not here). For my ſoul, being a real being as well as my body, is certainly as capable of changing diſtance with any other body or being, as body itſelf; and ſo is capable of motion. And if a mathematician can conſider a certain diſtance, or a change of that diſtance between two points, one may certainly conceive a diſtance, and a change of diſtance between two ſpirits; and ſo conceive their motion, their approach, or removal one from another.

§ 20.

EVERY one finds in himſelf, that his ſoul can think, will, and operate on his body in the place where that is, but cannot operate on a body, or in a place an hundred miles diſtant from it. Nobody can imagine that his ſoul can think, or move a body at Oxford, whilſt he is at London; and cannot but know, that being united to his body, it conſtantly changes place all the whole journey between Oxford and London, as the coach or horſe does that carries him, and, I think, may be ſaid to be truly all that while in motion; or, if that will not be allowed to afford us a clear *idea* enough of its motion, its being ſeparated from the body in death, I think, will: For to conſider it as going out of the body, or leaving it, and yet to have no *idea* of its motion, ſeems to me impoſſible.

§ 21.

IF it be ſaid by any one, that it cannot change place, becauſe it hath none; for ſpirits are not *in loco*, but *ubi*; I ſuppoſe that way of talking will not now be of much weight to many, in an age that is not much diſpoſed to admire, or ſuffer themſelves to be deceived by ſuch unintelligible ways of ſpeaking. But if any one thinks there is any ſenſe in that diſtinction, and that it is applicable to our preſent purpoſe, I deſire him to put it into intelligible Engliſh; and then from thence draw a reaſon to ſhow, that immaterial ſpirits are not capable of motion. Indeed motion cannot be attributed to God, not becauſe he is an immaterial, but becauſe he is an infinite Spirit.

§ 22. Idea *of Soul and Body compared.*

LET us *compare* then our complex *idea* of an immaterial ſpirit with our complex *idea* of body, and ſee whether there be any more obſcurity in one than in the other, and in which moſt. Our *idea* of body, as I think, is an extended ſolid ſubſtance, capable of communicating motion by impulſe: And our *idea* of ſoul, as an immaterial ſpirit, is of a ſubſtance that thinks, and has a power of exciting motion in body, by willing or thought. Theſe, I think, are *our complex* ideas *of ſoul and body, as contra-diſtinguiſhed;* and now let us examine which has moſt obſcurity in it, and difficultly to be apprehended. I know, that people, whoſe thoughts are immerſed in matter, and have ſo ſubjected their minds to their ſenſes, that they ſeldom reflect on any thing beyond them, are apt to ſay, they cannot comprehend a thinking thing; which perhaps is true: But I affirm, when they conſider it well, they can no more comprehend an extended thing.

§ 23. *Coheſion of ſolid Parts in Body, as hard to be conceived as Thinking in a Soul.*

IF any one ſay, he knows not what it is thinks in him; he means, he knows not what the ſubſtance is of that thinking thing: No more, ſay I, knows he what the ſubſtance is of that ſolid thing. Farther, if he ſays he knows not how he thinks, I anſwer, Neither knows he how he is extended; how the ſolid parts of body are united, or cohere together, to make extenſion. For though the preſſure of particles of air may account for the *coheſion of ſeveral parts of matter*, that are groſſer than the particles of air, and have pores leſs than the corpuſcles of air; yet the weight or preſſure of the air will not explain, nor can be a cauſe of the coherence of the particles of air themſelves. And, if the preſſure of the ether, or any ſubtiler matter than the air, may unite, and hold faſt together the parts of a particle of air, as well as other bodies, yet it cannot make bonds for itſelf, and hold together the parts that make up every the leaſt corpuſcle of that *materia ſubtilis.* So that that hypotheſis, how ingeniouſly ſoever explained, by ſhowing that the parts of ſenſible bodies are held together by the preſſure of other external inſenſible bodies, reaches not the parts of the ether itſelf: And by how much the more evident it proves, that the parts of other bodies are held together by the external preſſure of the ether, and can have no other conceivable cauſe of their coheſion and union, by ſo much the more it leaves us in the dark concerning the coheſion of the parts of the corpuſcles of the ether itſelf; which we can neither conceive without parts, they being bodies, and diviſible; nor yet how their parts cohere, they wanting that cauſe of coheſion which is given of the coheſion of all other bodies.

§ 24.

BUT in truth, *the preſſure of any ambient fluid,* how great ſoever, *can be no* intelligible *cauſe of the coheſion of the ſolid parts of matter.* For though ſuch a preſſure may hinder the avulſion of two poliſhed ſuperficies one from another, in a line perpendicular to them, as in the experiment of two poliſhed marbles; yet it can never, in the leaſt, hinder the ſeparation by a motion, in a line parallel to thoſe ſurfaces; becauſe the ambient fluid, having a full liberty to ſucceed in each point of ſpace, deſerted by a lateral motion, reſiſts ſuch a motion of bodies ſo joined, no more than it would reſiſt the motion of that body, were it on all ſides environed by that fluid, and touched no other body: And therefore, if there were no other cauſe of coheſion, all parts of bodies muſt be eaſily ſeparable by ſuch a lateral ſliding motion: For if the preſſure of the ether be the adequate cauſe of coheſion, wherever that cauſe operates not, there can be no coheſion. And ſince it cannot operate againſt ſuch a lateral ſeparation (as has been ſhown), therefore, in every imaginary plain, interſecting any maſs of matter, there could be no more coheſion, than of two poliſhed ſurfaces, which will always, notwithſtanding any imaginable preſſure of a fluid, eaſily ſlide one from another. So that perhaps, how clear an *idea* ſoever we think we have of the extenſion of body, which is nothing but the coheſion of ſolid parts, he that ſhall well conſider it in his mind, may have reaſon to conclude, that it is *as eaſy* for him *to have a clear* idea, *how the ſoul thinks, as how body is extended.* For ſince body is no farther, nor otherwiſe extended, than by the union and coheſion of its ſolid parts, we ſhall very ill comprehend the *extenſion* of body, without underſtanding wherein conſiſts the union and coheſion of its parts; which ſeems to me as incomprehenſible, as the manner of thinking, and how it is performed.

§ 25.

I ALLOW it is uſual for moſt people to wonder, how any one ſhould find a difficulty in what they think they every day obſerve. Do we not ſee (will they be ready to ſay) the parts of bodies ſtick firmly together? Is there any thing more common? And what doubt can there be made of it? And the like I ſay concerning *thinking* and *voluntary motion.* Do we not every moment experiment it in ourſelves; and therefore can it be doubted? The matter of fact is clear, I confeſs; but when we would a little nearer look into it, and conſider how it is done, there I think we are at a loſs, both in the one and the other; and can as little underſtand how the parts of body cohere, as how we ourſelves perceive, or move. I would have any one intelligibly explain to me, how the parts of gold, or braſs (that but now in fuſion were as looſe from one another, as the particles of water, or the ſands of an hour-glaſs), come in a few moments to be ſo united, and adhere ſo ſtrongly one to another, that the utmoſt force of mens arms cannot ſeparate them: A conſidering man will, I ſuppoſe, be here at a loſs to ſatisfy his own or another man's underſtanding.

§ 26.

THE little bodies that compoſe that fluid we call *water*, are ſo extremely ſmall, that I have never heard of any one, who, by a microſcope, (and yet I have heard of ſome that have magnified to 10,000, nay, to much above

100,000 times) pretended to perceive their diſtinct bulk, figure or motion: And the particles of *water* are alſo ſo perfectly looſe one from another, that the leaſt force ſenſibly ſeparates them. Nay, if we conſider their perpetual motion, we muſt allow them to have no coheſion one with another; and yet, let but a ſharp cold come, and they unite, they conſolidate, theſe little atoms cohere, and are not, without great force, ſeparable. He that could find the bonds that tie theſe heaps of looſe little bodies together ſo firmly; he that could make known the cement that makes them ſtick ſo faſt one to another, would diſcover a great, and yet unknown ſecret; and yet when that was done, would he be far enough from making the extenſion of body (which is the coheſion of its ſolid parts) intelligible, till he could ſhow wherein conſiſted the union, or conſolidation of the parts of thoſe bonds, or of that cement, or of the leaſt particle of matter that exiſts. Whereby it appears, that this primary and ſuppoſed obvious quality of body, will be found, when examined, to be as incomprehenſible as any thing belonging to our minds, and *a ſolid extended ſubſtance as hard to be conceived as a thinking immaterial one*, whatever difficulties ſome would raiſe againſt it.

§ 27.

FOR, to extend our thoughts a little farther, that preſſure which is brought to explain the coheſion of bodies, is as unintelligible as the coheſion itſelf. For if matter be conſidered, as no doubt it is, finite, let any one ſend his contemplation to the extremities of the univerſe, and there ſee what conceivable hoops, what bond he can imagine to hold this maſs of matter in ſo cloſe a preſſure together; from whence ſteel has its firmneſs, and the parts of a diamond their hardneſs and indiſſolubility. If matter be finite, it muſt have its extremes; and there muſt be ſomething to hinder it from ſcattering aſunder. If, to avoid this difficulty, any one will throw himſelf into the ſuppoſition and abyſs of infinite matter, let him conſider what light he thereby brings to the *coheſion* of body, and whether he be ever the nearer making it intelligible, by reſolving it into a ſuppoſition, the moſt abſurd and moſt incomprehenſible of all other:

So far is our extenſion of body (which is nothing but the coheſion of ſolid parts) from being clearer, or more diſtinct, when we would inquire into the nature, cauſe, or manner of it, than the *idea* of thinking.

§ 28. *Communication of Motion, by Impulſe or by Thought, equally intelligible.*

ANOTHER *idea* we have of body, is the power of *communication of motion by impulſe;* and of our ſouls, the power of *exciting motion by thought.* Theſe *ideas*, the one of body, the other of our minds, every day's experience clearly furniſhes us with; but if, here again, we inquire how this is done, we *are equally in the dark.* For in the communication of motion by impulſe, wherein as much motion is loſt to one body as is got to the other, which is the ordinarieſt caſe, we can have no other conception, but of the paſſing of motion out of one body into another; which, I think, is as obſcure and inconceivable, as how our minds move or ſtop our bodies by thought, which we every moment find they do. The increaſe of motion by impulſe, which is obſerved or believed ſometimes to happen, is yet harder to be underſtood. We have, by daily experience, clear evidence of motion produced both by impulſe and by thought; but the manner how, hardly comes within our comprehenſion; we are equally at a loſs in both. So that, however we conſider motion and its communication either from body or ſpirit, *the* idea *which belongs to ſpirit is at leaſt as clear as that which belongs to body.* And if we conſider the active power of moving, or, as I may call it, *motivity*, it is much clearer in ſpirit than body; ſince two bodies, placed by one another at reſt, will never afford us the *idea* of a power in the one to move the other, but by a borrowed motion: Whereas the mind, every day, affords us *ideas* of an active power of moving of bodies; and therefore it is worth our conſideration, whether active power be not the proper attribute of ſpirits, and paſſive power of matter. Hence may be conjectured, that created ſpirits are not totally ſeparate from matter, becauſe they are both active and paſſive. Pure ſpirit, *viz.* God, is only active; pure matter is only paſſive; thoſe beings that are both active and paſſive, we may judge to partake of both. But be that as it will, I think we have as many, and as clear *idea's* belonging to ſpirit, as we have belonging to body, the ſubſtance of each being equally unknown to us; and the *idea* of thinking in ſpirit, as clear as of extenſion in body; and the communication of motion by thought, which we attribute to ſpirit, is as evident as that by impulſe, which we aſcribe to body. Conſtant experience makes us ſenſible of both of theſe, though our narrow underſtandings can comprehend neither. For when the mind would look beyond thoſe original *ideas* we have from ſenſation or reflection, and penetrate into their cauſes and manner of production, we find ſtill it diſcovers nothing but its own ſhort-ſightedneſs.

§ 29.

To conclude, ſenſation convinces us, that there are ſolid extended ſubſtances; and reflection, that there are thinking ones: experience aſſures us of the exiſtence of ſuch beings; and that the one hath a power to move body by impulſe, the other by thought; this we cannot doubt of. Experience, I ſay, every moment furniſhes us with the clear *ideas*, both of the one and the other; but beyond theſe *ideas* as received from their proper ſources, our faculties will not reach. If we would inquire farther into their nature, cauſes, and manner, we perceive not the nature of extenſion clearer than we do of thinking. If we would explain them any farther, one is as eaſy as the other; and there is no more difficulty to conceive how a ſubſtance we know not, ſhould by thought, ſet body into motion, than how a ſubſtance we know not, ſhould by impulſe, ſet body into motion; ſo that we are no more able to diſcover wherein the *ideas* belonging to body conſiſt, than thoſe belonging to ſpirit. From whence it ſeems probable to me, that the ſimple *ideas* we receive from ſenſation and reflection, are the boundaries of our thoughts, beyond which the mind, whatever efforts it would make, is not able to advance one jot; nor can it make any diſcoveries, when it would pry into the nature and hidden cauſes of thoſe *ideas*.

§ 30. Idea *of Body and Spirit compared.*

So that, in ſhort, *the idea* we have *of ſpirit, compared with the idea* we have *of body,* ſtands thus: The ſubſtance of ſpirit is unknown to us; and ſo is the ſubſtance of body equally unknown to us. Two primary qualities or properties of body, *viz.* ſolid coherent parts and impulſe, we have diſtinct clear *ideas* of: ſo likewiſe we know, and have diſtinct clear *ideas* of two primary qualities or properties of ſpirit, *viz.* thinking, and a power of action; *i. e.* a power of beginning or ſtopping ſeveral thoughts or motions. We have alſo the *ideas* of ſeveral qualities inherent in bodies, and have the clear diſtinct *ideas* of them; which qualities are but the various modifications of the extenſion of cohering ſolid parts, and their motion. We have likewiſe the *ideas* of the ſeveral modes of thinking, *viz.* believing, doubting, intending, fearing, hoping; all which are but the ſeveral modes of thinking. We have alſo the *ideas* of willing, and moving the body conſequent to it, and with the body itſelf too; for, as has been ſhown, ſpirit is capable of motion.

§ 31. *The Notion of Spirit involves no more difficulty in it than that of Body.*

LASTLY, If this notion of immaterial ſpirit may have perhaps ſome difficulties in it, not eaſy to be explained, we have therefore no more reaſon to deny or doubt the exiſtence of ſuch ſpirits, than we have to deny or doubt the exiſtence of body; becauſe the notion of body is cumbered with ſome difficulties very hard, and perhaps impoſſible to be explained or underſtood by us. For I would fain have inſtanced any thing in our notion of ſpirit more perplexed, or nearer a contradiction, than the very notion of body includes in it; the diviſibility, *in infinitum,* of any finite extenſion, involving us, whether we grant or deny it, in conſequences impoſſible to be explicated, or made in our apprehenſions conſiſtent; conſequences that carry greater difficulty, and more apparent abſurdity, than any thing can follow from the notion of an immaterial knowing ſubſtance.

§ 32. *We know nothing beyond ſimple* Ideas.

WHICH we are not at all to wonder at, ſince we, having but ſome few ſuperficial *ideas* of things, diſcovered to us only by the ſenſes from without, or by the mind, reflecting on what it experiments in itſelf within, have no knowledge beyond that, much leſs of the internal conſtitution, and true nature of things, being deſtitute of faculties to attain it. And therefore, experimenting and diſcovering in ourſelves knowledge, and the power of voluntary motion, as certainly as we experiment, or diſcover in things without us, the coheſion and ſeparation of ſolid parts, which is the extenſion and motion of bodies; *we have as much reaſon to be ſatisfied with our notion of immaterial ſpirit, as with our notion of body, and the exiſtence of the one as well as the other.* For it being no more a contradiction, that thinking ſhould exiſt ſeparate and independent from ſolidity, than it is a contradiction that ſolidity ſhould exiſt, ſeparate and independent from thinking, they being both but ſimple *ideas*, independent one from another; and having as clear and diſtinct *ideas* in us of thinking as of ſolidity, I know not why we may not as well allow a thinking thing without ſolidity, *i. e. immaterial*, to exiſt, as a ſolid thing without thinking, *i. e. matter*, to exiſt; eſpecially ſince it is not harder to conceive how thinking ſhould exiſt without matter, than how matter ſhould think. For whenſoever we would proceed beyond theſe ſimple *ideas* we have from ſenſation and reflection, and dive farther into the nature of things, we fall preſently into darkneſs and obſcurity, perplexedneſs and difficulties, and can diſcover nothing farther but our own blindneſs and ignorance. But whichever of theſe complex *ideas* be cleareſt, that of body or immaterial ſpirit, this is evident, that the ſimple *ideas* that make them up, are no other than what we have received from ſenſation or reflection; and ſo is it of all our other *ideas* of ſubſtances, even of God himſelf.

§ 33. Idea *of God.*

FOR if we examine the *idea* we have of the incomprehenſible Supreme Being, we ſhall find, that we come by it the ſame way; and that the complex *ideas* we have both of God and ſeparate ſpirits, are made up of the ſimple *ideas* we receive from reflection; *v. g.* having from what we experiment in ourſelves got the *ideas* of exiſtence and duration; of knowledge and power, of pleaſure and happineſs, and of ſeveral other qualities and powers, which it is better to have than to be without; when we would frame an *idea* the moſt ſuitable we can to the Supreme Being, we enlarge every one of theſe with our *idea* of infinity, and ſo putting them together, make our complex *idea of God;* for that the mind has ſuch a power of enlarging ſome of its *ideas*, received from ſenſation and reflection, has been already ſhown.

§ 34.

If I find that I know ſome few things, and ſome of them, or all, perhaps, imperfectly, I can frame an *idea* of knowing twice as many, which I can double again, as often as I can add to number; and thus enlarge my *idea* of knowledge, by extending its comprehenſion to all things exiſting, or poſſible. The ſame alſo I can do of knowing them more perfectly, *i. e.* all their qualities, powers, cauſes, conſequences, and relations, &c. till all be perfectly known that is in them, or can any way relate to them; and thus frame the *idea* of infinite or boundleſs knowledge. The ſame may alſo be done of power, till we come to that we call infinite; and alſo of the duration of exiſtence, without beginning or end, and ſo frame the *idea* of an eternal Being. The degrees or extent wherein we aſcribe exiſtence, power, wiſdom, and all other perfections (which we can have any *ideas* of) to that Sovereign Being which we call God, being all boundleſs and infinite, we frame the beſt *idea* of him our minds are capable of: All which is done, I ſay, by enlarging thoſe ſimple *ideas* we have taken from the operations of our own minds by reflection, or by our ſenſes, from exterior things, to that vaſtneſs to which infinity can extend them.

§ 35. Idea *of God.*

For it is infinity, which joined to our *ideas* of exiſtence, power, knowledge, &c. makes that complex *idea*, whereby we repreſent to ourſelves the beſt we can, the Supreme Being. For though, in his own eſſence (which certainly we do not know, not knowing the real eſſence of a pebble, or a fly, or of our own ſelves) God be ſimple and uncompounded, yet I think I may ſay, we have no other *idea* of him but a complex one of exiſtence, knowledge, power, happineſs, &c. infinite and eternal; which are all diſtinct *ideas*, and ſome of them being relative, are again compounded of others; all which being, as has been ſhown, originally got from *ſenſation* and *reflection*, go to make up the *idea* or notion we have of God.

§ 36. *No* Ideas *in our complex one of Spirits but thoſe got from Senſation or Reflection.*

This farther is to be obſerved, that there is no *idea* we attribute to God, bating infinity, which is not alſo a part of our complex *idea* of other ſpirits; becauſe, being capable of no other ſimple *ideas*, belonging to any thing but body, but thoſe which by reflection we receive from the operation of our own minds, we can attribute to ſpirits no other but what we receive from thence; and all the difference we can put between them in our contemplation of ſpirits, is only in the ſeveral extents and degrees of their knowledge, power, duration, happineſs, &c. For that in our *ideas*, as well of *ſpirits* as of other things, we are *reſtrained to thoſe we receive from ſenſation and reflection*, is evident from hence, that, in our *ideas* of ſpirits, how much ſoever advanced in perfection beyond thoſe of bodies, even to that of infinite, we cannot yet have any *idea* of the manner wherein they diſcover their thoughts one to another; though we muſt neceſſarily conclude, that ſeparate ſpirits, which are beings that have perfecter knowledge and greater happineſs than we, muſt needs have alſo a perfecter way of communicating their thoughts than we have, who are fain to make uſe of corporeal ſigns and particular ſounds;

which are therefore of moſt general uſe, as being the beſt and quickeſt we are capable of. But of immediate communication, having no experiment in ourſelves, and conſequently no notion of it at all, we have no *idea* how ſpirits, which uſe not words, can with quickneſs, or much leſs how ſpirits, that have no bodies, can be maſters of their own thoughts, and communicate or conceal them at pleaſure, though we cannot but neceſſarily ſuppoſe they have ſuch a power.

§ 37. *Recapitulation.*

AND thus we have ſeen *what kinds of* ideas *we have of ſubſtances of all kinds*, wherein they conſiſt, and how we come by them: From whence, I think, it is very evident,

Firſt, That all our *ideas* of the ſeveral ſorts of ſubſtances, are nothing but collections of ſimple *ideas*, with a ſuppoſition of ſomething to which they belong, and in which they ſubſiſt; though of this ſuppoſed ſomething we have no clear diſtinct *idea* at all.

Secondly, That all the ſimple *ideas*, that thus united in one common *ſubſtratum*, make up our complex *ideas* of ſeveral ſorts of ſubſtances, are no other but ſuch as we have received from *ſenſation* or *reflection*: So that even in thoſe which we think we are moſt intimately acquainted with, and that come neareſt the comprehenſion of our moſt enlarged conceptions, we cannot go beyond thoſe ſimple *ideas*; and even in thoſe which ſeem moſt remote from all we have to do with, and do infinitely ſurpaſs any thing we can perceive in ourſelves by *reflection*, or diſcover by *ſenſation* in other things, we can attain to nothing but thoſe ſimple *ideas*, which we originally received from *ſenſation* or *reflection*; as is evident in the complex *ideas* we have of angels, and particularly of God himſelf.

Thirdly, That moſt of the ſimple *ideas* that make up our complex *ideas* of ſubſtances, when truly conſidered, are only powers, however we are apt to take them for poſitive qualities, *v. g.* the greateſt part of the *ideas* that make our complex *idea of gold*, are yellowneſs, great weight, ductility, fuſibility, and ſolubility in *aq.*

regia, &c. all united together in an unknown *ſubſtratum;* all which *ideas* are nothing elſe but ſo many relations to other ſubſtances, and are not really in the gold, conſidered barely in itſelf, though they depend on thoſe real and primary qualities of its internal conſtitution, whereby it has a fitneſs differently to operate, and be operated on by ſeveral other ſubſtances.

CHAP. XXIV.

OF COLLECTIVE *IDEAS* OF SUBSTANCES.

§ 1. *One* Idea.

BESIDES theſe complex *ideas* of ſeveral ſingle ſubſtances, as of man, horſe, gold, violet, apple, &c. the mind hath alſo *complex collective ideas* of ſubſtances, which I do ſo call, becauſe ſuch *ideas* are made up of many particular ſubſtances conſidered together, as united into one *idea*, and which ſo joined are looked on as one; *v. g.* the *idea* of ſuch a collection of men as make an army, though conſiſting of a great number of diſtinct ſubſtances, is as much one *idea* as the *idea* of a man; and the great collective *idea* of all bodies whatſoever, ſignified by the name world, is as much one *idea* as the *idea* of any the leaſt particle of matter in it; it ſufficing to the unity of any *idea*, that it be conſidered as one repreſentation or picture, though made up of ever ſo many particulars.

§ 2. *Made by the Power of compoſing in the Mind.* THESE collective *ideas* of ſubſtances the mind makes by its power of compoſition, and uniting ſeverally, either ſimple or complex *ideas* into one, as it does by the ſame faculty make the complex *ideas* of particular ſubſtances, conſiſting of an aggregate of divers ſimple *ideas* united in one ſubſtance; and as the mind, by putting together the repeated *ideas* of unity, makes the collective mode, or complex *idea* of any number, as a ſcore or a groſs, &c. ſo, by putting together ſeveral particular ſubſtances, it makes collective *ideas* of ſubſtances, as a troop, an army, a ſwarm, a city, a fleet; each of which every one finds that he repreſents to his own mind by one *idea*, in one view; and ſo under that notion conſiders thoſe ſeveral things as perfectly one, as one ſhip or one atom. Nor is it harder to conceive how an army of ten thouſand men ſhould make one *idea*, than how a man ſhould make one *idea*; it being as eaſy to the mind to unite into one the *idea* of a great number of men, and conſider it as one, as it is to unite into one particular all the diſtinct *ideas* that make up the compoſition of a man, and conſider them all together as one.

§ 3. *All artificial Things are collective* Ideas.

AMONGST ſuch kind of collective *ideas* are to be counted the moſt part of artificial things, at leaſt ſuch of them as are made up of diſtinct ſubſtances; and, in truth, if we conſider all theſe collective *ideas* aright, as *army*, *conſtellation*, *univerſe*, as they are united into ſo many ſingle *ideas*, they are but the artificial draughts of the mind, bringing things very remote, and independent on one another, into one view, the better to contemplate and diſcourſe of them, united into one conception, and ſignified by one name. For there are no things ſo remote, nor ſo contrary, which the mind cannot, by this art of compoſition, bring into one *idea*; as is viſible in that ſignified by the name *univerſe*.

CHAP. XXV.

OF RELATION.

§ 1. *Relation what.*

BESIDES the *ideas*, whether ſimple or complex, that the mind has of things as they are in themſelves, there are others it gets from their compariſon one with another. The underſtanding, in the conſideration of any thing, is not confined to that preciſe object: It can carry any *idea* as it were beyond itſelf, or at leaſt look beyond it, to ſee how it ſtands in conformity to any other. When the mind ſo conſiders one thing that it does, as it were, bring it to, and ſet it by another, and carry its view from one to the other, this is, as the words import, *relation* and *reſpect;* and the denominations given to poſitive things, intimating that reſpect, and ſerving as marks to lead the thoughts beyond the ſubject itſelf denominated to ſomething diſtinct from it, are what we call *relatives;* and the things ſo brought together, *related.* Thus, when the mind conſiders Caius as ſuch a poſitive being, it takes nothing into that *idea*, but what really exiſts in Caius; *v. g.* when I conſider him as man, I have nothing in my mind but the complex *idea* of the ſpecies man. So likewiſe, when I ſay Caius is a white man, I have nothing but the bare conſideration of man, who hath that white colour. But when I give Caius the name *huſband*, I intimate ſome other perſon; and when I give him the name *whiter*, I intimate ſome other thing: in both caſes my thought is led to ſomething beyond Caius, and there are two things brought into conſideration. And ſince any *idea*, whether ſimple or complex, may be the occaſion why the mind thus brings two things together, and, as it were, takes a view of them at once, though ſtill conſidered as diſtinct; therefore any of our *ideas* may be the foundation of relation; as in the above mentioned inſtance, the contract and ceremony of marriage with Sempronia is the occaſion of the denomination or relation of huſband; and the colour white, the occaſion why he is ſaid whiter than freeſtone.

§ 2. *Relations without corelative Terms, not eaſily perceived.*

THESE, and the like *relations expreſſed by relative terms that have others anſwering them, with a reciprocal intimation*, as father and ſon, bigger and leſs, cauſe and effect, *are very obvious* to every one, and every body at firſt ſight perceives the relation. For father and ſon, huſband and wife, and ſuch other corelative terms, ſeem ſo nearly to belong one to another, and through cuſtom do ſo readily chime and anſwer one another in people's memories, that, upon the naming of either of them, the thoughts are preſently carried beyond the thing ſo named; and nobody overlooks or doubts of a relation, where it is ſo plainly intimated. But where languages have failed to give corelative names, there the relation is not always ſo eaſily taken notice of. *Concubine* is, no doubt, a relative name, as well as wife; but, in languages where this, and the like words, have not a corelative term, there people are not ſo apt to take them to be ſo, as wanting that evident mark of relation which is between corelatives, which ſeem to explain one another, and not to be able to exiſt but together. Hence it is that many of thoſe names, which, duly conſidered, do include evident relations, have been called external denominations. But all names, that are more than empty ſounds, muſt ſignify ſome *idea* which is either in the thing to which the name is applied; and then it is poſitive, and is looked on as united to, and exiſting in the thing to which the denomination is given; or elſe it ariſes from the reſpect the mind finds in it to ſomething diſtinct from it, with which it conſiders it; and then it includes a relation.

§ 3. *Some ſeemingly abſolute Terms contain relations.* ANOTHER ſort of *relative terms* there is, which are not looked on to be either relative, or ſo much as external denominations; which yet, under the form and appearance of ſignifying ſomething abſolute in the ſubject, do conceal a tacit, though leſs obſervable relation. Such are the *ſeemingly poſitive* terms of *old*, *great*, *imperfect*, *&c.* whereof I ſhall have occaſion to ſpeak more at large in the following chapters.

§ 4. *Relation different from the Things related.* THIS farther may be obſerved, that the *ideas* of relation may be the ſame in men who have far different *ideas* of the things that are related, or that are thus compared; *v. g.* thoſe who have far different *ideas* of a *man*, may yet agree in the notion of a *father*; which is a notion ſuperinduced to the ſubſtance, or man, and refers only to an act of that thing called man, whereby he contributed to the generation of one of his own kind, let man be what he will.

§ 5. *Change of Relation may be without any Change in the Subject.*

THE *nature* therefore of *relation* consists in the referring or comparing two things one to another; from which comparison, one or both comes to be denominated. And if either of those things be removed or cease to be, the relation ceases, and the denomination consequent to it, though the other receive in itself no alteration at all; *v. g.* Caius, whom I considered to-day as a father, ceases to be so to-morrow only by the death of his son, without any alteration made in himself. Nay, barely by the mind's changing the object to which it compares any thing, the same thing is capable of having contrary denominations at the same time; *v. g.* Caius, compared to several persons, may truly be said to be older and younger, stronger and weaker, &c.

§ 6. *Relation only betwixt two Things.*

WHATSOEVER doth or can exist, or be considered as one thing, is positive: And so not only simple *ideas* and substances, but modes also are positive beings, though the parts of which they consist are very often relative one to another; but the whole together, considered as one thing, and producing in us the complex *idea* of one thing, which *idea* is in our minds, as one picture, though an aggregate of divers parts, and under one name, it is a positive or absolute thing or *idea*. Thus a triangle, though the parts thereof compared one to another be *relative*, yet the *idea* of the whole is a positive absolute *idea*. The same may be said of a family, a tune, &c.; for there can be no relation but betwixt two things considered as two things. There must always be in relation two *ideas*, or things, either in themselves really separate, or considered as distinct, and then a ground or occasion for their comparison.

§ 7. *All Things capable of Relation.*

CONCERNING relation in general, these things may be considered;

First, That there is *no one thing*, whether simple *idea*, substance, mode, or relation, or name of either of them, *which is not capable of almost an infinite number of* considerations, in reference to other things; and therefore this makes no small part of mens thoughts and words; *v. g.* one single man may at once be concerned in, and sustain all these following *relations*, and many more, viz. father, brother, son, grandfather grandson, father-in-law, son-in-law, husband, friend, enemy, subject, general, judge, patron, client, professor, European, Englishman, islander, servant, master, possessor, captain, superior, inferior, bigger, less, older, younger, contemporary, like, unlike, &c. to an almost infinite number; he being capable of as many relations, as there can be occasions of comparing him to other things, in any manner of agreement, disagreement, or respect whatsoever. For, as I said, *relation* is a way of comparing or considering two things together, and giving one or both of them some appellation from that comparison, and sometimes giving even the relation itself a name.

§ 8. *The* Ideas *of Relations clearer often than of the Subjects related.*

SECONDLY, This farther may be considered concerning *relation*, that though it be not contained in the real existence of things, but something extraneous and superinduced; yet the *ideas* which relative words stand for, are often clearer and more distinct than those substances to which they do belong. The notion we have of a father or brother is a great deal clearer and more distinct than that we have of a man; or, if you will, *paternity* is a thing whereof it is easier to have a clear *idea* than of *humanity*: And I can much easier conceive what a friend is, than what God; because the knowledge of one action, or one simple *idea*, is oftentimes sufficient to give me the notion of a relation; but to the knowing of any substantial being, an accurate collection of sundry *ideas* is necessary. A man, if he compares two things together, can hardly be supposed not to know what it is wherein he compares them: so that, when he compares any things together, he cannot but have a very clear *idea* of that relation. The *ideas* then of *relations are capable* at leaſt *of being more perfect and diſtinct in our minds than thoſe of ſubſtances;* becauſe it is commonly hard to know all the ſimple *ideas* which are really in any ſubſtance, but for the moſt part eaſy enough to know the ſimple *ideas* that make up any relation I think on, or have a name for; *v. g.* comparing two men, in reference to one common parent, it is very eaſy to frame the *ideas* of brothers, without having yet the perfect *idea* of a man; or ſignificant relative words, as well as others, ſtanding only for *ideas*, and thoſe being all either ſimple, or made up of ſingle ones, it ſuffices for the knowing the preciſe *idea* the relative term ſtands for, to have a clear conception of that which is the foundation of the relation, which may be done without having a perfect and clear *idea* of the thing it is attributed to. Thus having the notion that one laid the egg out of which the other was hatched, I have a clear *idea* of the relation of *dam* and *chick*, between the two caſſiowaries in St. James's Park, though perhaps I have but a very obſcure and imperfect *idea* of thoſe birds themſelves.

§ 9. *Relations all terminate in ſimple* Ideas.

THIRDLY, Though there be a great number of conſiderations, wherein things may be compared one with another, and ſo a multitude of *relations*, yet they *all terminate in*, and are concerned about thoſe *ſimple ideas*, either of ſenſation or reflection, which I think to be the whole materials of all our knowledge. To clear this, I ſhall ſhow it in the moſt conſiderable relations that we have any notion of, and in ſome that ſeem to be the moſt remote from *ſenſe* or *reflection;* which yet will appear to have their *ideas* from thence, and leave it paſt doubt, that the notions we have of them are but certain ſimple *ideas*, and ſo originally derived from ſenſe or reflection.

§ 10. *Terms leading the Mind beyond the Subject denominated, are relative.*

FOURTHLY, That *relation*, being the conſidering of one thing with another, which is extrinſical to it, it is evident that all words that neceſſarily lead the mind to any other *ideas* than are ſuppoſed really to exiſt in that thing, to which the word is applied, are *relative words*, *v. g.* a *man black*, *merry*, *thoughtful*, *thirſty*, *angry*, *extended;* theſe, and the like, are all abſolute, becauſe they neither ſignify nor intimate any thing, but what does, or is ſuppoſed really to exiſt in the man thus denominated; but *father*, *brother*, *king*, *huſband*, *blacker*, *merrier*, &c. are words, which, together with the thing they denominate, imply alſo ſomething elſe ſeparate and exterior to the exiſtence of that thing.'

§ 11. *Concluſion.*

HAVING laid down theſe premiſes concerning *relation* in general, I ſhall now proceed to ſhow, in ſome inſtances, how all the *ideas* we have of *relation* are made up, as the others are, only of ſimple *ideas*, and that they all, how refined and remote from ſenſe ſoever they ſeem, terminate at laſt in ſimple *ideas*. I ſhall begin with the moſt comprehenſive relation, wherein all things that do or can exiſt are concerned, and that is the relation of *cauſe* and *effect*, the *idea* whereof, how derived from the two fountains of all our knowledge, *ſenſation* and *reflection*, I ſhall in the next place conſider.

CHAP. XXVI.

OF CAUSE AND EFFECT, AND OTHER RELATIONS.

§ 1. *Whence their* Ideas *got.*

IN the notice that our ſenſes take of the conſtant viciſſitude of things, we cannot but obſerve, that ſeveral particular, both qualities and ſubſtances, begin to exiſt, and that they receive this their exiſtence from the due application and operation of ſome other being. From this obſervation we get our *ideas* of *cauſe* and *effect*. That which produces any ſimple or complex *idea*, we denote by the general name *cauſe*, and that which is produced, *effect*. Thus, finding that in that ſubſtance which we call wax, fluidity, which is a ſimple *idea* that was not in it before, is conſtantly produced by the application of a certain degree of heat; we call the ſimple *idea* of heat, in relation to fluidity in wax, the cauſe of it, and fluidity the effect. So alſo, finding that the ſubſtance wood, which is a certain collection of ſimple *ideas* ſo called, by the application of fire is turned into another ſubſtance called aſhes, *i. e.* another complex *idea*, conſiſting of a collection of ſimple *ideas*, quite different from that complex *idea* which we call wood; we conſider fire, in relation to aſhes, as cauſe, and the aſhes as effect: So that, whatever is conſidered by us to conduce or operate to the producing any particular ſimple *idea*, or collection of ſimple *ideas*, whether ſubſtance or mode, which did not before exiſt, hath thereby in our minds the relation of a cauſe, and ſo is denominated by us.

§ 2. *Creation, Generation, making Alteration.*

HAVING thus, from what our ſenſes are able to diſcover in the operations of bodies on one another, got the notion of *cauſe* and *effect*, viz. that a *cauſe* is that which makes any other thing, either ſimple *idea*, ſubſtance, or mode, begin to be; and an *effect* is that which had its beginning from ſome other thing; the mind finds no great difficulty to diſtinguiſh the ſeveral originals of things into two ſorts:

Firſt, When the thing is wholly made new, ſo that no part thereof did ever exiſt before, as when a new particle of matter doth begin to exiſt *in rerum natura*, which had before no being, and this we call *creation*.

Secondly, When a thing is made up of particles, which did all of them before exiſt, but that very thing ſo conſtituted of pre-exiſting particles, which, conſidered altogether, make up ſuch a collection of ſimple *ideas*, had not any *exiſtence* before, as this man, this egg, roſe, or cherry, &c.; and this, when referred to a ſubſtance, produced in the ordinary courſe of nature by an internal principle, but ſet on work by, and received from ſome external agent or cauſe, and working by inſenſible ways, which we perceive not, we call *generation*: When the cauſe is extrinſical, and the effect produced by a ſenſible ſeparation, or *juxta*-poſition of diſcernible parts, we call it *making;* and ſuch are all artificial things. When any ſimple *idea* is produced, which was not in that ſubject before, we call it *alteration.* Thus, a man is generated, a picture made, and either of them altered, when any new ſenſible quality or ſimple *idea* is produced in either of them, which was not there before; and the things thus made to exiſt, which were not there before, are *effects,* and thoſe things which operated to the exiſtence, *cauſes;* in which, and all other caſes, we may obſerve, that the notion of *cauſe* and *effect,* has its riſe from *ideas,* received by ſenſation or reflection, and that this relation, how comprehenſive ſoever, terminates at laſt in them; for to have the *idea* of *cauſe* and *effect,* it ſuffices to conſider any ſimple *idea* or ſubſtance as beginning to exiſt by the operation of ſome other, without knowing the manner of that operation.

§ 3. *Relations of Time.*

TIME and *place* are alſo the foundations of very large relations, and all finite beings at leaſt are concerned in them. But having already ſhown, in another place, how we get theſe *ideas,* it may ſuffice here to intimate, that moſt of the denominations of things, received from time, are only relations. Thus, when any one ſays, that Queen Elizabeth lived ſixty-nine, and reigned forty five years, theſe words import only the relation of that duration to ſome other, and mean no more than this, that the duration of her exiſtence was equal to ſixty-nine, and the duration of her government to forty-five annual revolutions of the ſun, and ſo are all words anſwering *how long.* Again, William the Conqueror invaded England about the year 1070, which means this, that taking the duration from our Saviour's time till now, for one entire great length of time, it ſhows at what diſtance this invaſion was from the two extremes; and ſo do all words of time, anſwering to the queſtion *when,* which ſhow only the diſtance of any point of time from the period of a longer duration from which we meaſure, and to which we thereby conſider it as related.

§ 4.

There are yet, besides those, other words of time, that ordinarily are thought to stand for positive *ideas*, which yet will, when considered, be found to be relative, such as are *young*, *old*, &c. which include and intimate the relation any thing has to a certain length of duration, whereof we have the *idea* in our minds. Thus, having settled in our thoughts the *idea* of the ordinary duration of a man to be seventy years, when we say a man is *young*, we mean that his age is yet but a small part of that which usually men attain to; and when we denominate him *old*, we mean that his duration is run out almost to the end of that which men do not usually exceed; and so it is but comparing the particular age, or duration of this or that man, to the *idea* of that duration which we have in our minds, as ordinarily belonging to that sort of animals, which is plain, in the application of these names to other things; for a man is called young at twenty years, and very young at seven years old: But yet a horse we call old at twenty, and a dog at seven years; because, in each of these, we compare their age to different *ideas* of duration, which are settled in our minds, as belonging to these several sorts of animals, in the ordinary course of nature. But the sun and stars, though they have outlasted several generations of men, we call not old, because we do not know what period God hath set to that sort of beings; this term belonging properly to those things which we can observe, in the ordinary course of things, by a natural decay, to come to an end in a certain period of time; and so have, in our minds as it were, a standard to which we can compare the several parts of their duration; and by the relation they bear thereunto, call them young or old; which we cannot therefore do to a ruby or a diamond, things whose usual periods we know not.

§ 5. *Relations of Place and Extension.*

The *relation* also that things have to one another in their places and distances, is very obvious to observe; as above, below, a mile distant from Charing-cross in

England, and in London. But as in duration, ſo in extenſion and bulk, there are ſome *ideas* that are relative, which we ſignify by names that are thought poſitive; as *great* and *little* are truly *relations*. For here alſo having, by obſervation, ſettled in our minds the *ideas* of the bigneſs of ſeveral ſpecies of things, from thoſe we have been moſt accuſtomed to, we make them as it were the ſtandards whereby to denominate the bulk of others. Thus we call a great apple, ſuch a one as is bigger than the ordinary ſort of thoſe we have been uſed to; and a little horſe, ſuch a one as comes not up to the ſize of that *idea* which we have in our minds to belong ordinarily to horſes; and that will be a great horſe to a Welſhman, which is but a little one to a Fleming; they two having, from the different breed of their countries, taken ſeveral ſized *ideas* to which they compare, and in relation to which they denominate their great and their little.

§ 6. *Abſolute Terms often ſtand for Relations.* So likewiſe *weak* and *ſtrong* are but *relative denominations* of power compared to ſome *ideas* we have at that time, of greater or leſs power. Thus, when we ſay a weak man, we mean one that has not ſo much ſtrength or power to move, as uſually men have, or uſually thoſe of his ſize have; which is a comparing his ſtrength to the *idea* we have of the uſual ſtrength of men, or men of ſuch a ſize. The like, when we ſay the creatures are all weak things; weak, there, is but a relative term, ſignifying the diſproportion there is in the power of God and the creatures. And ſo abundance of words, in ordinary ſpeech, ſtand only for relations (and perhaps the greateſt part) which at firſt ſight ſeem to have no ſuch ſignification; *v. g.* the ſhip has neceſſary ſtores. *Neceſſary* and *ſtores* are both relative words; one having a relation to the accompliſhing the voyage intended, and the other to future uſe. All which relations, how they are confined to and terminate in *ideas* derived from *ſenſation* and *reflection*, is too obvious to need any explication.

CHAP. XXVII.

OF IDENTITY AND DIVERSITY.

§ 1. *Wherein Identity consists.*

ANOTHER occasion the mind often takes of comparing, is the very being of things, when considering any thing as existing at any determined time and place, we compare it with its self-existing at another time, and thereon form the *ideas* of *identity* and *diversity*. When we see any thing to be in any place in any instant of time, we are sure (be it what it will) that it is that very thing, and not another, which at that same time exists in another place, how like and undistinguishable soever it may be in all other respects: And in this consists *identity*, when the *ideas* it is attributed to vary not at all from what they were that moment wherein we consider their former existence, and to which we compare the present. For we never finding nor conceiving it possible, that two things of the same kind should exist in the same place at the same time, we rightly conclude, that whatever exists any where at any time, excludes all of the same kind, and is there itself alone. When therefore we demand, whether any thing be the same or no, it refers always to something that existed such a time in such a place, which it was certain at that instant was the same with itself, and no other. From whence it follows, that one thing cannot have two beginnings of existence, nor two things one beginning; it being impossible for two things of the same kind to be or exist in the same instant, in the very same place, or one and the same thing in different places. That therefore that had one beginning, is the same thing; and that which had a different beginning in time and place from that, is not the same, but diverse. That which has made the difficulty about this relation, has been the little care and attention used in having precise notions of the things to which it is attributed.

§ 2. *Identity of Subſtances.*

We have the *ideas* but of three ſorts of ſubſtances; 1. God. 2. Finite intelligences. 3. *Bodies*. Firſt, God is without beginning, eternal, unalterable, and every where; and therefore, concerning his identity there can be no doubt. Secondly, Finite ſpirits having had each its determinate time and place of beginning to exiſt, the relation to that time and place will always determine to each of them its identity, as long as it exiſts. Thirdly, The ſame will hold of every particle of matter, to which no addition or ſubtraction of matter being made, it is the ſame. For though theſe three ſorts of ſubſtances, as we term them, do not exclude one another out of the ſame place, yet we cannot conceive but that they muſt neceſſarily each of them exclude any of the ſame kind out of the ſame place: or elſe the notions and names of identity and diverſity would be in vain, and there could be no ſuch diſtinction of ſubſtances, or any thing elſe one from another. For example: Could two bodies be in the ſame place at the ſame time, then thoſe two parcels of matter muſt be one and the ſame, take them great or little. Nay, all bodies muſt be one and the ſame; for, by the ſame reaſon that two particles of matter may be in one place, all bodies may be in one place; which, when it can be ſuppoſed, takes away the diſtinction of identity and diverſity of one and more, and renders it ridiculous. But it being a contradiction that two or more ſhould be one, identity and diverſity are relations and ways of comparing well founded, and of uſe to the underſtanding. All other things being but modes or relations ultimately terminated in ſubſtances, the identity and diverſity of each particular exiſtence of them too will be by the ſame way determined: only as to things whoſe exiſtence is in ſucceſſion; ſuch as are the actions of finite beings, *v. g* *motion* and *thought*, both which conſiſt in a continued train of ſucceſſion: Concerning their diverſity, there can be no queſtion, becauſe each periſhing the moment it begins, they cannot exiſt in different times, or in different places, as permanent beings can at different times exiſt in diſtant places; and therefore no motion or thought, conſidered as at different times, can be the ſame, each part thereof having a different beginning of exiſtence.

§ 3. Principium Individuationis.

FROM what has been ſaid, it is eaſy to diſcover what is ſo much inquired after, the *principium individuationis;* and that, it is plain, is exiſtence itſelf, which determines a being of any ſort to a particular time and place incommunicable to two beings of the ſame kind. This, though it ſeems eaſier to conceive in ſimple ſubſtances or modes, yet when reflected on, is not more difficult in compounded ones, if care be taken to what it is applied: *v. g.* Let us ſuppoſe an atom, *i. e.* a continued body, under one immutable ſuperficies, exiſting in a determined time and place; it is evident that, conſidered in any inſtant of its exiſtence, it is in that inſtant the ſame with itſelf; for being at that inſtant what it is, and nothing elſe, it is the ſame, and ſo muſt continue as long as its exiſtence is continued; for ſo long it will be the ſame, and no other. In like manner, if two or more atoms be joined together into the ſame maſs, every one of thoſe atoms will be the ſame, by the foregoing rule; and whilſt they exiſt united together, the maſs, conſiſting of the ſame atoms, muſt be the ſame maſs, or the ſame body, let the parts be ever ſo differently jumbled; but if one of theſe atoms be taken away, or one new one added, it is no longer the ſame maſs, or the ſame body. In the ſtate of living creatures, their identity depends not on a maſs of the ſame particles, but on ſomething elſe; for in them the variation of great parcels of matter alters not the identity: An oak growing from a plant to a great tree, and then lopped, is ſtill the ſame oak; and a colt grown up to a horſe, ſometimes fat, ſometimes lean, is all the while the ſame horſe; though in both theſe caſes, there may be a manifeſt change of the parts; ſo that truly they are not either of them the ſame maſſes of matter, though they be truly one of them the ſame oak, and the other the ſame horſe. The reaſon whereof is, that in theſe two caſes of a maſs of matter, and a living body, *identity* is not applied to the ſame thing.

§ 4. *Identity of Vegetables.*

WE muſt therefore conſider wherein an oak differs from a maſs of matter, and that ſeems to me to be in this, that the one is only the cohesion of particles of matter any how united, the other ſuch a diſpoſition of them as conſtitutes the parts of an oak; and ſuch an organization of thoſe parts as is fit to receive and diſtribute nouriſhment, ſo as to continue and frame the wood, bark, and leaves, &c. of an oak, in which conſiſts the vegetable life. That being then one plant which has ſuch an organization of parts in one coherent body partaking of one common life, it continues to be the ſame plant as long as it partakes of the ſame life, though that life be communicated to new particles of matter vitally united to the living plant, in a like continued organization conformable to that ſort of plants. For this organization being at any one inſtant in any one collection of *matter*, is in that particular concrete diſtinguiſhed from all other, and is that individual life, which exiſting conſtantly from that moment both forwards and backwards, in the ſame continuity of inſenſibly ſucceeding parts united to the living body of the plant, it has that identity which makes the ſame plant, and all the parts of it, parts of the ſame plant, during all the time that they exiſt united in that continued organization, which is fit to convey that common life to all the parts ſo united.

§ 5. *Identity of Animals.*

THE caſe is not ſo much different in *brutes*, but that any one may hence ſee what makes an animal, and continues it the ſame. Something we have like this in machines, and may ſerve to illuſtrate it. For example, What is a watch? It is plain it is nothing but a fit organization, or conſtruction of parts, to a certain end, which when a ſufficient force is added to it, it is capable to attain. If we would ſuppoſe this machine one continued body, all whoſe organized parts were repaired, increaſed or diminiſhed, by a conſtant addition or ſeparation of inſenſible parts, with one common life, we ſhould have ſomething very much like the body of an animal, with this difference, that in an animal the fitneſs of the organization, and the motion wherein life conſiſts, begin together, the motion coming from within; but in machines, the force coming ſenſibly from without, is often away when the organ is in order, and well fitted to receive it.

§ 6. *Identity of Man.*

THIS alſo ſhows wherein the identity of the ſame *man* conſiſts, *viz.* in nothing but a participation of the ſame continued life, by conſtantly fleeting particles of matter, in ſucceſſion vitally united to the ſame organized body. He that ſhall place the *identity* of man in any thing elſe, but, like that of other animals, in one fitly organized body, taken in any one inſtant, and from thence continued under one organization of life in ſeveral ſucceſſively fleeting particles of matter united to it, will find it hard to make an *embryo*, one of years, mad and ſober, the ſame man, by any ſuppoſition, that will not make it poſſible for Seth, Iſmael, Socrates, Pilate, St. Auſtin, and Cæſar Borgia, to be the ſame man. For if the *identity* of ſoul alone makes the ſame man, and there be nothing in the nature of matter, why the ſame individual ſpirit may not be united to different bodies, it will be poſſible that thoſe men living in diſtant ages, and of different tempers, may have been the ſame man; which way of ſpeaking muſt be, from a very ſtrange uſe of the word *man*, applied to an *idea*, out of which body and ſhape is excluded: And that way of ſpeaking would agree yet worſe with the notions of thoſe philoſophers who allow of tranſmigration, and are of opinion that the ſouls of men may, for their miſcarriages, be detruded into the bodies of beaſts, as fit habitations, with organs ſuited to the ſatisfaction of their brutal inclinations. But yet, I think, nobody, could he be ſure that the ſoul of Heliogabalus were in one of his hogs, would yet ſay, that hog were a man or Heliogabalus.

§ 2. *Identity ſuited to the* Idea.

IT is not therefore unity of ſubſtance that comprehends

all ſorts of *identity*, or will determine it in every caſe; but to conceive and judge of it aright, we muſt conſider what *idea* the word it is applied to ſtands for; it being one thing to be the ſame *ſubſtance*, another the ſame *man*, and a third the ſame *perſon*, if *perſon*, *man*, and *ſubſtance* are three names ſtanding for three different *ideas*; for ſuch as is the *idea* belonging to that name, ſuch muſt be the *identity*: which, if it had been a little more carefully attended to, would poſſibly have prevented a great deal of that confuſion, which often occurs about this matter, with no ſmall ſeeming difficulties, eſpecially concerning *perſonal identity*, which therefore we ſhall in the next place a little conſider.

§ 8. *Same Man.*

An animal is a living organized body; and conſequently the ſame animal, as we have obſerved, is the ſame continued life communicated to different particles of matter, as they happen ſucceſſively to be united to that organized living body. And whatever is talked of other definitions, ingenious obſervation puts it paſt doubt, that the *idea* in our minds, of which the ſound *man* in our mouths is the ſign, is nothing elſe but of an animal of ſuch a certain form: ſince I think I may be confident, that whoever ſhould ſee a creature of his own ſhape and make, though it had no more reaſon all its life than a *cat* or a *parrot*, would call him ſtill a *man*; or whoever ſhould hear a *cat* or a *parrot* diſcourſe, reaſon and philoſophiſe, would call or think it nothing but a *cat* or a *parrot*, and ſay, the one was a dull irrational *man*, and the other a very intelligent rational *parrot*. A relation we have in an author of great note, is ſufficient to countenance the ſuppoſition of a rational *parrot*. His words * are:

" I had a mind to know from Prince Maurice's own " mouth, the account of a common, but much credited " ſtory, that I had heard ſo often from many others, of " an old *parrot* he had in Braſil during his government " there, that ſpoke, and aſked and anſwered common

* Memoirs of what paſſed in Chriſtendom, from 1672 to 1679, p. 57—392.

" questions like a reasonable creature; so that those of " his train there generally concluded it to be witchery " or possession; and one of his chaplains, who lived " long afterwards in Holland, would never from that " time endure a *parrot*, but said they all had a devil in " them. I had heard many particulars of this story, " and assevered by people hard to be discredited, which " made me ask Prince Maurice what there was of it. " He said, with his usual plainness and dryness in talk, " there was something true, but a great deal false, of " what had been reported. I desired to know of him " what there was of the first? He told me short and " coldly, that he had heard of such an old *parrot* " when he came to Brasil; and though he believ- " ed nothing of it, and it was a good way off, yet " he had so much of curiosity as to send for it: That " it was a very great and a very old one; and when it " came first into the room where the prince was, with " a great many Dutchmen about him, it said present- " ly, *What a company of white men are here!* They " asked it, what he thought that man was, pointing " to the prince? It answered, *Some general or other.* " When they brought it close to him, he asked it, * *D'ou venes vous?* It answered, *De Marinnan.* The prince, " *A qui estes vous?* The parrot, *A un Portugais.* Prince, " *Que fais tu la?* Parrot, *Je garde les poulles.* The " prince laughed, and said, *Vous gardes les poulles?* " The parrot answered, *Ouy moy, & je scay bien faire;* " and made the chuck four or five times that people " use to make to chickens when they call them. I set " down the words of this worthy dialogue in French " just as Prince Maurice said them to me. I asked " him in what language the *parrot* spoke, and he said " in Brasilian; I asked, whether he understood Brasi- " lian? He said no; but he had taken care to have

* "Whence come ye?" It answered, "From Marinnan." The prince, "To whom do you belong?" The parrot, "To a Portuguese." Prince, "What do you there?" Parrot, "I look after the chickens." The prince laughed, and said, "You look after the chickens?" The parrot answered, "Yes I, and I know well enough how to do it."

" two interpreters by him, the one a Dutchman that " ſpoke Braſilian, and the other a Braſilian that ſpoke " Dutch; that he aſked them ſeparately and privately, " and both of them agreed in telling him juſt the ſame " thing that the *parrot* ſaid. I could not but tell this " odd ſtory, becauſe it is ſo much out of the way, " and from the firſt hand, and what may paſs for a " good one; for, I dare ſay, this prince at leaſt be- " lieved himſelf in all he told me, having ever paſſed for " a very honeſt and pious man: I leave it to naturaliſts " to reaſon, and to other men to believe as they pleaſe " upon it. However, it is not perhaps amiſs to relieve " or enliven a buſy ſcene ſometimes with ſuch digreſ- " ſions, whether to the purpoſe or no."

Same Man.

I HAVE taken care that the reader ſhould have the ſtory at large, in the author's own words, becauſe he ſeems to me not to have thought it incredible; for it cannot be imagined that ſo able a man as he, who had ſufficiency enough to warrant all the teſtimonies he gives of himſelf, ſhould take ſo much pains in a place where it had nothing to do, to pin ſo cloſe not only on a man whom he mentions as his friend, but on a prince in whom he acknowledges very great honeſty and piety, a ſtory which, if he himſelf thought incredible, he could not but alſo think ridiculous. The prince, it is plain, who vouches this ſtory, and our author, who relates it from him, both of them call this talker a *parrot;* and I aſk any one elſe, who thinks ſuch a ſtory fit to be told, whether if this *parrot*, and all of its kind, had always talked, as we have a prince's word for it, as this one did, whether, I ſay, they would not have paſſed for a race of *rational animals:* but yet whether, for all that, they would have been allowed to be men, and not *parrots?* For I preſume it is not the *idea* of a thinking or rational being alone that makes the *idea* of a *man* in moſt people's ſenſe, but of a body, ſo and ſo ſhaped, joined to it: and if that be the *idea* of a *man*, the ſame ſucceſſive body not ſhifted all at once, muſt, as well as the same immaterial spirit, go to the making of same *man*.

§ 9. *Personal Identity.*

THIS being premised to find wherein *personal identity* consists, we must consider what *person* stands for; which, I think, is a thinking intelligent being, that has reason and reflection, and can consider itself as itself, the same thinking thing in different times and places; which it does by that consciousness which is inseparable from thinking, and, as it seems to me, essential to it; it being impossible for any one to perceive, without perceiving that he does perceive. When we see, hear, smell, taste, feel, meditate, or will any thing, we know that we do so. Thus it is always as to our present sensations and perceptions: And by this every one is to himself that which he calls *self*; it not being considered in this case, whether the same *self* be continued in the same or divers substances: For, since consciousness always accompanies thinking, and it is that that makes every one to be what he calls *self*, and thereby distinguishes himself from all other thinking things; in this alone consists *personal identity*, *i. e.* the sameness of a rational being: And as far as this consciousness can be extended backwards to any past action or thought, so far reaches the identity of that *person*: it is the same *self* now it was then; and it is by the same *self* with this present one that now reflects on it, that that action was done.

§ 10. *Consciousness makes personal Identity.*

BUT it is farther inquired, whether it be the same identical substance? This few would think they had reason to doubt of, if these perceptions, with their consciousness, always remained present in the mind whereby the same thinking thing would be always consciously present, and as would be thought evidently the same to itself. But that which seems to make the difficulty is this, that this consciousness being interrupted always by forgetfulness, there being no moment of our lives wherein we have the whole train of all our past actions before our eyes in one view, but even the best memories losing the sight of one part whilst they are viewing another; and we sometimes, and that the greatest part of our lives, not reflecting on our past selves, being intent on our present thoughts, and in sound sleep, having no thoughts at all, or at least none with that consciousness which remarks our waking thoughts; I say, in all these cases, our consciousness being interrupted, and we losing the sight of our past *selves*, doubts are raised whether we are the same thinking thing, *i. e.* the same substance or no; which, however reasonable or unreasonable, concerns not *personal identity* at all; the question being, what makes the same *person*, and not whether it be the same identical substance, which always thinks in the same person; which in this case matters not at all: Different substances by the same consciousness (where they do partake in it) being united into one person, as well as different bodies by the same life are united into one animal, whose *identity* is preserved, in that change of substances, by the unity of one continued life; for it being the same consciousness that makes a man be himself to himself, *personal identity* depends on that only, whether it be annexed only to one individual substance, or can be continued in a succession of several substances: For as far as any intelligent being can repeat the *idea* of any past action with the same consciousness it had of it at first, and with the same consciousness it has of any present action; so far it is the same *personal self;* for it is by the consciousness it has of its present thoughts and actions that it is *self* to *itself* now, and so will be the same *self*, as far as the same consciousness can extend to actions past or to come; and would be by distance of time, or change of substance, no more two *persons*, than a man be two men by wearing other clothes to-day than he did yesterday, with a long or short sleep between; the same consciousness uniting those distant actions into the same *person*, whatever substances contributed to their production.

§ 11. *Personal Identity in Change of Substances.*

THAT this is so, we have some kind of evidence in our

very bodies, all whose particles, whilst vitally united to this same thinking conscious self, so that we feel when they are touched, and are affected by, and conscious of good or harm that happens to them, are a part of our *selves*, *i. e.* of our thinking conscious *self*. Thus the *limbs* of his body is to every one a part of *himself*: he sympathises and is concerned for them. Cut off an hand, and thereby separate it from that consciousness he had of its heat, cold, and other affections, and it is then no longer a part of that which is *himself*, any more than the remotest part of matter. Thus we see the *substance* whereof *personal self* consisted at one time, may be varied at another, without the change of personal *identity*; there being no question about the same person, though the limbs, which but now were a part of it, be cut off.

§ 12. *Whether in the Change of thinking Substances.* BUT the question is, whether if the same substance which thinks be changed, it can be the same person; or remaining the same, it can be different persons?

And to this I answer, first, This can be no question at all to those who place thought in a purely material animal constitution, void of an immaterial substance; for whether their supposition be true or no, it is plain they conceive personal identity preserved in something else than identity of substance; as animal identity is preserved in identity of life, and not of substance: And therefore those who place thinking in an immaterial substance only before they can come to deal with these men, must show why personal identity cannot be preserved in the change of immaterial substances or variety of particular immaterial substances, as well as animal identity is preserved in the change of material substances, or variety of particular bodies; unless they will say, it is one immaterial spirit that makes the same life in brutes, as it is one immaterial spirit that makes the same person in men; which the Cartesians at least will not admit, for fear of making brutes thinking things too.

§ 13.

But next, as to the firſt part of the queſtion, whether if the ſame thinking ſubſtance (ſuppoſing immaterial ſubſtances only to think) be changed, it can be the ſame perſon? I anſwer, That cannot be reſolved but by thoſe who know what kind of ſubſtances they are that do think, and whether the conſciouſneſs of paſt actions can be transferred from one thinking ſubſtance to another. I grant, were the ſame conſciouſneſs the ſame individual action, it could not; but it being but a preſent repreſentation of a paſt action, why it may not be poſſible that that may be repreſented to the mind to have been, which really never was, will remain to be ſhown. And therefore, how far the conſciouſneſs of paſt actions is annexed to any individual agent, ſo that another cannot poſſibly have it, will be hard for us to determine, till we know what kind of action it is that cannot be done without a reflex act of perception accompanying it, and how performed by thinking ſubſtances, who cannot think without being conſcious of it. But that which we call the *ſame conſciouſneſs*, not being the ſame individual act, why one intellectual ſubſtance may not have repreſented to it, as done by itſelf, what it never did, and was perhaps done by ſome other agent; why, I ſay, ſuch a repreſentation may not poſſibly be without reality of matter of fact, as well as ſeveral repreſentations in dreams are, which yet, whilſt dreaming, we take for true, will be difficult to conclude from the nature of things; and that it is never ſo, will by us, till we have clearer views of the nature of thinking ſubſtances, be beſt reſolved into the goodneſs of God, who, as far as the happineſs or miſery of any of his ſenſible creatures is concerned in it, will not by a fatal error of theirs transfer from one to another that conſciouſneſs which draws reward or puniſhment with it. How far this may be an argument againſt thoſe who would place thinking in a ſyſtem of fleeting animal ſpirits, I leave to be conſidered. But yet to return to the queſtion before us, it muſt be allowed, that if the ſame conſciouſneſs (which, as has been ſhown, is quite a different thing from the ſame numerical figure or motion in body) can be transferred from one thinking ſubſtance to another, it will be poſſible that two thinking ſubſtances may make but one perſon; for the ſame conſciouſneſs being preſerved, whether in the ſame or different ſubſtances, the perſonal identity is preſerved.

§ 14.

As to the ſecond part of the queſtion, whether the ſame immaterial ſubſtance remaining, there may be two diſtinct perſons? which queſtion ſeems to me to be built on this, whether the ſame immaterial being, being conſcious of the actions of its paſt duration, may be wholly ſtripped of all the conſciouſneſs of its paſt exiſtence, and loſe it beyond the power of ever retrieving again, and ſo as it were beginning a new account from a new period, have a conſciouſneſs that cannot reach beyond this new ſtate? All thoſe who hold pre-exiſtence are evidently of this mind, ſince they allow the ſoul to have no remaining conſciouſneſs of what it did in that pre-exiſtent ſtate, either wholly ſeparate from body, or informing any other body; and if they ſhould not, it is plain experience would be againſt them: So that perſonal identity reaching no farther than conſciouſneſs reaches, a pre-exiſtent ſpirit not having continued ſo many ages in a ſtate of ſilence, muſt needs make different perſons. Suppoſe a *Chriſtian Platoniſt*, or *Pythagorean* ſhould, upon God's having ended all his works of creation the ſeventh day, think his ſoul hath exiſted ever ſince; and ſhould imagine it has revolved in ſeveral human bodies, as I once met with one, who was perſuaded his had been the ſoul of *Socrates* (how reaſonably I will not diſpute; this I know, that in the poſt he filled, which was no inconſiderable one, he paſſed for a very rational man, and the preſs has ſhown that he wanted not parts or learning): would any one ſay, that he being not conſcious of any of *Socrates's* actions or thoughts, could be the ſame perſon with *Socrates?* Let any one reflect upon himſelf, and conclude that he has in himſelf an immaterial ſpirit, which is that which thinks in him, and in the conſtant change of his body keeps him the ſame, and is that which he calls himſelf: let him alſo ſuppoſe it to be the ſame ſoul that was in *Neſtor* or *Therſites*, at the ſiege of *Troy* (for ſouls being, as far as we know any thing of them in their nature, indifferent to any parcel of matter, the ſuppoſition has no apparent abſurdity in it), which it may have been, as well as it is now, the ſoul of any other man: but he now having no conſciouſneſs of any of the actions either of Neſtor or Therſites, does or can he conceive himſelf the ſame perſon with either of them? can he be concerned in either of their actions? attribute them to himſelf, or think them his own more than the actions of any other man that ever exiſted? So that this conſciouſneſs not reaching to any of the actions of either of thoſe men, he is no more one *ſelf* with either of them, than if the ſoul or immaterial ſpirit that now informs him, had been created, and began to exiſt, when it began to inform his preſent body; though it were ever ſo true, that the ſame ſpirit that informed Neſtor's or Therſites's body, were numerically the ſame that now informs his; for this would no more make him the ſame perſon with Neſtor, than if ſome of the particles of matter that were once a part of Neſtor, were now a part of this man; the ſame immaterial ſubſtance, without the ſame conſciouſneſs, no more making the ſame perſon by being united to any body, than the ſame particle of matter, without conſciouſneſs united to any body, makes the ſame perſon: But let him once find himſelf conſcious of any of the actions of Neſtor, he then finds himſelf the ſame perſon with Neſtor.

§ 15.

AND thus we may be able, without any difficulty, to conceive the ſame perſon at the reſurrection, though in a body not exactly in make or parts the ſame which he had here, the ſame conſciouſneſs going along with the ſoul that inhabits it: But yet the ſoul alone, in the change of bodies, would ſcarce to any one, but to him that makes the ſoul the *man*, be enough to make the ſame *man*; for ſhould the ſoul of a prince, carrying with it the conſciouſneſs of the prince's paſt life, enter and inform the body of a cobler, as ſoon as deſerted by his own ſoul, every one ſees he would be the ſame perſon with the prince, accountable only for the prince's actions: but who would ſay it was the ſame man? The body too goes to the making the man, and I would gueſs, to every body determine the man in this caſe; wherein the ſoul, with all its princely thoughts about it, would not make another man; but he would be the ſame cobler to every one beſides himſelf. I know that, in the ordinary way of ſpeaking, the ſame perſon, and the ſame man, ſtand for one and the ſame thing. And indeed every one will always have a liberty to ſpeak as he pleaſes, and to apply what articulate ſounds to what *ideas* he thinks fit, and change them as often as he pleaſes. But yet when we will inquire what makes the ſame *ſpirit*, *man*, or *perſon*, we muſt fix the *ideas* of *ſpirit*, *man*, or *perſon* in our minds; and having reſolved with ourſelves what we mean by them, it will not be hard to determine in either of them, or the like, when it is the *ſame*, and when not.

§ 16. *Conſciouſneſs makes the ſame Perſon.*

BUT though the ſame immaterial ſubſtance or ſoul does not alone, wherever it be, and in whatſoever ſtate, make the ſame man; yet it is plain, conſciouſneſs, as far as ever it can be extended, ſhould it be to ages paſt, unites exiſtences and actions very remote in time into the ſame perſon, as well as it does the exiſtence and actions of the immediately preceding moment: ſo that whatever has the conſciouſneſs of preſent and paſt actions, is the ſame perſon to whom they both belong. Had I the ſame conſciouſneſs that I ſaw the ark and Noah's flood, as that I ſaw an overflowing of the *Thames* laſt winter, or as that I write now; I could no more doubt that I who write this now, that ſaw the *Thames* overflowed laſt winter, and that viewed the flood at the general deluge, was the ſame *ſelf*, place that *ſelf* in what ſubſtance you pleaſe, than that I who write this am the ſame *myſelf* now whilſt I write (whether I conſiſt of all the ſame ſubſtance, material or immaterial, or no) that I was yesterday. For as to this point of being the same *self*, it matters not whether this present *self* be made up of the same or other substances; I being as much concerned, and as justly accountable for any action was done a thousand years since, appropriated to me now by this self-consciousness, as I am for what I did the last moment.

§ 17. *Self depends on Consciousness.*

SELF is that conscious thinking thing (whatever substance made up of, whether spiritual or material, simple or compounded, it matters not) which is sensible, or conscious of pleasure and pain, capable of happiness or misery, and so is concerned for *itself*, as far as that consciousness extends. Thus every one finds, that whilst comprehended under that consciousness, the little finger is as much a part of *itself*, as what is most so. Upon separation of this little finger, should this consciousness go along with the little finger, and leave the rest of the body, it is evident the little finger would be the *person*, the *same person*; and self then would have nothing to do with the rest of the body. As in this case it is the consciousness that goes along with the substance, when one part is separate from another, which makes the same *person*, and constitutes this inseparable *self*; so it is in reference to substances remote in time. That with which the *consciousness* of this present thinking thing can join itself, makes the same *person*, and is one *self* with it, and with nothing else; and so attributes to it *self*, and owns all the actions of that thing as its own, as far as that consciousness reaches, and no farther: as every one who reflects will perceive.

§ 18. *Objects of Reward and Punishment.*

IN this *personal identity* is founded all the right and justice of reward and punishment; happiness and misery being that for which every one is concerned for *himself*, not mattering what becomes of any substance, not joined to or affected with that consciousness: For as it is evident in the instance I gave but now, if the consciousness went along with the little finger when it was cut off, that would be the same *self* which was concerned for the whole body yeſterday, as making a part of it*ſelf*, whoſe actions then it cannot but admit as its own now: Though if the ſame body ſhould ſtill live, and immediately, from the ſeparation of the little finger, have its own peculiar conſciouſneſs, whereof the little finger knew nothing; it would not at all be concerned for it, as a part of *itſelf*, or could own any of its actions, or have any of them imputed to him.

§ 19.

THIS may ſhow us wherein *perſonal identity* conſiſts, not in the identity of ſubſtance, but, as I have ſaid, in the identity of *conſciouſneſs*; wherein if Socrates and the preſent Mayor of Queenborough agree, they are the ſame perſon: If the ſame Socrates waking and ſleeping do not partake of the ſame *conſciouſneſs*, Socrates waking and ſleeping is not the ſame perſon; and to puniſh Socrates waking for what ſleeping Socrates thought, and waking Socrates was never conſcious of, would be no more of right, than to puniſh one twin for what his brother-twin did, whereof he knew nothing, becauſe their outſides were ſo like, that they could not be diſtinguiſhed; for ſuch twins have been ſeen.

§ 20.

BUT yet poſſibly it will ſtill be objected, Suppoſe I wholly loſe the memory of ſome parts of my life, beyond a poſſibility of retrieving them, ſo that perhaps I ſhall never be conſcious of them again; yet am I not the ſame perſon that did thoſe actions, had thoſe thoughts that I once was conſcious of, though I have now forgot them? To which I anſwer, That we muſt here take notice what the word *I* is applied to; which, in this caſe, is the man only; and the ſame man being preſumed to be the ſame perſon, *I* is eaſily here ſuppoſed to ſtand alſo for the ſame perſon. But if it be poſſible for the ſame man to have diſtinct incommunicable conſciouſneſſes at different times, it is paſt doubt the ſame man would at different times make different perſons; which, we ſee, is the ſenſe of mankind in the ſolemneſt declaration of their opinions, human laws not puniſhing the *mad man* for the *ſober man's* actions, nor the *ſober man* for what the *mad man* did, thereby making them two perſons: which is ſomewhat explained by our way of ſpeaking *Engliſh*, when we ſay ſuch an one *is not himſelf*, or is *beſides himſelf;* in which phraſes it is inſinuated, as if thoſe who now, or at leaſt firſt uſed them, thought that *ſelf* was changed, the *ſelf*-ſame perſon was no longer in that man.

§ 21. *Difference between Identity of Man and Perſon.* BUT yet it is hard to conceive that Socrates, the ſame individual man, ſhould be two perſons. To help us a little in this, we muſt conſider what is meant by Socrates, or the ſame individual man.

Firſt, It muſt be either the ſame individual, immaterial thinking ſubſtance; in ſhort, the ſame numerical ſoul and nothing elſe.

Secondly, Or the ſame animal, without any regard to an immaterial ſoul.

Thirdly, Or the ſame immaterial ſpirit united to the ſame animal.

Now take which of theſe ſuppoſitions you pleaſe, it is impoſſible to make perſonal identity to conſiſt in any thing but conſciouſneſs, or reach any farther than that does.

For by the firſt of them, it muſt be allowed poſſible, that a man born of different women, and in diſtant times, may be the ſame man; a way of ſpeaking, which whoever admits, muſt allow it poſſible for the ſame man to be two diſtinct perſons, as any two that have lived in different ages, without the knowledge of one another's thoughts.

By the ſecond and third, Socrates in this life, and after it, cannot be the ſame man any way, but by the ſame conſciouſneſs; and ſo making *human identity* to conſiſt in the ſame thing wherein we place *perſonal identity*, there will be no difficulty to allow the ſame man to be the ſame perſon: But then they who place *human identity* in conſciouſneſs only, and not in ſomething elſe, muſt conſider how they will make the infant Socrates the ſame man with Socrates after the reſurrection. But whatſoever to ſome men makes a *man*, and conſequently the ſame individual man, wherein perhaps few are agreed, perſonal identity can by us be placed in nothing but conſciouſneſs (which is that alone which makes what we call *ſelf*) without involving us in great abſurdities.

§ 22.

But is not a man drunk and ſober the ſame perſon? why elſe is he puniſhed for the fact he commits when drunk, though he be never afterwards conſcious of it? Juſt as much the ſame perſon, as a man that walks, and does other things in his ſleep, is the ſame perſon, and is anſwerable for any miſchief he ſhall do in it. Human laws puniſh both with a juſtice ſuitable to their way of knowledge, becauſe in theſe caſes they cannot diſtinguiſh certainly what is real what counterfeit; and ſo the ignorance in drunkenneſs or ſleep, is not admitted as a plea: For though puniſhment be annexed to perſonality, and perſonality to conſciouſneſs, and the drunkard perhaps be not conſcious of what he did; yet human judicatures juſtly puniſh him, becauſe the fact is proved againſt him, but want of conſciouſneſs cannot be proved for him. But in the great day, wherein the ſecrets of all hearts ſhall be laid open, it may be reaſonable to think, no one ſhall be made to anſwer for what he knows nothing of, but ſhall receive his doom, his conſcience accuſing or excuſing him.

§ 23. *Conſciouſneſs alone makes Self.*

Nothing but conſciouſneſs can unite remote exiſtences into the ſame perſon, the identity of ſubſtance will not do it; for whatever ſubſtance there is, however framed, without conſciouſneſs there is no perſon; and a carcaſe may be a perſon, as well as any ſort of ſubſtance be ſo without conſciouſneſs.

Could we ſuppoſe two diſtinct incommunicable conſciouſneſſes acting the ſame body, the one conſtantly by day, the other by night; and, on the other ſide, the ſame conſciouſneſs acting by intervals two diſtinct bodies: I aſk in the firſt caſe, whether the *day* and the *night-man* would not be two as diſtinct perſons, as *Socrates* and *Plato*? And whether, in the ſecond caſe, there would not be one perſon in two diſtinct bodies, as much as one man is the ſame in two diſtinct clothings? Nor is it at all material to ſay, that this ſame, and this diſtinct conſciouſneſs, in the caſes abovementioned, is owing to the ſame and diſtinct immaterial ſubſtances, bringing it with them to thoſe bodies; which, whether true or no, alters not the caſe; ſince it is evident the *perſonal identity* would equally be determined by the conſciouſneſs, whether that conſciouſneſs were annexed to ſome individual immaterial ſubſtance or no: For granting that the thinking ſubſtance in man muſt be neceſſarily ſuppoſed immaterial, it is evident that immaterial thinking thing may ſometimes part with its paſt conſciouſneſs, and be reſtored to it again, as appears in the forgetfulneſs men often have of their paſt actions: and the mind many times recovers the memory of a paſt conſciouſneſs, which it had loſt for twenty years together. Make theſe intervals of memory and forgetfulneſs to take their turns regularly by day and night, and you have two perſons with the ſame immaterial ſpirit, as much as in the former inſtance two perſons with the ſame body: So that *ſelf* is not determined by identity or diverſity of ſubſtance, which it cannot be ſure of, but only by identity of conſciouſneſs.

§ 24.

INDEED it may conceive the ſubſtance, whereof it is now made up, to have exiſted formerly, united in the ſame conſcious being; but conſciouſneſs removed, that ſubſtance is no more it *ſelf*, or makes no more a part of it, than any other ſubſtance; as is evident in the inſtance we have already given of a limb cut off, of whoſe heat, or cold, or other affections, having no longer any conſciouſneſs, it is no more of a man's ſelf, than any other matter of the univerſe. In like manner it will be in reference to any immaterial ſubſtance, which is void of that conſciouſneſs, whereby I am my *ſelf* to my *ſelf*: if there be any part of its exiſtence, which I cannot upon recollection join with that preſent conſciouſneſs whereby I am now my *ſelf*, it is in that part of its exiſtence no more my *ſelf*, than any other immaterial being; for whatſoever any ſubſtance has thought or done, which I cannot recollect, and by my consciousness make my own thought and action, it will no more belong to me, whether a part of me thought or did it, than if it had been thought or done by any other immaterial being any where existing.

§ 25.

I AGREE, the more probable opinion is, that this consciousness is annexed to, and the affection of one individual immaterial substance.

But let men, according to their diverse hypotheses, resolve of that as they please. This every intelligent being, sensible of happiness or misery, must grant, that there is something that is *himself* that he is concerned for, and would have happy; that this *self* has existed in a continued duration more than one instant, and therefore it is possible may exist, as it has done, months and years to come, without any certain bounds to be set to its duration, and may be the same *self*, by the same consciousness continued on for the future: And thus, by this consciousness, he finds himself to be the *same self* which did such or such an action some years since, by which he comes to be happy or miserable now. In all which account of *self*, the same numerical substance is not considered as making the same *self*; but the same continued consciousness, in which several substances may have been united, and again separated from it, which, whilst they continued in a vital union with that, wherein this consciousness then resided, made a part of that same *self*. Thus any part of our bodies vitally united to that which is conscious in us, makes a part of our *selves*: but upon separation from the vital union, by which that consciousness is communicated, that which a moment since was part of our *selves*, is no more so, than a part of another man's *self* is a part of me, and it is not impossible, but in a little time may become a real part of another person; and so we have the same numerical substance become a part of two different persons, and the same person preserved under the change of various substances. Could we suppose any spirit wholly stripped of all its memory or consciousness of paſt actions, as we find our minds always are of a great part of ours, and ſometimes of them all, the union or ſeparation of ſuch a ſpiritual ſubſtance would make no variation of perſonal identity, any more than that of any particle of matter does. Any ſubſtance vitally united to the preſent thinking being, is a part of that very *ſame ſelf* which now is: any thing united to it by a conſciouſneſs of former actions, makes alſo a part of the *ſame ſelf*, which is the ſame both then and now.

§ 26. *Perſon, a Forenſic Term.*

PERSON, as I take it, is the name of this *ſelf*. Wherever a man finds what he calls *himſelf*, there I think another may ſay is the *ſame perſon*. It is a forenſic term appropriating actions and their merit; and ſo belongs only to intelligent agents capable of a law, and happineſs and miſery. This perſonality extends it *ſelf* beyond preſent exiſtence to what is paſt, only by conſciouſneſs, whereby it becomes concerned and accountable, owns and imputes to it *ſelf* paſt actions, juſt upon the ſame ground, and for the ſame reaſon that it does the preſent: All which is founded in a concern for happineſs, the unavoidable concomitant of conſciouſneſs; that which is conſcious of pleaſure and pain, deſiring that that ſelf that is conſcious ſhould be happy. And therefore whatever paſt actions it cannot reconcile or appropriate to that preſent *ſelf* by conſciouſneſs, it can be no more concerned in, than if they had never been done: and to receive pleaſure or pain, *i. e.* reward or puniſhment, on the account of any ſuch action, is all one as to be made happy or miſerable in its firſt being, without any demerit at all: For ſuppoſing a man puniſhed now for what he had done in another life, whereof he could be made to have no conſciouſneſs at all, what difference is there between that puniſhment, and being created miſerable? And therefore conformable to this the Apoſtle tells us, that at the great day, when every one ſhall *receive according to his doings, the ſecrets of all hearts ſhall be laid open*, the ſentence ſhall be juſtified by the conſciouſneſs all perſons ſhall have, that they *themſelves*, in what bodies ſoever they appear, or what ſubſtances ſoever that conſciouſneſs adheres to, are the *ſame* that committed thoſe actions, and deſerve that puniſhment for them.

§ 27.

I AM apt enough to think I have, in treating of this ſubject, made ſome ſuppoſitions that will look ſtrange to ſome readers, and poſſibly they are ſo in themſelves; but yet, I think, they are ſuch as are pardonable in this ignorance we are in of the nature of that thinking thing that is in us, and which we look on as our *ſelves.* Did we know what it was, or how it was tied to a certain ſyſtem of fleeting animal ſpirits; or whether it could or could not perform its operations of thinking and memory out of a body organized as ours is; and whether it has pleaſed God, that no one ſuch ſpirit ſhall ever be united to any but one ſuch body, upon the right conſtitution of whoſe organs its memory ſhould depend; we might ſee the abſurdity of ſome of thoſe ſuppoſitions I have made. But taking, as we ordinarily now do (in the dark concerning theſe matters), the ſoul of a man, for an immaterial ſubſtance, independent from matter, and indifferent alike to it all, there can from the nature of things be no abſurdity at all to ſuppoſe, that the ſame ſoul may, at different times, be united to different bodies, and with them make up, for that time, one man: as well as we ſuppoſe a part of a ſheep's body yeſterday ſhould be a part of a man's body to-morrow, and in that union make up a vital part of *Melibæus* himſelf, as well as it did of his ram.

§ 28. *The Difficulty from ill uſe of Names.*

To conclude, whatever ſubſtance begins to exiſt, it muſt, during its exiſtence, neceſſarily be the ſame; whatever compoſitions of ſubſtances begin to exiſt during the union of thoſe ſubſtances, the concrete muſt be the ſame; whatſoever mode begins to exiſt, during its exiſtence, it is the ſame: and ſo if the compoſition be of diſtinct ſubſtances and different modes, the ſame rule holds. Whereby it will appear, that the difficulty or obſcurity that has been about this matter, rather riſes from the names ill uſed, than from any obſcurity in things themſelves. For whatever makes the ſpecific *idea* to which the name is applied, if that *idea* be ſteadily kept to, the diſtinction of any thing into the ſame, and divers, will eaſily be conceived, and there can ariſe no doubt about it.

§ 29. *Continued Exiſtence makes Identity.*

For ſuppoſing a rational ſpirit be the *idea* of a *man*, it is eaſy to know what is the *ſame man*, viz. the *ſame ſpirit*, whether ſeparate or in a body, will be the *ſame man*. Suppoſing a rational ſpirit vitally united to a body, of a certain conformation of parts to make a *man*, whilſt that rational ſpirit, with that vital conformation of parts, though continued in a fleeting ſucceſſive body, remains, it will be the *ſame man*. But if to any one the *idea* of a *man* be but the vital union of parts in a certain ſhape, as long as that vital union and ſhape remains, in a concrete no otherwiſe the ſame, but by a continued ſucceſſion of fleeting particles, it will be the ſame *man*: For whatever be the compoſition, whereof the complex *idea* is made, whenever exiſtence makes it one particular thing under any denomination, the ſame exiſtence continued, preſerves it the ſame individual under the ſame denomination.

CHAP. XXVIII.

OF OTHER RELATIONS.

§ 1. *Proportional.*

BESIDES the before-mentioned occaſions of time, place, and cauſality of comparing, or referring things one to another, there are, as I have ſaid, infinite others, ſome whereof I ſhall mention.

Firſt, The firſt I ſhall name, is ſome one ſimple *idea*; which being capable of parts or degrees, affords an occaſion of comparing the ſubjects wherein it is to one another, in reſpect of that ſimple *idea*, v. g. *whiter*, *ſweeter*, *bigger*, *equal*, *more*, &c. Theſe relations depending on the equality and exceſs of the ſame ſimple *idea*, in ſeveral ſubjects, may be called, if one will, *proportional*; and that these are only conversant about those simple *ideas* received from sensation or reflection, is so evident, that nothing need be said to evince it.

§ 2. *Natural.*

SECONDLY, Another occasion of comparing things together, or considering one thing, so as to include in that consideration some other thing, is the circumstances of their origin or beginning; which being not afterwards to be altered, make the relations depending thereon as lasting as the subjects to which they belong; *v. g. father* and *son, brothers, cousin-germans,* &c. which have their relations by one community of blood, wherein they partake in several degrees; *country-men, i. e.* those who were born in the same country, or track of ground; and these I call *natural relations:* wherein we may observe that mankind have fitted their notions and words to the use of common life, and not to the truth and extent of things: For it is certain that in reality the relation is the same betwixt the begetter and the begotten, in the several races of other animals as well as men: but yet it is seldom said, this bull is the grandfather of such a calf; or that two pigeons are cousin-germans. It is very convenient, that by distinct names these relations should be observed and marked out in mankind; there being occasion, both in laws, and other communications one with another, to mention and take notice of men under these relations: from whence also arise the obligations of several duties amongst men. Whereas in brutes, men having very little or no cause to mind these relations, they have not thought fit to give them distinct and peculiar names. This, by the way, may give us some light into the different state and growth of languages; which being suited only to the convenience of communication, are proportioned to the notions men have, and the commerce of thoughts familiar amongst them, and not to the reality or extent of things, nor to the various respects might be found among them, nor the different abstract considerations might be framed about them. Where they had no philosophical notions, there they had no terms to express them; and it is no wonder men should have framed no names for thofe things they found no occafion to difcourfe of: From whence it is eafy to imagine why, as in fome countries, they may not have fo much as the name for a horfe; and in others, where they are more careful of the pedigrees of their horfes than of their own, that there they may have not only names for particular horfes, but alfo of their feveral relations of kindred one to another.

§ 3. *Inftituted.*

THIRDLY, Sometimes the foundation of confidering things, with reference to one another, is fome act whereby any one comes by a moral right, power, or obligation to do fomething. Thus a *general* is one that hath power to command an army; and an army under a general is a collection of armed men obliged to obey one man. A *citizen*, or a *burgher*, is one who has a right to certain privileges in this or that place. All this fort depending upon mens wills, or agreement in fociety, I call *inftituted* or *voluntary*; and may be diftinguifhed from the natural, in that they are moft, if not all of them, fome way or other alterable, and feparable from the perfons to whom they have fometimes belonged, though neither of the fubftances, fo related, be deftroyed. Now, though thefe are all reciprocal, as well as the reft, and contain in them a reference of two things one to the other; yet, becaufe one of the two things often wants a relative name, importing that reference, men ufually take no notice of it, and the relation is commonly overlooked: *v. g.* a *patron* and *client* are eafily allowed to be relations, but a *conftable* or *dictator*, are not fo readily, at firft hearing, confidered as fuch; becaufe there is no peculiar name for thofe who are under the command of a dictator, or conftable, expreffing a relation to either of them; though it be certain, that either of them hath a certain power over fome others; and fo is fo far related to them, as well as a patron is to his client, or general to his army.

§ 4. *Moral.*

FOURTHLY, There is another fort of relation, which is the conformity, or difagreement, mens voluntary actions have to a rule to which they are referred, and by whic they are judged of; which, I think, may be called *Mo ral* relation, as being that which denominates our mor actions, and deserves well to be examined, there bein no part of knowledge wherein we should be more care ful to get determined *ideas*, and avoid, as much as ma be, obscurity and confusion. Human actions, whe with their various ends, objects, manners, and circum stances, they are framed into distinct complex *ideas*, are as has been shown, so many *mixed modes*, a great pai whereof have names annexed to them. Thus, supposin gratitude to be a readiness to acknowledge and retur kindness received, polygamy to be the having mor wives than one at once; when we frame these notion thus in our minds, we have there so many determine *ideas* of mixed modes: But this is not all that concern our actions; it is not enough to have determined *idea* of them, and to know what names belong to such an such combinations of *ideas*; we have a farther an greater concernment, and that is, to know whether suc actions so made up are morally good or bad.

§ 5. *Moral Good and Evil.*

Good and evil, as hath been shown, B. II. Ch. 20. § 2 and Ch 21. § 42. are nothing but pleasure or pain, c that which occasions, or procures pleasure or pain to us Moral good and evil then is only the conformity or dis agreement of our voluntary actions to some law, where by good or evil is drawn on us by the will and powe of the law-maker; which good and evil, pleasure c pain, attending our observance, or breach of the law, b the decree of the law-maker, is that we call reward an punishment.

§ 6. *Moral Rules.*

Of these moral rules, or laws, to which men generall refer, and by which they judge of the rectitude or pra vity of their actions, there seem to me to be *three sort* with their three different enforcements, or rewards an punishments: For since it would be utterly in vain t suppose a rule set to the free actions of man, withou annexing to it some enforcement of good and evil to de termine his will, we muſt, wherever we ſuppoſe a law, ſuppoſe alſo ſome reward or puniſhment annexed to that law. It would be in vain for one intelligent being to ſet a rule to the actions of another, if he had it not in his power to reward the compliance with, and puniſh deviation from his rule, by ſome good and evil, that is not the natural product and conſequence of the action itſelf; for that being a natural convenience, or inconvenience, would operate of itſelf without a law: This, if I miſtake not, is the true nature of all *law*, properly ſo called.

§ 7. *Laws.*

THE laws that men generally refer their actions to, to judge of their rectitude or obliquity, ſeem to me to be theſe three: 1. The divine law; 2. The civil law; 3. The law of *opinion* or *reputation*, if I may ſo call it. By the relation they bear to the firſt of theſe, men judge whether their actions are ſins or duties; by the ſecond, whether they be criminal or innocent; and by the third, whether they be virtues or vices.

§ 8. *Divine Law, the Meaſure of Sin and Duty.*

FIRST, The *divine* law, whereby I mean that law which God has ſet to the actions of men, whether promulgated to them by the light of nature or the voice of revelation. That God has given a rule whereby men ſhould govern themſelves, I think there is nobody ſo brutiſh as to deny: He has a right to do it; we are his creatures: He has goodneſs and wiſdom to direct our actions to that which is beſt; and he has a power to inforce it by rewards and puniſhments, of infinite weight and duration, in another life; for nobody can take us out of his hands. This is the only true touchſtone of *moral rectitude*, and by comparing them to this law, it is that men judge of the moſt conſiderable *moral good* or *evil* of their actions; that is, whether as *duties* or *ſins* they are like to procure them happineſs or miſery from the hands of the Almighty.

§ 9. *Civil Law, the Meaſure of Crimes and Innocence.*

SECONDLY, The *civil* law, the rule ſet by the commonwealth to the actions of thoſe who belong to it, is another rule to which men refer their actions, to judge whether they be *criminal* or no; this law nobody overlooks; the rewards and punishments that inforce it being ready at hand, and suitable to the power that makes it, which is the force of the commonwealth, engaged to protect the lives, liberties, and possessions of those who live according to its laws, and has power to take away life, liberty, or goods from him who disobeys; which is the punishment of offences committed against this law.

§ 10. *Philosophical Law, the Measure of Virtue and Vice.*

THIRDLY, The *law of opinion or reputation.* Virtue and vice are names pretended and supposed every where to stand for actions in their own nature right or wrong; and as far as they really are so applied, they so far are coincident with the *divine law* above mentioned: But yet whatever is pretended, this is visible, that these names *Virtue* and *Vice*, in the particular instances of their application, through the several nations and societies of men in the world, are constantly attributed only to such actions, as in each country and society are in reputation or discredit: Nor is it to be thought strange, that men every where should give the name of *Virtue* to those actions, which amongst them are judged praiseworthy, and call that *Vice*, which they account blameable; since otherwise they would condemn themselves, if they should think any thing *right*, to which they allowed not commendation, any thing *wrong*, which they let pass without blame. Thus the measure of what is every where called and esteemed *Virtue* and *Vice*, is this approbation of dislike, praise, or blame, which by a secret and tacit consent establishes itself in the several societies, tribes, and clubs of men in the world; whereby several actions come to find credit or disgrace amongst them, according to the judgment, maxims, or fashions of that place: For though men, uniting into politic societies, have resigned up to the public the disposing of all their force, so that they cannot employ it against any fellow-citizens any farther than the law of the country directs, yet they retain still the power of thinking well or ill, approving or disapproving of the actions of those whom they live amongst, and converse with: And by this approbation and dislike, they establish among themselves what they will call *Virtue* and *Vice*.

§ 11.

THAT this is the common *measure of virtue and vice*, will appear to any one who considers, that though that passes for *vice* in one country, which is counted a *virtue*, or at least not *vice* in another, yet every where *virtue* and praise, *vice* and blame go together. *Virtue* is every where that which is thought praise-worthy; and nothing else but that which has the allowance of public esteem, is called *Virtue**. *Virtue* and praise are so united, that they

* *Our author, in his preface to the fourth edition, taking notice how apt men have been to mistake him, added what here follows:* Of this the ingenious author of the *Discourse concerning the Nature of Man* has given me a late instance, to mention no other. For the civility of his expressions, and the candour that belongs to his order, forbid me to think, that he would have closed his preface with an insinuation, as if in what I had said, *Book II. Chap.* 28. concerning the third rule which men refer their actions to, I went about to make *virtue vice*, and *vice virtue*, unless he had mistaken my meaning, which he could not have done, if he had but given himself the trouble to consider what the argument was I was then upon, and what was the chief design of that chapter, plainly enough set down in the fourth section, and those following. For I was there not laying down moral rules, but showing the original and nature of moral *ideas*, and enumerating the rules men make use of in moral relations, whether those rules were true or false; and pursuant thereunto, I tell what has every where that denomination, which in the language of that place answers to *virtue* and *vice* in ours, which *alters not the nature of things*, though men do generally judge of, and denominate their actions according to the esteem and fashion of the place, or sect they are of.

If he had been at the pains to reflect on what I had said, *B.* I. *c.* 3. § 18. and in this present chapter, § 13, 14, 15, and 20. he would have known what I think of the eternal and unalterable nature of right and wrong, and what I call *virtue* and *vice*, and if he had observed, that in the place he quotes, I only report, as matter of fact, what others call *virtue* and *vice*, he would not have found it liable to any great exception: For I think I am not much out in saying, that one of the rules made use of in the world for a ground or measure of a moral relation, is that esteem and reputation which several sorts of actions find variously in the several societies of men, according to which they are called *virtues* or *vices*; and whatever authority the learned Mr. *Lowde* places in his *Old English Dictionary*, I dare say it no where tells him (if I should are called often by the same name. *Sunt sua præmia laudi*, says *Virgil*; and so *Cicero*, *Nihil habet natura præstantius, quam honestatem, quam laudem, quam dignitatem*,

appeal to it) that the same action is not in credit, called and counted a *virtue* in one place, which being in disrepute, passes for and under the name of *vice* in another. The taking notice that men bestow the names of *virtue* and *vice* according to this rule of reputation, is all I have done, or can be laid to my charge to have done, towards making *vice virtue*, and *virtue vice*: But the good man does well, and as becomes his calling, to be watchful in such points, and to take the alarm, even at expressions, which standing alone by themselves might sound ill, and be suspected.

It is to this zeal, allowable in his function, that I forgive his citing, as he does these words of mine, in § 11. of this chapter: *The exhortations of inspired teachers have not feared to appeal to common repute; whatsoever things are lovely, whatsoever things are of good report, if there be any virtue, if there be any praise*, &c. Phil. iv. 8. without taking notice of those immediately preceding, which introduce them, run thus: *Whereby in the corruption of manners, the true boundaries of the law of nature, which ought to be the rule of virtue and vice, were pretty well preserved; so that even the exhortations of inspired teachers*, &c. By which words, and the rest of that section, it is plain that I brought that passage of St. *Paul*, not to prove that the general measure of what men call *virtue* and *vice*, throughout the world, was the reputation and fashion of each particular society within itself; but to show, that though it were so, yet, for reasons I there give, men, in that way of denominating their actions, did not for the most part much vary from the law of nature; which is that standing and unalterable rule, by which they ought to judge of the moral rectitude and pravity of their actions, and accordingly denominate them *virtues* or *vices*. Had Mr. *Lowde* considered this, he would have found it little to his purpose, to have quoted that passage in a sense I used it not; and would, I imagine, have spared the explication he subjoins to it, as not very necessary. But I hope this second edition will give him satisfaction in the point, and that this matter is now so expressed, as to show him there was no cause of scruple.

Though I am forced to differ from him in those apprehensions he has expressed in the latter end of his preface, concerning what I had said about *virtue* and *vice*, yet we are better agreed than he thinks, in what he says in his third chapter, p. 78. concerning *natural inscription* and *innate notions*. I shall not deny him the privilege he claims, p. 52. to state the question as he pleases, especially when he states it so as to leave nothing in it contrary to what I have said: For, according to him, *innate notions being conditional things, depending upon the concurrence of several other circumstances, in order to the soul's exerting them*, all that he says for *innate, imprinted, impressed notions* (for of *innate ideas* he says nothing at all) amounts at last only to this; that there are certain propositions, which though the soul from the beginning, or when a man is born, does not know, yet by *assistance from the outward senses, and the help of some previous cultivation*, it may afterwards come certainly to know the truth of; which is no more than what I have affirmed in my first book: For I suppose, by the *soul's* exerting them, he means its be-

quam decus; which, he tells, you, are all names for the ſame thing, *Tuſc. l.* 2. This is the language of the heathen philoſophers, who well underſtood wherein their notions of *virtue* and *vice* conſiſted. And though perhaps, by the different temper, education, faſhion, maxims, or intereſt of different ſorts of men, it fell out that what was thought praiſe-worthy in one place, eſcaped not cenſure in another; and ſo in different ſocieties, *virtues* and *vices* were changed; yet, as to the main, they for the moſt part kept the ſame every where: For ſince nothing can be more natural, than to encourage with eſteem and reputation that wherein every one finds his advantage, and to blame and diſcountenance the contrary; it is no wonder, that eſteem and diſcredit, virtue and vice, ſhould in a great meaſure every where correſpond with the unchangeable rule of right or wrong, which the law of God hath eſtabliſhed; there being nothing that ſo directly and viſibly ſecures and advances the general good of mankind, in this world, as obedience to the laws he has ſet them; and nothing that breeds ſuch miſchiefs and confuſion, as the neglect of them: And therefore men, without renouncing all

ginning to know them, or elſe the *ſoul's exerting of notions* will be to me a very unintelligible expreſſion, and I think at beſt is a very unfit one in this caſe, it miſleading mens thoughts by an inſinuation, as if theſe notions were in the mind before the *ſoul exerts them*, i. e before they are known; whereas truly before they are known, there is nothing of them in the mind but a capacity to know them, when the *concurrence of thoſe circumſtances*, which this ingenious author thinks neceſſary *in order to the ſoul's exerting them*, brings them into our knowledge.

P. 52. I find him expreſs it thus: *Theſe natural notions are not ſo imprinted upon the ſoul, as that they naturally and neceſſarily exert themſelves (even in children and idiots) without any aſſiſtance from the outward ſenſes, or without the help of ſome previous cultivation.* Here he ſays *they exert themſelves*, as p. 78. that the *ſoul exerts them.* When he has explained to himſelf or others, what he means by the *ſoul's exerting innate notions*, or *their exerting themſelves*, and what that *previous cultivation*, and *circumſtances, in order* to their being *exerted*, are, he will, I ſuppoſe, find there is ſo little of controverſy between him and me in the point, bating that he calls that *exerting of notions*, which I in a more vulgar ſtyle call *knowing*, that I have reaſon to think he brought in my name upon this occaſion, only out of the pleaſure he has to ſpeak civilly of me; which I muſt gratefully acknowledge he has done every where he mentions me, not without conferring on me, as ſome others have done, a title I have no right to.

ſenſe and reaſon, and their own intereſt, which they are ſo conſtantly true to, could not generally miſtake in placing their commendation and blame on that ſide that really deſerved it not: Nay, even thoſe men, whoſe practice was otherwiſe, failed not to give their approbation right; few being depraved to that degree, as not to condemn, at leaſt in others, the faults they themſelves were guilty of; whereby, even in the corruption of manners, the true boundaries of the law of nature, which ought to be the rule of virtue and vice, were pretty well preſerved: So that even the exhortations of inſpired teachers have not feared to appeal to common repute: *Whatſoever is lovely, whatſoever is of good report, if there be any virtue, if there be any praiſe*, &c. Phil. iv. 8.

§ 12. *Its Inforcements, Commendation, and Diſcredit.*

If any one ſhall imagine that I have forgot my own notion of a law, when I make the *law*, whereby men judge of *virtue* and *vice*, to be nothing elſe but the conſent of private men, who have not authority enough to make a law; eſpecially wanting that which is ſo neceſſary and eſſential to a law, a power to inforce it; I think I may ſay, that he who imagines commendation and diſgrace not to be ſtrong motives on men, to accommodate themſelves to the opinions and rules of thoſe with whom they converſe, ſeems little ſkilled in the nature or hiſtory of mankind, the greateſt part whereof he ſhall find to govern themſelves chiefly, if not ſolely, by this law of faſhion; and ſo they do that which keeps them in reputation with their company, little regarding the laws of God, or the magiſtrate. The penalties that attend the breach of God's laws, ſome, nay perhaps moſt men, ſeldom ſeriouſly reflect on; and amongſt thoſe that do, many, whilſt they break that law, entertain thoughts of future reconciliation, and making their peace for ſuch breaches: And as to the puniſhments due from the laws of the commonwealth, they frequently flatter themſelves with the hopes of impunity; but no man eſcapes the puniſhment of their cenſure and diſlike, who offends againſt the faſhion and opinion of the company he keeps, and would recommend himſelf to; nor is there one of ten thousand, who is stiff and insensible enough to bear up under the constant dislike and condemnation of his own club. He must be of a strange and unusual constitution who can content himself to live in constant disgrace and disrepute with his own particular society. Solitude many men have sought, and been reconciled to; but nobody, that has the least thought or sense of a man about him, can live in society under the constant dislike and ill opinion of his familiars, and those he converses with: This is a burden too heavy for human sufferance: And he must be made up of irreconcileable contradictions, who can take pleasure in company, and yet be insensible of contempt and disgrace from his companions.

§ 13. *These three Laws the Rules of Moral Good and Evil.* THESE three then, *First*, the law of God; *Secondly*, The law of politic societies; *Thirdly*, the law of fashion or private censure, are those to which men variously compare their actions: And it is by their conformity to one of these laws, that they take their measures, when they would judge of their moral rectitude, and denominate their actions good or bad.

§ 14. *Morality is the Relation of Actions to these Rules.* WHETHER the rule, to which, as to a touchstone, we bring our voluntary actions to examine them by, and try their goodness, and accordingly to name them, which is, as it were, the mark of the value we set upon them; whether, I say, we take that rule from the fashion of the country, or the will of a law-maker, the mind is easily able to observe the relation any action hath to it, and to judge whether the action agrees or disagrees with the rule; and so hath a notion of *moral goodness* or *evil*, which is either conformity or not conformity of any action to that rule; and therefore is often called moral rectitude. This rule being nothing but a collection of several simple *ideas*, the conformity thereto is but so ordering the action, that the simple *ideas* belonging to it may correspond to those which the law requires; And thus we see how moral beings and notions are founded on, and terminated in these simple *ideas* we have received from ſenſation or reflection. For example, let us conſider the complex *idea* we ſignify by the word murder; and when we have taken it aſunder, and examined all the particulars, we ſhall find them to amount to a collection of ſimple *ideas* derived from reflection or ſenſation, *viz.* *Firſt*, From reflection on the operations of our minds, we have the *ideas* of willing, conſidering, purpoſing before-hand, malice, or wiſhing ill to another; and alſo of life, or perception, and ſelf-motion. *Secondly*, From ſenſation we have the collection of thoſe ſimple ſenſible *ideas* which are to be found in a man, and of ſome action, whereby we put an end to perception and motion in the man; all which ſimple *ideas* are comprehended in the word murder. This collection of ſimple *ideas* being found by me to agree or diſagree with the eſteem of the country I have been bred in, and to be held by moſt men there worthy praiſe or blame, I call the action virtuous or vicious: If I have the will of a ſupreme inviſible law-maker for my rule; then, as I ſuppoſed the action commanded or forbidden by God, I call it good or evil, ſin or duty: And if I compare it to the civil law, the rule made by the legiſlative power of the country, I call it lawful or unlawful, a crime or no crime. So that whenceſoever we take the rule of moral actions, or by what ſtandard ſoever we frame in our minds the *ideas* of virtues or vices, they conſiſt only, and are made up of collections of ſimple *ideas*, which we originally received from ſenſe or reflection; and their rectitude or obliquity conſiſts in the agreement or diſagreement with thoſe patterns preſcribed by ſome law.

§ 15.

To conceive rightly of *moral actions*, we muſt take notice of them under this twofold conſideration. *Firſt*, as they are in themſelves each made up of ſuch a collection of ſimple *ideas*. Thus *drunkenneſs*, or *lying*, ſignify ſuch or ſuch a collection of ſimple *ideas*, which I call mixed modes; and in this ſenſe they are as much *poſitive abſolute ideas*, as the drinking of a horſe, or ſpeaking of a parrot. *Secondly*, our actions are conſidered as good, bad, or indifferent; and in this reſpect they are *relative*, it being their conformity to, or difagreement with fome rule that makes them to be regular or irregular, good or bad; and fo, as far as they are compared with a rule, and thereupon denominated, they come under relation. Thus the challenging and fighting with a man, as it is a certain pofitive mode, or particular fort of action, by particular *ideas*, diftinguifhed from all others, is called *duelling*; which when confidered, in relation to the law of God, will deferve the name fin; to the law of fafhion, in fome countries, valour and virtue; and to the municipal laws of fome governments, a capital crime. In this cafe, when the pofitive mode has one name, and another name as it ftands in relation to the law, the diftinction may as eafily be obferved, as it is in fubftances, where one name, *v. g. man*, is ufed to fignify the thing; another, *v. g. father*, to fignify the relation.

§ 16. *The Denominations of Actions often miflead us.* BUT becaufe very frequently the pofitive *idea* of the action, and its moral relation, are comprehended together under one name, and the fame word made ufe of to exprefs both the mode or action, and its moral rectitude or obliquity; therefore the relation itfelf is lefs taken notice of, and there is often no *diftinction* made *between the pofitive* idea of the action, *and the reference it has to a rule.* By which confufion of thefe two diftinct confiderations under one term, thofe who yield too eafily to the impreffions of founds, and are forward to take names for things, are often mifled in their judgment of actions. Thus, the taking from another what is his, without his knowledge or allowance, is properly called *ftealing*; but that name being commonly underftood to fignify alfo the moral pravity of the action, and to denote its contrariety to the law, men are apt to condemn whatever they hear called ftealing, as an ill action, difagreeing with the rule of right. And yet the private taking away his fword from a madman, to prevent his doing mifchief, though it be properly denominated *ftealing*, as the name of fuch a *mixed mode*, yet when compared to the law of God, and confidered in its relation to that fupreme rule, it is no ſin or tranſgreſſion, though the name *ſtealing* ordinarily carries ſuch an intimation with it.

§ 17. *Relations innumerable.*

AND thus much for the relation of human actions to a law, which therefore I call *moral relations.*

It would make a volume to go over all ſorts of *relations;* it is not therefore to be expected, that I ſhould here mention them all. It ſuffices to our preſent purpoſe, to ſhow by theſe, what the *ideas* are we have of this comprehenſive conſideration, called *relation:* Which is ſo *various,* and the occaſions of it ſo *many,* (as many as there can be of comparing things one to another) that it is not very eaſy to reduce it to rules, or under juſt heads. Thoſe I have mentioned, I think, are ſome of the moſt conſiderable, and ſuch as may ſerve to let us ſee from whence we get our *ideas* of relations, and wherein they are founded. But before I quit this argument, from what has been ſaid, give me leave to obſerve:

§ 18. *All Relations terminate in ſimple* Ideas.

FIRST, that it is evident, that *all relation terminates in,* and is ultimately founded on thoſe *ſimple ideas* we have *got from ſenſation or reflection;* ſo that all we have in our thoughts ourſelves, (if we think of any thing, or have any meaning) or would ſignify to others, when we uſe words ſtanding for relations, is nothing but ſome ſimple *ideas,* or collections of ſimple *ideas,* compared one with another: This is ſo manifeſt in that ſort called *proportional,* that nothing can be more; for when a man ſays, honey is ſweeter than wax, it is plain that his thoughts in this relation terminate in this ſimple *idea,* ſweetneſs; which is equally true of all the reſt, though where they are compounded or decompounded, the ſimple *ideas* they are made up of, are, perhaps, ſeldom taken notice of; *v. g.* when the word father is mentioned; *firſt,* there is meant that particular ſpecies, or collective *idea,* ſignified by the word man; *ſecondly,* thoſe ſimple *ideas* ſignified by the word generation; and *thirdly,* the effects of it, and all the ſimple *ideas* ſignified by the word child. So the word friend being taken for a man who loves, and is ready to do good to another, has all these following *ideas* to the making of it up; *first*, All the simple *ideas* comprehended in the word man, or intelligent being; *secondly*, The *idea* of love; *thirdly*, The *idea* of readiness or disposition; *fourthly*, The *idea* of action, which is any kind of thought or motion; *fifthly*, The *idea* of good, which signifies any thing that may advance his happiness, and terminates at last, if examined, in particular simple *ideas*; of which the word *good* in general signifies any one, but if removed from all simple *ideas* quite, it signifies nothing at all. And thus also all moral words terminate at last, though perhaps more remotely, in a collection of simple *ideas*; the immediate signification of relative words, being very often other supposed known relations, which, if traced one to another, still end in simple *ideas*.

§ 19. *We have ordinarily as clear (or clearer) a Notion of the Relation as of its Foundation.*

SECONDLY, That in relations, we have for the most part, if not always, *as clear a notion of the relation, as we have of those simple* ideas *wherein it is founded*; agreement or disagreement, whereon relation depends, being things whereof we have commonly as clear *ideas*, as of any other whatsoever; it being but the distinguishing simple *ideas*, or their degrees one from another, without which we could have no distinct knowledge at all: For if I have a clear *idea* of sweetness, light or extension, I have too, of equal, or more or less of each of these: If I know what it is for one man to be born of a woman, *viz*. *Sempronia*, I know what it is for another man to be born of the same woman, *Sempronia*; and so have as clear a notion of brothers as of births, and perhaps clearer: For if I believed that *Sempronia* dug *Titus* out of the parsley-bed (as they use to tell children) and thereby became his mother; and that afterwards, in the same manner, she dug *Caius* out of the parsley-bed, I had as clear a notion of the relation of brothers between them, as if I had all the skill of a midwife: the notion that the same woman contributed, as mother, equally to their births (though I were ignorant or mistaken in the manner of it) being that on which I grounded the relation, and that they agreed in that circumſtance of birth, let it be what it will. The comparing them then in their deſcent from the ſame perſon, without knowing the particular circumſtances of that deſcent, is enough to found my notion of their having or not having the relation of brothers: But though the *ideas* of particular *relations* are capable of being as clear and diſtinct in the minds of thoſe who will duly conſider them, as thoſe of mixed modes, and more determinate than thoſe of ſubſtances, yet the names belonging to *relation* are often of as doubtful and uncertain ſignification, as thoſe of ſubſtances or mixed modes, and much more than thoſe of ſimple *ideas*; becauſe relative words being the marks of this compariſon which is made only by mens thoughts, and is an *idea* only in mens minds, men frequently apply them to different compariſons of things, according to their own imaginations, which do not always correſpond with thoſe of others uſing the ſame names.

§ 20. *The Notion of the Relation is the ſame, whether the Rule any Action is compared to be true or falſe.*

THIRDLY, That in theſe I call *moral relations*, I have a true notion of relation, by comparing the action with the rule, whether the rule be true or falſe: For if I meaſure any thing by a yard, I know whether the thing I meaſure be longer or ſhorter than that ſuppoſed yard, though perhaps the yard I meaſure by be not exactly the ſtandard; which indeed is another inquiry: For though the rule be erroneous, and I miſtaken in it, yet the agreement or diſagreement obſervable in that which I compare with it, makes me perceive the relation; though meaſuring by a wrong rule, I ſhall thereby be brought to judge amiſs of its moral rectitude, becauſe I have tried it by that which is not the true rule; but I am not miſtaken in the relation which that action bears to that rule I compare it to, which is agreement or diſagreement.

CHAP. XXIX.

OF CLEAR AND OBSCURE, DISTINCT AND CONFUSED IDEAS.

§ 1. Ideas *some clear and distinct, others obscure and confused.*

HAVING shown the original of our *ideas*, and taken a view of their several sorts, considered the difference between the simple and the complex, and observed how the complex ones are divided into those of modes, substances, and relations; all which, I think, is necessary to be done by any one who would acquaint himself thoroughly with the progress of the mind in its apprehension and knowledge of things; it will perhaps be thought I have dwelt long enough upon the examination of *ideas*. I must, nevertheless, crave leave to offer some few other considerations concerning them. The first is, that some are *clear* and others *obscure*; some *distinct* and others *confused*.

§ 2. *Clear and obscure, explained by Sight.*

THE perception of the mind being most aptly explained by words relating to the sight, we shall best understand what is meant by *clear* and *obscure* in our *ideas*, by reflecting on what we call *clear* and *obscure* in the objects of sight. Light being that which discovers to us visible objects, we give the name of *obscure* to that which is not placed in a light sufficient to discover minutely to us the figure and colours which are observable in it, and which, in a better light, would be discernible: In like manner, our *simple ideas* are *clear*, when they are such as the objects themselves, from whence they were taken, did or might, in a well-ordered sensation or perception, present them. Whilst the memory retains them thus, and can produce them to the mind, whenever it has occasion to consider them, they are *clear ideas*; so far as they either want any thing of that original exactness, or have lost any of their first freshness, and are, as it were, faded or tarnished by time, so far are they *obscure*.

Complex ideas, as they are made up of ſimple ones, ſo they are *clear*, when the *ideas* that go to their compoſition are clear; and the number and order of thoſe ſimple *ideas*, that are the ingredients of any complex one, is determinate and certain.

§ 3. *Cauſes of Obſcurity.*

THE *cauſes* of *obſcurity* in ſimple *ideas*, ſeem to be either dull organs, or very ſlight and tranſient impreſſions made by the objects, or elſe a weakneſs in the memory not able to retain them as received: For to return again to viſible objects, to help us to apprehend this matter; if the organs or faculties of perception, like wax over-hardened with cold, will not receive the impreſſion of the ſeal, from the uſual impulſe wont to imprint it; or, like wax of a temper too ſoft, will not hold it well when well imprinted; or elſe ſuppoſing the wax of a temper fit, but the ſeal not applied with a ſufficient force to make a clear impreſſion; in any of theſe caſes, the print left by the ſeal will be *obſcure*: This, I ſuppoſe, needs no application to make it plainer.

§ 4. *Diſtinct and Confuſed, what.*

As a *clear idea* is that whereof the mind has ſuch a full and evident perception, as it does receive from an outward object operating duly on a well-diſpoſed organ, ſo a *diſtinct idea* is that wherein the mind perceives a difference from all other; and a *confuſed idea* is ſuch an one, as is not ſufficiently diſtinguiſhable from another, from which it ought to be different.

§ 5. *Objection.*

IF no *idea* be *confuſed* but ſuch as is not ſufficiently diſtinguiſhable from another, from which it ſhould be different, it will be hard, may any one ſay, to find any where a *confuſed idea*; for let any *idea* be as it will, it can be no other but ſuch as the mind perceives it to be, and that very perception ſufficiently diſtinguiſhes it from all other *ideas*, which cannot be other, *i. e.* different, without being perceived to be ſo. No *idea* therefore can be undiſtinguiſhable from another, from which it ought to be different, unleſs you would have it different from itſelf; for from all other it is evidently different.

§ 6. *Confuſion of* Ideas, *is in reference to their Names.*

To remove this difficulty, and to help us to conceive aright what it is that makes the *confuſion ideas* are at any time chargeable with, we muſt conſider that things ranked under diſtinct names, are ſuppoſed different enough to be diſtinguiſhed, that ſo each ſort by its peculiar name may be marked and diſcourſed of apart upon any occaſion; and there is nothing more evident, than that the greateſt part of different names are ſuppoſed to ſtand for different things. Now, every *idea* a man has, being viſibly what it is, and diſtinct from all other *ideas* but itſelf, that which makes it *confuſed* is, when it is ſuch, that it may as well be called by another name, as that which it is expreſſed by. the difference which keeps the things (to be ranked under thoſe two different names) diſtinct, and makes ſome of them belong rather to the one, and ſome of them to the other of thoſe names, being left out; and ſo the diſtinction, which was intended to be kept up by thoſe different names, is quite loſt.

§ 7. *Defaults which make Confuſion.*

The *defaults which* uſually *occaſion* this *confuſion*, I think, are chiefly theſe following:

Firſt, complex Ideas *made up of too few ſimple ones.*

First, When any complex *idea* (for it is complex *ideas* that are moſt liable to confuſion) is made up of *too ſmall a number of ſimple ideas*, and ſuch only as are common to other things, whereby the differences that make it deſerve a different name, are left out. Thus he that has an *idea* made up of barely the ſimple ones of a beaſt with ſpots, has but a confuſed *idea* of a leopard; it not being thereby ſufficiently diſtinguiſhed from a lynx, and ſeveral other ſorts of beaſts that are ſpotted: So that ſuch an *idea*, though it hath the peculiar name leopard, is not diſtinguiſhable from thoſe deſigned by the names lynx or panther, and may as well come under the name lynx as leopard. How much the cuſtom of defining of words by general terms, contributes to make the *ideas* we would expreſs by them confuſed and undetermined, I leave others to conſider: This is evident, that confuſed *ideas*, are ſuch as render the uſe of words uncertain, and take away the benefit of distinct names; when the *ideas*, for which we use different terms, have not a difference answerable to their distinct names, and so cannot be distinguished by them, there it is that they are truly confused.

§ 8. *Secondly, or its simple ones jumbled disorderly together.*

SECONDLY, Another default which makes our *ideas* confused, is, when though the particulars that make up any *idea* are in number enough, yet they are so *jumbled together*, that it is not easily discernible, whether it more belongs to the name that is given it, than to any other. There is nothing properer to make us conceive this confusion, than a sort of pictures usually shown as surprising pieces of art, wherein the colours, as they are laid by the pencil on the table itself, mark out very odd and unusual figures, and have no discernible order in their position. This draught, thus made up of parts wherein no symmetry nor order appears, is in itself no more a confused thing, than the picture of a cloudy sky, wherein though there be as little order of colours or figures to be found, yet nobody thinks it a confused picture. What is it then that makes it be thought confused, since the want of symmetry does not? as it is plain it does not; for another draught made, barely in imitation of this could not be called confused. I answer, That which makes it be thought confused, is, the applying it to some name, to which it does no more discernibly belong, than to some other: *v. g.* When it is said to be the picture of a man, or *Cæsar*, then any one with reason counts it confused; because it is not discernible, in that state, to belong more to the name man, or *Cæsar*, than to the name baboon, or *Pompey*, which are supposed to stand for different *ideas* from those signified by man or *Cæsar*: But when a cylindrical mirror placed right, hath reduced those irregular lines on the table into their due order and proportion, then the confusion ceases, and the eye presently sees that it is a man, or *Cæsar*, i. e. that it belongs to those names, and that it is sufficiently distinguishable from a baboon, or *Pompey*, i. e.

from the *ideas* signified by those names. Just thus it is with our *ideas*, which are as it were the pictures of things. No one of these mental draughts, however the parts are put together, can be called confused (for they are plainly discernible as they are) till it be ranked under some ordinary name, to which it cannot be discerned to belong, any more than it does to some other name of an allowed different signification.

§ 9. *Thirdly, or are mutable and undetermined.*

THIRDLY, A third defect that frequently gives the name of confused to our *ideas*, is, when any one of them is *uncertain* and *undetermined*. Thus we may observe men, who not forbearing to use the ordinary words of their language, till they have learned their precise signification, change the *idea* they make this or that term stand for, almost as often as they use it: He that does this out of uncertainty of what he should leave out, or put into his *idea* of *church* or *idolatry*, every time he thinks of either, and holds not steady to any one precise combination of *ideas* that makes it up, is said to have a confused *idea* of idolatry or the church; though this be still for the same reason that the former, *viz.* because a mutable *idea* (if we will allow it to be one *idea*) cannot belong to one name rather than another, and so loses the distinction that distinct names are designed for.

§ 10. *Confusion without reference to Names, hardly conceivable.*

BY what has been said, we may observe how much names, as supposed steady signs of things, and by their difference to stand for and keep things distinct that in themselves are different, are the *occasion of denominating* ideas *distinct or confused*, by a secret and unobserved reference the mind makes of its *ideas* to such names. This perhaps will be fuller understood, after what I say of words, in the third book, has been read and considered: But without taking notice of such a reference of *ideas*, to distinct names as the signs of distinct things, it will be hard to say what a *confused idea* is; and therefore when a man designs, by any name, a sort of things, or any one particular thing, distinct from all others, the complex *idea* he annexes to that name, is the more distinct, the more particular the *ideas* are, and the greater and more determinate the number and order of them is, whereof it is made up; for the more it has of these, the more has it still of the perceivable differences, whereby it is kept separate and distinct from all *ideas* belonging to other names, even those that approach nearest to it, and thereby all confusion with them is avoided.

§ 11. *Confusion concerns always two* Ideas.

CONFUSION, making it a difficulty to separate two things that should be separated, *concerns always two ideas;* and those most, which most approach one another: Whenever therefore, we suspect any *idea* to be *confused*, we must examine what other it is in danger to be confounded with, or which it cannot easily be separated from; and that will always be found an *idea* belonging to another name, and so should be a different thing; from which yet it is not sufficiently distinct, being either the same with it, or making a part of it, or at least as properly called by that name, as the other it is ranked under; and so keeps not that difference from that other *idea* which the different names import.

§ 12. *Causes of Confusion.*

THIS, I think, is the *confusion* proper to *ideas*, which still carries with it a secret reference to names: At least if there be any other confusion of *ideas*, this is that which most of all disorders mens thoughts and discourses, *ideas* as ranked under names, being those that for the most part men reason of within themselves, and always those which they commune about with others; and therefore where there are supposed two different *ideas* marked by two different names, which are not as distinguishable as the sounds that stand for them, there never fails to be *confusion:* And where any *ideas* are distinct, as the *ideas* of those two sounds they are marked by, there can be between them no *confusion*. *The way to prevent it*, is to collect and unite into our complex *idea*, as precisely as is possible, all those ingredients whereby it is differenced from others; and to them so united in a determinate number and order, apply steadily the same name; but this neither accommodating mens ease or vanity, or serving any design but that of naked truth, which is not always the thing aimed at, such exactness is rather to be wished than hoped for. And since the loose application of names to undetermined, variable, and almost no *ideas*, serve both to cover our own ignorance, as well as to perplex and confound others, which goes for learning and superiority in knowledge, it is no wonder that most men should use it themselves, whilst they complain of it in others. Though, I think, no small part of the *confusion* to be found in the notions of men, might by care and ingenuity be avoided, yet I am far from concluding it every where wilful. Some *ideas* are so complex, and made up of so many parts, that the memory does not easily retain the very same precise combination of simple *ideas* under one name; much less are we able constantly to divine for what precise complex *idea* such a name stands in another man's use of it. From the first of these follows *confusion* in a man's own reasonings and opinions within himself; from the latter, frequent *confusion* in discoursing and arguing with others. But having more at large treated of words, their defects and abuses in the following book, I shall here say no more of it.

§ 13. *Complex* Ideas *may be distinct in one part, and confused in another.*

OUR *complex ideas* being made up of collections, and so variety of simple ones, *may* accordingly *be very clear and distinct in one part, and very obscure and confused in another.* In a man who speaks of a *chiliaedron*, or a body of a thousand sides, the *idea* of the figure may be very confused, though that of the number be very distinct; so that he being able to discourse and demonstrate concerning that part of his complex *idea* which depends upon the number of a thousand, he is apt to think he has a distinct *idea* of a *chiliaedron*; though it be plain he has no precise *idea* of its figure, so as to distinguish it by that, from one that has but 999 sides; the not obſerving whereof, cauſes no ſmall error in mens thoughts, and confuſion in their diſcourſes.

§ 14. *This, if not heeded, cauſes Confuſion in our Arguings.* He that thinks he has a diſtinct *idea* of the figure of a *chiliaedron*, let him for trial-ſake take another parcel of the ſame uniform matter *viz.* gold or wax, of an equal bulk, and make it into a figure of 999 ſides; he will, I doubt not, be able to diſtinguiſh theſe two *ideas* one from another, by the number of ſides, and reaſon and argue diſtinctly about them, whilſt he keeps his thoughts and reaſoning to that part only of theſe *ideas*, which is contained in their numbers, as, that the ſides of the one could be divided into two equal numbers, and of the other not, *&c.*: But when he goes about to diſtinguiſh them by their figure, he will there be preſently at a loſs, and not able, I think, to frame in his mind two *ideas*, one of them diſtinct from the other, by the bare figure of theſe two pieces of gold, as he could, if the ſame parcels of gold were made one into a cube, the other a figure of five ſides; in which incomplete *ideas*, we are very apt to impoſe on ourſelves, and wrangle with others, eſpecially where they have particular and familiar names: For being ſatisfied in that part of the *idea* which we have clear, and the name which is familiar to us being applied to the whole, containing that part alſo which is imperfect and obſcure, we are apt to uſe it for that confuſed part, and draw deductions from it, in the obſcure part of its ſignification, as confidently as we do from the other.

§ 15. *Inſtance in Eternity.*

Having frequently in our mouths the name *eternity*, we are apt to think we have a poſitive comprehenſive *idea* of it, which is as much as to ſay, that there is no part of that duration which is not clearly contained in our *idea*: It is true, that he that thinks ſo may have a clear *idea* of duration; he may alſo have a very clear *idea* of a very great length of duration; he may alſo have a clear *idea* of the compariſon of that great one with ſtill a greater; but it not being poſſible for him to include in his *idea* of any duration, let it be as great as it will, the whole extent together of a duration where he ſuppoſes no end, that part of his *idea*, which is ſtill beyond the bounds of that large duration he repreſents to his own thoughts, is very obſcure and undetermined. And hence it is that in diſputes and reaſonings concerning eternity, or any other *infinite*, we are apt to blunder, and involve ourſelves in manifeſt abſurdities.

§ 16. *Diviſibility of Matter.*

IN matter we have no clear *ideas* of the ſmallneſs of parts much beyond the ſmalleſt that occur to any of our ſenſes; and therefore when we talk of the diviſibility of matter *in infinitum*, though we have clear *ideas* of diviſion and diviſibility, and have alſo clear *ideas* of parts made out of a whole by diviſion; yet we have but very obſcure and confuſed *ideas* of corpuſcles, or minute bodies ſo to be divided, when by former diviſions they are reduced to a ſmallneſs much exceeding the perception of any of our ſenſes; and ſo all that we have clear and diſtinct *ideas* of, is of what diviſion in general or abſtractly is, and the relation of *totum* and *pars*: But of the bulk of the body, to be thus infinitely divided after certain progreſſions, I think, we have no clear nor diſtinct *idea* at all: For I aſk any one, whether taking the ſmalleſt atom of duſt he ever ſaw, he has any diſtinct *idea* (bating ſtill the number which concerns not extenſion) betwixt the 100,000, and the 1,000,000 part of it; or if he thinks he can refine his *ideas* to that degree, without loſing ſight of them, let him add ten cyphers to each of thoſe numbers. Such a degree of ſmallneſs is not unreaſonable to be ſuppoſed, ſince a diviſion carried on ſo far, brings it no nearer the end of infinite diviſion, than the firſt diviſion into two halves does. I muſt confeſs, for my part, I have no clear diſtinct *ideas* of the different bulk or extenſion of theſe bodies, having but a very obſcure one of either of them; ſo that I think, when we talk of diviſion of bodies *in infinitum*, our *idea* of their diſtinct bulks, which is the ſubject and foundation of diviſion, comes, after a little progreſſion, to be confounded, and almoſt loſt in obſcurity: For that *idea*, which is to repreſent only bigneſs, muſt be very obſcure and confused, which we cannot distinguish from one ten times as big, but only by number; so that we have clear distinct *ideas*, we may say, of ten and one, but no distinct *ideas* of two such extensions. It is plain from hence, that when we talk of infinite divisibility of body, or extension, our distinct and clear *ideas* are only of numbers; but the clear distinct *ideas* of extension, after some progress of division, is quite lost, and of such minute parts we have no distinct *ideas* at all; but it returns, as all our *ideas* of infinite do, at last to that of number always to be added, but thereby never amounts to any distinct *idea* of actual infinite parts. We have, it is true, a clear *idea* of division, as often as we think of it; but thereby we have no more a clear *idea* of infinite parts in matter, than we have a clear *idea* of an infinite number, by being able still to add new numbers to any assigned number we have; endless divisibility giving us no more a clear and distinct *idea* of actually infinite parts, than endless addibility (if I may so speak) gives us a clear and distinct *idea* of an actually infinite number; they both being only in a power still increasing the number, be it already as great as it will: So that of what remains to be added (wherein consists the infinity) we have but an obscure, imperfect, and confused *idea*, from or about which we can argue or reason with no certainty or clearness, no more than we can in arithmetic, about a number of which we have no such distinct *idea* as we have of 4 or 100, but only this relative obscure one, that, compared to any other, it is still bigger: And we have no more a clear positive *idea* of it when we say or conceive it is bigger, or more than 400,000,000, than if we should say it is bigger than 40 or 4; 400,000,000, having no nearer a proportion to the end of addition, or number, than 4: For he that adds only 4 to 4, and so proceeds, shall as soon come to the end of all addition, as he that adds 400,000,000, to 400,000,000. And so likewise in eternity, he that has an *idea* of but four years, has as much a positive complete *idea* of eternity, as he that has one of 400,000,000 of years; for what remains of eternity beyond either of theſe two numbers of years, is as clear to the one as the other; *i. e.* neither of them has any clear poſitive *idea* of it at all: For he that adds only 4 years to 4, and ſo on, ſhall as ſoon reach eternity, as he that adds 400,000,000 of years, and ſo on, or if he pleaſe, doubles the increaſe as often as he will; the remaining abyſs being ſtill as far beyond the end of all theſe progreſſions, as it is from the length of a day or an hour; for nothing finite bears any proportion to infinite; and therefore our *ideas*, which are all finite, cannot bear any. Thus it is alſo in our *idea* of *extenſion*, when we increaſe it by addition, as well as when we diminiſh it by diviſion, and would enlarge our thoughts to infinite ſpace. After a few doublings of thoſe *ideas* of extenſion, which are the largeſt we are accuſtomed to have, we loſe the clear diſtinct *idea* of that ſpace; it becomes a confuſedly great one, with a ſurplus of ſtill greater; about which, when we would argue or reaſon, we ſhall always find ourſelves at a loſs; confuſed *ideas* in our arguings and deductions from that part of them which is confuſed, always leading us into confuſion.

CHAP. XXX.

OF REAL AND FANTASTICAL IDEAS.

§ 1. *Real* Ideas *are conformable to their Archetypes.*

BESIDES what we have already mentioned concerning *ideas*, other conſiderations belong to them, in reference to things from whence they are taken, or which they may be ſuppoſed to repreſent: and thus, I think, they may come under a threefold diſtinction; and are,

Firſt, Either real or fantaſtical.

Secondly, Adequate or inadequate.

Thirdly, True or falſe.

Firſt, By *real ideas*, I mean ſuch as have a foundation in nature; ſuch as have a conformity with the real being and exiſtence of things, or with their archetypes. *Fantaſtical* or *chimerical*, I call ſuch as have no foundation in nature, nor have any conformity with that reality of being to which they are tacitly referred as to their archetypes. If we examine the several sorts of *ideas* before mentioned, we shall find that,

§ 2. *Simple* Ideas *all real.*

FIRST, Our *simple* ideas *are all real*, all agree to the reality of things: Not that they are all of them the images or representations of what does exist; the contrary whereof, in all but the primary qualities of bodies, hath been already shown. But though whiteness and coldness are no more in snow than the pain is, yet those *ideas* of whiteness and coldness, pain, *&c.* being in us the effects of powers in things without us, ordained by our Maker to produce in us such sensations, they are real *ideas* in us, whereby we distinguish the qualities that are really in things themselves. For these several appearances being designed to be the marks whereby we are to know and distinguish things which we have to do with, our *ideas* do as well serve us to that purpose, and are as real distinguishing characters, whether they be only constant effects, or else exact resemblances of something in the things themselves; the reality lying in that steady correspondence they have with the distinct constitutions of real beings. But whether they answer to those constitutions, as to causes or patterns, it matters not; it suffices that they are constantly produced by them. And thus our simple *ideas* are all real and true, because they answer and agree to those powers of things which produce them in our minds, that being all that is requisite to make them real, and not fictions at pleasure. For in simple *ideas* (as has been shown) the mind is wholly confined to the operation of things upon it, and can make to itself no simple *idea*, more than what it has received.

§ 3. *Complex* Ideas *are voluntary Combinations.*

THOUGH the mind be wholly passive, in respect of its simple *ideas*, yet, I think, we may say it is not so in respect of its complex *ideas*; for those being combinations of simple *ideas* put together, and united under one general name, it is plain that the mind of man uses some kind of liberty, in forming those complex *ideas*:

How elſe comes it to paſs, that one man's *idea* of gold or juſtice is different from another's, but becauſe he has put in or left out of his ſome ſimple *idea*, which the other has not. The queſtion then is, which of theſe are real, and which barely imaginary combinations? What collections agree to the reality of things, and what not? And to this I ſay, That,

§ 4. *Mixed Modes, made of conſiſtent* Ideas, *are real.* *SECONDLY*, *Mixed modes and relations* having no other *reality* but what they have in the minds of men, there is nothing more required to thoſe kind of *ideas*, to make them *real*, but that they be ſo framed, that there be a poſſibility of exiſting conformable to them. Theſe *ideas* themſelves being archetypes, cannot differ from their archetypes, and ſo *cannot be chimerical*, unleſs any one will jumble together in them inconſiſtent *ideas*. Indeed, as any of them have the names of a known language aſſigned to them, by which he that has them in his mind would ſignify them to others, ſo bare poſſibility of exiſting is not enough; they muſt have a conformity to the ordinary ſignification of the name that is given them, that they may not be thought fantaſtical, as if a man would give the name of juſtice to that *idea*, which common uſe calls liberality. But this fantaſticalneſs relates more to propriety of ſpeech than reality of *ideas*; for a man to be undiſturbed in danger, ſedately to conſider what is fitteſt to be done, and to execute it ſteadily, is a mixed mode, or a complex *idea* of an action which may exiſt; but to be undiſturbed in danger, without uſing one's reaſon or induſtry, is what is alſo poſſible to be, and ſo is as real an *idea* as the other; though the firſt of theſe, having the name *courage* given to it, may, in reſpect of that name, be a right or wrong *idea*; but the other, whilſt it has not a common received name of any known language aſſigned to it, is not capable of any deformity, being made with no reference to any thing but itſelf.

§ 5. Ideas *of Subſtances are real, when they agree with the Exiſtence of Things.*

THIRDLY, Our *complex* ideas *of ſubſtances* being made all of them in reference to things existing without us, and intended to be representations of substances as they really are, are no farther *real* than as they are such combinations ot simple *ideas* as are really united, and coexist in things without us. On the contrary, those are *fantastical* which are made up of such collections of simple *ideas* as were never really united, never were found together in any substance; *v. g.* a rational creature, consisting of a horse's head, joined to a body of human shape, or such as the *Centaurs* are described; or a body yellow, very malleable, fusible, and fixed, but lighter than common water; or an uniform unorganized body, consisting, as to sense, all of similar parts, with perception and voluntary motion joined to it. Whether such substances as these can possibly exist or no, it is probable we do not know; but be that as it will, these *ideas* of substances being made conformable to no pattern existing that we know, and consisting of such collections of *ideas* as no substance ever showed us united together, they ought to pass with us for barely imaginary; but much more are those complex *ideas* so, which contain in them any inconsistency or contradiction of their parts.

CHAP. XXXI.

OF ADEQUATE AND INADEQUATE IDEAS.

§ 1. *Adequate* Ideas *are such as perfectly represent their Archetypes.*

OF our real *ideas*, some are adequate, and some are inadequate. Those I call *adequate*, which perfectly represent those archetypes which the mind supposes them taken from, which it intends them to stand for, and to which it refers them. *Inadequate ideas* are such, which are but a partial or incomplete representation of those archetypes to which they are referred. Upon which account it is plain,

§ 2. *Simple* Ideas *all adequate.*

FIRST, That *all our simple* ideas *are adequate;* because being nothing but the effects of certain powers in things fitted and ordained by God to produce ſuch ſenſations in us, they cannot but be correſpondent and adequate to thoſe powers, and we are ſure they agree to the reality of things; for if ſugar produce in us the *ideas* which we call whiteneſs and ſweetneſs, we are ſure there is a power in ſugar to produce thoſe *ideas* in our minds, or elſe they could not have been produced by it; and ſo each ſenſation anſwering the power that operates on any of our ſenſes, the *idea* ſo produced is a real *idea* (and not a fiction of the mind, which has no power to produce any ſimple *idea)*, and cannot but be adequate, ſince it ought only to anſwer that power; and ſo all ſimple *ideas* are adequate. It is true, the things producing in us theſe ſimple *ideas* are but few of them denominated by us, as if they were only the cauſes of them, but as if thoſe *ideas* were real beings in them; for though fire be called painful to the touch, whereby is ſignified the power of producing in us the *idea* of pain, yet it is denominated alſo light and hot, as if light and heat were really ſomething in the fire more than a power to excite theſe *ideas* in us, and therefore are called *qualities* in or of the fire: But theſe being nothing, in truth, but powers to excite ſuch *ideas* in us, I muſt, in that ſenſe, be underſtood, when I ſpeak of ſecondary *qualities* as being in things, or of their *ideas*, as being in the objects that excite them in us. Such ways of ſpeaking, though accommodated to the vulgar notions, without which one cannot be well underſtood, yet truly ſignify nothing but thoſe powers which are in things to excite certain ſenſations or *ideas* in us; ſince were there no fit organs to receive the impreſſions fire makes on the ſight and touch, nor a mind joined to thoſe organs to receive the *ideas* of light and heat by thoſe impreſſions from the fire or the ſun, there would yet be no more light or heat in the world, than there would be pain, if there were no ſenſible creature to feel it, though the ſun ſhould continue juſt as it is now, and Mount *Ætna* flame higher than ever it did. Solidity and extenſion, and the termination of it, figure, with motion and reſt, whereof we have the *ideas*, would be really in the world as they are, whether there were any sensible being to perceive them or no: and therefore we have reason to look on those as the real modifications of matter, and such as are the exciting causes of all our various sensations from bodies. But this being an inquiry not belonging to this place, I shall enter no farther into it, but proceed to show what complex *ideas* are *adequate*, and what not.

§ 3. *Modes are all adequate.*

SECONDLY, Our *complex* ideas *of modes*, being voluntary collections of simple *ideas* which the mind puts together without reference to any real archetypes or standing patterns existing any where, *are* and cannot but be *adequate ideas*; because they not being intended for copies of things really existing, but for archetypes made by the mind to rank and denominate things by, cannot want any thing, they having each of them that combination of *ideas*, and thereby that perfection which the mind intended they should; so that the mind acquiesces in them and can find nothing wanting. Thus by having the *idea* of a figure with three sides meeting in three angles, I have a complete *idea*, wherein I require nothing else to make it perfect. That the mind is satisfied with the perfection of this its *idea*, is plain in that it does not conceive that any understanding hath or can have a more complete or perfect *idea* of that thing it signifies by the word *triangle*, supposing it to exist, than itself has in that complex *idea* of three sides, and three angles; in which is contained all that is, or can be essential to it or necessary to complete it, wherever or however it exists. But in our *ideas* of *substances* it is otherwise; for there, desiring to copy things as they really do exist, and to represent to ourselves that constitution on which all their properties depend, we perceive our *ideas* attain not that perfection we intend; we find they still want something we should be glad were in them; and so are all *inadequate*. But *mixed modes* and *relations*, being archetypes without patterns, and so having nothing to represent but themselves, cannot but be adequate, every thing being so to itself. He that at first put together the *idea* of danger, perceived absence of disorder from fear, sedate consideration from what was justly to be done, and executing of that without disturbance, or being deterred by the danger of it, had certainly in his mind that complex *idea* made up of that combination; and intending to be nothing else but what it is, nor to have in it any other simple *ideas* but what it hath, it could not also but be an *adequate idea*; and laying this up in his memory, with the name *courage* annexed to it, to signify it to others, and denominate from thence any action he should observe to agree with it, had thereby a standard to measure and denominate actions by, as they agreed to it. This *idea* thus made, and laid up for a pattern, must necessarily be *adequate*, being referred to nothing else but itself, nor made by any other original, but the good-liking and will of him that first made this combination.

§ 4. *Modes, in reference to settled Names, may be inadequate.*

INDEED another coming after, and in conversation learning from him the word *courage*, may make any *idea*, to which he gives that name *courage*, different from what the first author applied it to, and has in his mind, when he uses it. And in this case, if he designs that his *idea* in thinking should be conformable to the other's *idea*, as the name he uses in speaking is conformable in sound to his from whom he learned it, his *idea* may be very wrong and *inadequate*; because in this case, making the other man's *idea* the pattern of his *idea* in thinking, as the other man's word or sound is the pattern of his in speaking, his *idea* is so far defective and *inadequate*, as it is distant from the archetype and pattern he refers it to, and intends to express and signify by the name he uses for it; which name he would have to be a sign of the other man's *idea* (to which, in its proper use, it is primarily annexed) and of his own, as agreeing to it; to which, if his own does not exactly correspond, it is faulty and inadequate.

§ 5.

THEREFORE these *complex* ideas *of modes*, when they are referred by the mind, and intended to correspond to the *ideas* in the mind of ſome other intelligent being, expreſſed by the names we apply to them, they *may be* very deficient, wrong and *inadequate*, becauſe they agree not to that which the mind deſigns to be their archetype and pattern: in which reſpect only, any *idea* of *modes* can be wrong, imperfect or *inadequate*. And on this account our *ideas* of *mixed modes* are the moſt liable to be faulty of any other; but this refers more to proper ſpeaking, than knowing right.

§ 6. Ideas *of Subſtances, as referred to real Eſſences, not adequate.*

THIRDLY, What *ideas we have of ſubſtances*, I have above ſhown. Now thoſe *ideas* have in the mind a double reference: 1. Sometimes they are referred to a ſuppoſed real eſſence of each ſpecies of things; 2. Sometimes they are only deſigned to be pictures and repreſentations in the mind, of things that do exiſt by *ideas* of thoſe qualities that are diſcoverable in them. In both which ways, theſe copies of thoſe originals and archetypes, are imperfect and *inadequate*.

Firſt, It is uſual for men to make the names of ſubſtances ſtand for things, as ſuppoſed to have certain real eſſences, whereby they are of this or that ſpecies: and names ſtanding for nothing but the *ideas* that are in mens minds, they muſt conſequently refer their *ideas* to ſuch real eſſences, as to their archetypes. That men (eſpecially ſuch as have been bred up in the learning taught in this part of the world) do ſuppoſe certain ſpecific eſſences of ſubſtances, which each individual, in its ſeveral kinds, is made conformable to, and partakes of, is ſo far from needing proof, that it will be thought ſtrange if any one ſhould do otherwiſe; and thus they ordinarily apply the ſpecific names they rank particular ſubſtances under, to things as diſtinguiſhed by ſuch ſpecific real eſſences. Who is there almoſt, who would not take it amiſs, if it ſhould be doubted, whether he called himſelf man, with any other meaning, than as having the real eſſence of a man? And yet if you demand what thoſe real eſſences are, it is plain men are ignorant, and know them not. From whence it follows, that the *ideas* they have in their minds, being referred to real effences, as to archetypes which are unknown, muft be fo far from being *adequate*, that they cannot be fuppofed to be any reprefentation of them at all. The complex *ideas* we have of fubftances, are, as it has been fhown, certain collections of fimple *ideas* that have been obferved or fuppofed conftantly to exift together: But fuch a complex *idea* cannot be the real effence of any fubftance; for then the properties we difcover in that body, would depend on that complex *idea*, and be deducible from it, and their neceffary connection with it be known; as all properties of a triangle depend on, and as far as they are difcoverable, are deducible from the complex *idea* of three lines, including a fpace. But it is plain, that in our complex *ideas* of fubftances, are not contained fuch *ideas*, on which all the other qualities that are to be found in them, do depend. The common *idea* men have of *iron*, is a body of a certain colour, weight and hardnefs; and a property that they look on as belonging to it, is malleablenefs; but yet this property has no neceffary connection with that complex *idea*, or any part of it; and there is no more reafon to think that malleablenefs depends on that colour, weight and hardnefs, than that that colour, or that weight depends on its malleablenefs; and yet, though we know nothing of thefe real effences, there is nothing more ordinary, than that men fhould attribute the forts of things to fuch effences. The particular parcel of matter, which makes the ring I have on my finger, is forwardly, by moft men, fuppofed to have a real effence, whereby it is *gold*; and from whence thofe qualities flow which I find in it, *viz.* its peculiar colour, weight, hardnefs, fufibility, fixednefs, and change of colour upon a flight touch of mercury, &c. This effence, from which all thefe properties flow, when I inquire into it, and fearch after it, I plainly perceive I cannot difcover; the fartheft I can go, is only to prefume, that it being nothing but body, its real effence, or internal conftitution, on which thefe qualities depend, can be nothing but the figure, fize and connection of its folid parts, of neither of which having any diſtinct perception at all, can I have any *idea* of its eſſence, which is the cauſe that it has that particular ſhining yellowneſs, a greater weight than any thing I know of the ſame bulk, and a fitneſs to have its colour changed by the touch of quickſilver. If any one will ſay, that the real eſſence and internal conſtitution, on which theſe properties depend, is not the figure, ſize and arrangement or connection of its ſolid parts, but ſomething elſe, called its particular *form*; I am farther from having any *idea* of its real eſſence, than I was before: for I have an *idea* of a figure, ſize and ſituation of ſolid parts in general, though I have none of the particular figure, ſize, or putting together of parts, whereby the qualities above-mentioned are produced; which qualities I find in that particular parcel of matter that is on my finger, and not in another parcel of matter, with which I cut the pen I write with. But when I am told, that ſomething beſides the figure, ſize and poſture of the ſolid parts of that body, is its eſſenee, ſomething called *ſubſtantial form*; of that, I confeſs, I have no *idea* at all, but only of the ſound *form*, which is far enough from an *idea* of its real eſſence, or conſtitution. The like ignorance as I have of the real eſſence of this particular ſubſtance, I have alſo of the real eſſence of all other natural ones; of which eſſences, I confeſs I have no diſtinct *ideas* at all; and I am apt to ſuppoſe others, when they examine their own knowledge, will find in themſelves, in this one point, the ſame ſort of ignorance.

§ 7.

Now then, when men apply to this particular parcel of matter on my finger a general name already in uſe, and denominate it *gold*, do they not ordinarily, or are they not underſtood to give it that name as belonging to a particular ſpecies of bodies, having a real internal eſſence; by having of which eſſence, this particular ſubſtance comes to be of that ſpecies, and to be called by that name? If it be ſo, as it is plain it is, the name, by which things are marked, as having that eſſence, muſt be referred primarily to that eſſence; and conſequently the *idea* to which that name is given, muſt be referred alſo to that eſſence, and be intended to repreſent it; which eſſence, ſince they who ſo uſe the names know not, their ideas *of ſubſtances* muſt be *all adequate* in that reſpect, as not containing in them that real eſſence which the mind intends they ſhould.

§ 8. Ideas *of Subſtances, as Collections of their Qualities, are all inadequate.*

SECONDLY, Thoſe who neglecting that uſeleſs ſuppoſition of unknown real eſſences, whereby they are diſtinguiſhed, endeavour to copy the ſubſtances that exiſt in the world, by putting together the *ideas* of thoſe ſenſible qualities which are found co-exiſting in them, though they come much nearer a likeneſs of them, than thoſe who imagine they know not what real ſpecific eſſences; yet they arrive not at perfectly adequate *ideas* of thoſe ſubſtances they would thus copy into their minds, nor do thoſe copies exactly and fully contain all that is to be found in their archetypes; becauſe thoſe qualities and powers of ſubſtances whereof we make their complex *ideas,* are ſo many and various, that no man's complex *idea* contains them all. That our abſtract *ideas* of ſubſtances do not contain in them all the ſimple *ideas* that are united in the things themſelves, is evident, in that men do rarely put into their complex *idea* of any ſubſtance, all the ſimple *ideas* they do know to exiſt in it; becauſe endeavouring to make the ſignification of their ſpecific names as clear and as little cumberſome as they can, they make their ſpecific *ideas* of the ſorts of ſubſtances, for the moſt part, of a few of thoſe ſimple *ideas* which are to be found in them; but theſe having no original precedency or right to be put in, and make the ſpecific *idea* more than others that are left out, it is plain, that both theſe ways *our* ideas *of ſubſtances* are deficient and *inadequate.* The ſimple *ideas,* whereof we make our complex ones of ſubſtances, are all of them (bating only the figure and bulk of ſome ſorts) powers, which being relations to other ſubſtances, we can never be ſure that we know all the powers that are in any one body, till we have tried what changes it is fitted to give to or receive from other ſubſtances, in their ſeveral ways of application, which being impoſſible to be tried upon any one body, much leſs upon all, it is impoſſible we ſhould have adequate *ideas* of any ſubſtance made up of a collection of all its properties.

§ 9.

WHOSOEVER firſt lit on a parcel of that ſort of ſubſtance we denote by the word *gold*, could not rationally take the bulk and figure he obſerved in that lump to depend on its real eſſence or internal conſtitution; therefore thoſe never went into his *idea* of that ſpecies of body, but its peculiar colour, perhaps, and weight, were the firſt he abſtracted from it, to make the complex *idea* of that ſpecies, which both are but powers, the one to affect our eyes after ſuch a manner, and to produce in us that idea we call yellow, and the other to force upwards any other body of equal bulk, they being put into a pair of equal ſcales, one againſt another. Another, perhaps, added to theſe the *ideas* of fuſibility and fixedneſs, two other paſſive powers, in relation to the operation of fire upon it; another, its ductility and ſolubility in *aq. regia*, two other powers relating to the operation of other bodies, in changing its outward figure or ſeparation of it into inſenſible parts. Theſe, or part of theſe, put together, uſually make the complex *idea* in mens minds, of that ſort of body we call *gold*.

§ 10.

BUT no one who hath conſidered the properties of bodies in general, or this ſort in particular, can doubt that this called *gold* has infinite other properties not contained in that *complex idea*. Some who have examined this ſpecies more accurately, could, I believe, enumerate ten times as many properties in *gold*, all of them as inſeparable from its internal conſtitution, as its colour or weight; and it is probable, if any one knew all the properties that are by divers men known of this metal, there would an hundred times as many *ideas* go to the complex *idea* of *gold*, as any one man yet has in his, and yet perhaps that not be the thouſandth part of what is to be diſcovered in it; the changes which that one body is apt to receive, and make in other bodies, upon a due application, exceeding far not only what we know, but what we are apt to imagine; which will not appear so much a paradox to any one, who will but confider how far men are yet from knowing all the properties of that one, no very compound figure, a *triangle*, though it be no fmall number that are already by mathematicians difcovered of it.

§ 11. Ideas *of Subftances, as Collections of their Qualities, are all inadequate.*

So that *all our complex* ideas *of fubftances are* imperfect and *inadequate*, which would be fo alfo in mathematical figures, if we were to have our complex *ideas* of them, only by collecting their properties in reference to other figures. How uncertain and imperfect would our *ideas* be of an *ellipfis*, if we had no other *idea* of it, but fome few of its properties? Whereas, having in our plain *idea* the whole effence of that figure, we from thence difcover thofe properties, and demonftratively fee how they flow, and are infeparable from it.

§ 12. *Simple* Ideas *ἔκτυπα, and adequate.*

Thus the mind has three forts of abftract *ideas*, or nominal effences:

First, Simple ideas, which are *ἔκτυπα*, or *copies*, but yet certainly *adequate;* becaufe being intended to exprefs nothing but the power in things to produce in the mind fuch a fenfation, that fenfation, when it is produced, cannot but be the effect of that power. So the paper I write on having the power, in the light, (I fpeak according to the common notion of light) to produce in me the fenfation which I call white, it cannot but be the effect of fuch a power in fomething without the mind, fince the mind has not the power to produce any fuch *idea* in itfelf; and being meant for nothing elfe but the effect of fuch a power, that fimple *idea* is real and *adequate;* the fenfation of white, in my mind, being the effect of that power which is in the paper to produce it, is perfectly *adequate* to that power, or elfe that power would produce a different *idea*.

§ 13. Ideas *of Subſtances are* ἔκτυπα, *inadequate.*

SECONDLY, The *complex* ideas *of ſubſtances are ectypes, copies* too, but not perfect ones, not *adequate,* which is very evident to the mind, in that it plainly perceives that whatever collection of ſimple *ideas* it makes of any ſubſtance that exiſts, it cannot be ſure that it exactly anſwers all that are in that ſubſtance, ſince not having tried all the operations of all other ſubſtances upon it, and found all the alterations it would receive from or cauſe in other ſubſtances, it cannot have an exact *adequate* collection of all its active and paſſive capacities, and ſo *not* have an *adequate* complex *idea* of the powers of any ſubſtance exiſting, and its relations, which is that ſort of complex *idea* of ſubſtances we have; and after all, if we could have, and actually had, in our complex *idea,* an exact collection of all the ſecondary qualities or powers of any ſubſtance, we ſhould not yet thereby have an *idea* of the eſſence of that thing; for ſince the powers or qualities that are obſervable by us, are not the real eſſence of that ſubſtance, but depend on it, and flow from it, any collection whatſoever of theſe qualities cannot be the real eſſence of that thing; whereby it is plain, that our *ideas* of ſubſtances are not *adequate,* are not what the mind intends them to be. Beſides, a man has no *idea* of ſubſtance in general, nor knows what ſubſtance is in itſelf.

§ 14. Ideas *of Modes and Relations are Archetypes, and cannot but be adequate.*

THIRDLY, Complex ideas *of modes and relations are* originals and archetypes, are not copies, nor made after the pattern of any real exiſtence, to which the mind intends them to be conformable, and exactly to anſwer; theſe being ſuch collections of ſimple *ideas,* that the mind itſelf puts together, and ſuch collections, that each of them contains in it preciſely all that the mind intends it ſhould, they are archetypes and eſſences of modes that may exiſt, and ſo are deſigned only for, and belong only to ſuch modes, as when they do exiſt, have an exact conformity with thoſe complex *ideas.* The *ideas,* therefore, of modes and relations, cannot but be *adequate.*

CHAP. XXXII.

OF TRUE AND FALSE IDEAS.

§ 1. *Truth and Falſehood properly belong to Propoſitions.*

THOUGH truth and falſehood belong, in propriety of ſpeech, only to propoſitions; yet *ideas* are oftentimes termed *true* or *falſe* (as what words are there, that are not uſed with great latitude, and with ſome deviation from their ſtrict and proper ſignifications?) Though, I think, that when the *ideas* themſelves are termed true or falſe, there is ſtill ſome ſecret or tacit propoſition, which is the foundation of that denomination; as we ſhall ſee, if we examine the particular occaſions wherein they come to be called true or falſe: In all which, we ſhall find ſome kind of affirmation or negation, which is the reaſon of that denomination: For our *ideas* being nothing but bare appearances or perceptions in our minds, cannot properly and ſimply in themſelves be ſaid to be *true* or *falſe*, no more than a ſingle name of any thing can be ſaid to be *true* or *falſe*.

§ 2. *Metaphyſical Truth contains a tacit Propoſition.*

INDEED both *ideas* and words *may* be ſaid to be *true in a metaphyſical ſenſe* of the word truth, as all other things, that any way exiſt, are ſaid to be true; *i. e.* really to be ſuch as they exiſt: Though in things called *true*, even in that ſenſe, there is perhaps a ſecret reference to our *ideas*, looked upon as the ſtandards of that truth, which amounts to a mental propoſition, though it be uſually not taken notice of.

§ 3. *No* Idea, *as an Appearance in the mind, true or falſe.*

BUT it is not in that metaphyſical ſenſe of truth which we inquire here, when we examine whether our *ideas* are capable of being *true* or *falſe*, but in the more ordinary acceptation of thoſe words: And ſo I ſay, that the *ideas* in our minds being only ſo many perceptions, or appearances there, none of them are *falſe*; the *idea* of a centaur having no more falſehood in it, when it appears in our minds, than the name centaur has falſehood in it, when it is pronounced by our mouths or written on paper: For truth or falsehood lying always in some affirmation, or negation, mental or verbal, our *ideas* are *not capable*, any of them, *of being false*, till the mind passes some judgment on them; that is, affirms or denies something of them.

§ 4. Ideas *referred to any thing, may be true or false.* WHENEVER the mind refers any of its *ideas* to any thing extraneous to them, they are then *capable to be called true or false;* because the mind in such a reference makes a tacit supposition of their conformity to that thing; which supposition, as it happens to be *true* or *false*, so the *ideas* themselves come to be denominated. The most usual cases wherein this happens, are these following:-

§ 5. *Other Mens* Ideas, *real Existence, and supposed real Essences, are what men usually refer their* Ideas *to.*

First, When the mind supposes any *idea* it has *conformable to* that in *other mens* minds, called by the same common name; *v. g.* when the mind intends or judges its *ideas* of *justice, temperance, religion*, to be the same with what other men give those names to.

Secondly, When the mind supposes any *idea* it has in itself, to be *conformable to some real existence*. Thus the two *ideas* of a man and a centaur, supposed to be the ideas of real substances, are the one *true*, and the other *false;* the one having a conformity to what has really existed, the other not.

Thirdly, When the mind *refers* any of its *ideas* to that real constitution and *essence* of any thing, whereon all its properties depend; and thus the greatest part, if not all our *ideas* of substances, are *false*.

§ 6. *The Cause of such References.*

THESE suppositions the mind is very apt tacitly to make concerning its own *ideas:* But yet if we will examine it, we shall find it is chiefly, if not only, concerning its abstract complex *ideas:* For the natural tendency of the mind being towards knowledge, and finding that, if it should proceed by and dwell upon only particular things, its progress would be very slow, and its work endless; therefore, to shorten its way to knowledge, and make each perception more comprehenſive, the firſt thing it does, as the foundation of the eaſier enlarging its knowledge, either by contemplation of the things themſelves that it would know, or conference with others about them, is to bind them into bundles, and rank them ſo into ſorts, that what knowledge it gets of any of them, it may thereby with aſſurance extend to all of that ſort; and ſo advance by larger ſteps in that, which is its great buſineſs, knowledge. This, as I have elſewhere ſhowed, is the reaſon why we collect things under comprehenſive *ideas*, with names annexed to them, into *genera* and *ſpecies*, *i. e.* into kinds and ſorts.

§ 7.

If therefore we will warily attend to the motions of the mind, and obſerve what courſe it uſually takes in its way to knowledge, we ſhall, I think, find that the mind having got any *idea*, which it thinks it may have uſe of, either in contemplation or diſcourſe, the firſt thing it does, is to abſtract it, and then get a name to it, and ſo lay it up in its ſtorehouſe, the memory, as containing the eſſence of a ſort of things, of which that name is always to be the mark. Hence it is, that we may often obſerve, that when any one ſees a new thing of a kind that he knows not, he preſently aſks what it is, meaning by that inquiry nothing but the name; as if the name carried with it the knowledge of the ſpecies, or the eſſence of it; whereof it is indeed uſed as the mark, and is generally ſuppoſed annexed to it.

§ 8.

But this abſtract *idea* being ſomething in the mind between the thing that exiſts, and the name that is given it, it is in our *ideas*, that both the rightneſs of our knowledge, and the propriety or intelligibleneſs of our ſpeaking conſiſts. And hence it is, that men are ſo forward to ſuppoſe, that the abſtract *ideas* they have in their minds, are ſuch as agree to the things exiſting without them, to which they are referred, and are the ſame alſo, to which the names they give them do, by the uſe and propriety of that language, belong: For without this *double conformity* of their *ideas*, they find they ſhould both think amiſs of things in themſelves, and talk of them unintelligibly to others.

§ 9. *Simple* Ideas *may be falſe, in reference to others of the ſame Name, but are leaſt liable to be ſo.*

FIRST, then, I ſay, That *when the truth of our* ideas *is judged of, by the conformity they have to the* ideas *which other men have, and commonly ſignify by the ſame name, they may be any of them falſe:* But yet *ſimple ideas are leaſt of all liable to be ſo miſtaken;* becauſe a man by his ſenſes, and every day's obſervation, may eaſily ſatisfy himſelf what the ſimple *ideas* are, which their ſeveral names that are in common uſe ſtand for, they being but few in number, and ſuch as, if he doubts or miſtakes in, he may eaſily rectify by the objects they are to be found in. Therefore it is ſeldom that any one miſtakes in his names of ſimple *ideas*, or applies the name *red* to the *idea green*, or the name *ſweet* to the *idea bitter;* much leſs are men apt to confound the names of *ideas* belonging to different ſenſes, and call a colour by the name of a taſte, &c. whereby it is evident, that the ſimple *ideas* they call by any name, are commonly the ſame that others have and mean when they uſe the ſame names.

§ 10. Ideas *of mixed Modes moſt liable to be falſe in this Senſe.*

COMPLEX ideas *are much more liable to be falſe in this reſpect; and the complex* ideas *of mixed modes, much more than thoſe of ſubſtances;* becauſe in ſubſtances (eſpecially thoſe which the common and unborrowed names of any language are applied to) ſome remarkable ſenſible qualities, ſerving ordinarily to diſtinguiſh one ſort from another, eaſily preſerve thoſe, who take any care in the uſe of their words, from applying them to ſorts of ſubſtances, to which they do not at all belong: But in mixed modes we are much more uncertain; it being not ſo eaſy to determine of ſeveral actions, whether they are to be called *juſtice* or *cruelty*, *liberality* or *prodigality*. And ſo in referring our *ideas* to thoſe of other men, called by the ſame names, ours may be *falſe;* and the *idea* in our minds, which we expreſs by the word *juſtice*, may perhaps be that which ought to have another name.

§ 11. *Or at least to be thought false.*

But whether or no our *ideas* of mixed modes are more liable than any sort to be different from those of other men, which are marked by the same names; this at least is certain, That *this sort of falsehood is much more familiarly attributed to our* ideas *of mixed modes, than to any other.* When a man is thought to have a false *idea* of *justice*, or *gratitude*, or *glory*, it is for no other reason, but that his agrees not with the *ideas* which each of those names are the signs of in other men.

§ 12. *And why.*

The *reason* whereof seems to me to be this; That the abstract *ideas* of mixed modes, being mens voluntary combinations of such a precise collection of simple *ideas*; and so the essence of each species being made by men alone, whereof we have no other sensible standard existing any where, but the name itself, or the definition of that name; we have nothing else to refer these our *ideas* of mixed modes to, as a standard to which we would conform them, but the *ideas* of those who are thought to use those names in their most proper significations; and so as our *ideas* conform or differ from them, they pass for true or false. And thus much concerning the *truth* and *falsehood* of our *ideas*, in reference to their names.

§ 13. *As referred to real Existences, none of our* Ideas *can be false, but those of Substances.*

Secondly, As to the truth and falsehood of our *ideas*, in reference to the *real existence* of things, when that is made the standard of their truth, none of them can be termed false, but only our complex *ideas* of substances.

§ 14. *First, Simple* Ideas *in this sense not false, and why.*

First, Our simple *ideas* being barely such perceptions as God has fitted us to receive, and given power to external objects to produce in us by established laws and ways, suitable to his wisdom and goodness, though incomprehensible to us, their truth consists in nothing else but in such appearances as are produced in us, and must be suitable to those powers he has placed in external objects, or else they could not be produced in us; and thus anſwering thoſe powers, they are what they ſhould be, *true ideas*: Nor do they become liable to any imputation of *falſehood*, if the mind (as in moſt men I believe it does) judges theſe *ideas* to be in the things themſelves; for God, in his wiſdom, having ſet them as marks of diſtinction in things, whereby we may be able to diſcern one thing from another, and ſo chooſe any of them for our uſes, as we have occaſion, it alters not the nature of our ſimple *idea*, whether we think that the *idea* of blue be in the violet itſelf, or in our mind only, and only the power of producing it by the texture of its parts, reflecting the particles of light, after a certain manner, to be in the violet itſelf; for that texture in the object, by a regular and conſtant operation, producing the ſame *idea* of blue in us, it ſerves us to diſtinguiſh, by our eyes, that from any other thing, whether that diſtinguiſhing mark, as it is really in the *violet*, be only a peculiar texture of parts, elſe that very colour, the *idea* whereof (which is in us) is the exact reſemblance: And it is equally from that appearance to be denominated *blue*, whether it be that real colour, or only a peculiar texture in it, that cauſes in us that *idea*; ſince the name *blue* notes properly nothing, but that mark of diſtinction that is in a *violet*, diſcernible only by our eyes, whatever it conſiſts in, that being beyond our capacities diſtinctly to know, and perhaps would be of leſs uſe to us, if we had faculties to diſcern.

§ 15. *Though one Man's* Idea *of blue ſhould be different from another's.*

NEITHER would it carry any imputation of *falſehood* to our ſimple *ideas*, if by the different ſtructure of our organs it were ſo ordered, that *the ſame object ſhould produce in ſeveral mens minds different ideas* at the ſame time; *v. g.* if the *idea* that a *violet* produced in one man's mind by his eyes were the ſame that a *marigold* produced in another man's, and *vice verſa*: For ſince this could never be known, becauſe one man's mind could not paſs into another man's body, to perceive what appearances were produced by thoſe organs; neither the *ideas* hereby, nor the names, would be at all confounded, or any *falsehood* be in either; for all things that had the texture of a *violet*, producing constantly the *idea* which he called *blue*, and those which had the texture of a *marigold*, producing constantly the *idea* which he has constantly called *yellow*; whatever those appearances were in his mind, he would be able as regularly to distinguish things for his use by those appearances, and understand and signify those distinctions marked by the name *blue* and *yellow*, as if the appearances, or *ideas* in his mind, received from those two flowers, were exactly the same with the *ideas* in other mens minds. I am nevertheless very apt to think, that the sensible *ideas* produced by any object in different mens minds, are most commonly very near and undiscernibly alike: For which opinion I think there might be many reasons offered; but that being besides my present business, I shall not trouble my reader with them, but only mind him, that the contrary supposition, if it could be proved, is of little use, either for the improvement of our knowledge, or conveniency of life; and so we need not trouble ourselves to examine it.

§ 16. *First, Simple* Ideas *in this Sense not false, and why.* FROM what has been said concerning our simple *ideas*, I think it evident, that our *simple* ideas can *none of them* be *false in respect of things* existing without us: For the truth of these appearances, or perceptions in our minds, consisting, as has been said, only in their being answerable to the powers in external objects, to produce by our senses such appearances in us, and each of them being in the mind, such as it is, suitable to the power that produced it, and which alone it represents; it cannot upon that account, or as referred to such a pattern, be *false*. *Blue* or *yellow*, *bitter* or *sweet*, can never be false *ideas*; these perceptions in the mind are just such as they are there, answering the powers appointed by God to produce them, and so are truly what they are and are intended to be. Indeed the names may be misapplied, but that in this respect makes no falsehood in the *ideas*, as if a man ignorant in the *English* tongue should call *purple scarlet*.

§ 17. *Secondly, Modes not false.*

SECONDLY, Neither can our *complex* ideas *of modes in reference to the essence of any thing really existing, be false;* because whatever complex *idea* I have of any mode, it hath no reference to any pattern existing, and made by nature; it is not supposed to contain in it any other *ideas* than what it hath, nor to represent any thing but such a complication of *ideas* as it does: Thus when I have the *idea* of such an action of a man, who forbears to afford himself such meat, drink and clothing, and other conveniencies of life as his riches and estate will be sufficient to supply, and his station requires, I have no *false ideas*, but such an one as represents an action, either as I find or imagine it, and so is capable of neither *truth* or *falsehood:* But when I give the name *frugality*, or *virtue*, to this action, then it may be called a *false idea*, if thereby it be supposed to agree with that *idea*, to which, in propriety of speech, the name of *frugality* doth belong, or to be conformable to that law, which is the standard of virtue and vice.

§ 18. *Thirdly*, Ideas *of Substances when false.*

THIRDLY, Our *complex* ideas *of substances, being all referred to patterns in things themselves, may be false:* That they are all *false*, when looked upon as the representations of the unknown essences of things, is so evident, that there needs nothing to be said of it: I shall therefore pass over that chimerical supposition, and consider them as collections of simple *ideas* in the mind, taken from combinations of simple *ideas* existing together constantly in things, of which patterns they are the supposed copies; and in this reference of them, to the existence of things, they *are false* ideas: 1. *When* they put together simple *ideas*, which in the real existence of things have no union; as when to the shape and size that exist together in a horse, is joined, in the same complex *idea*, the power of barking like a dog; which three *ideas*, however put together into one in the mind, were never united in nature; and this therefore may be called a *false idea* of an horse. 2. *Ideas* of substances are, in this respect, also *false*, when from any collection of simple *ideas* that do always exiſt together, there is ſeparated, by a direct negation, any other ſimple *idea* which is conſtantly joined with them. Thus, if to extenſion, ſolidity, fuſibility, the peculiar weightineſs, and yellow colour of gold, any one join in his thoughts the negation of a greater degree of fixedneſs than is in lead or copper, he may be ſaid to have a falſe complex *idea*, as well as when he joins to thoſe other ſimple ones the *idea* of perfect abſolute fixedneſs: For either way, the complex *idea* of gold being made up of ſuch ſimple ones as have no union in nature, may be termed falſe; but if he leave out of this his complex *idea*, that of fixedneſs quite, without either actually joining to, or ſeparating of it from the reſt in his mind, it is, I think, to be looked on as an inadequate and imperfect *idea* rather than a falſe one; ſince though it contains not all the ſimple *ideas* that are united in nature, yet it puts none together but what do really exiſt together.

§ 19. *Truth or Falſehood always ſuppoſes Affirmation or Negation.*

THOUGH, in compliance with the ordinary way of ſpeaking, I have ſhowed in what ſenſe, and upon what ground our *ideas* may be ſometimes called *true* or *falſe*, yet if we will look a little nearer into the matter, in all caſes where any *idea* is called *true* or *falſe*, it is from ſome judgment that the mind makes, or is ſuppoſed to make, that is *true* or *falſe*: For *truth* or *falſehood*, being *never without ſome affirmation or negation*, expreſs or tacit, it is not to be found but when ſigns are joined or ſeparated, according to the agreement or diſagreement of the things they ſtand for. The ſigns we chiefly uſe are either *ideas* of words, wherewith we make either mental or verbal propoſitions. *Truth* lies in ſo joining or ſeparating theſe repreſentatives, as the things they ſtand for do in themſelves agree or diſagree; and *falſehood* in the contrary, as ſhall be more fully ſhowed hereafter.

§ 20. Ideas *in themſelves neither true nor falſe.*

ANY *idea* then which we have in our minds, whether conformable or not to the exiſtence of things, or to any *ideas* in the minds of other men, cannot properly for this alone be called *falſe*: For theſe repreſentations, if they have nothing in them but what is really exiſting in things without, cannot be thought *falſe*, being exact repreſentations of ſomething: Nor yet if they have any thing in them differing from the reality of things, can they properly be ſaid to be falſe repreſentations, or *ideas* of things they do not repreſent: But the miſtake and *falſehood* is,

§ 21. *But are falſe; 1. When judged agreeable to another man's* Idea, *without being ſo.*

FIRST, *When the mind*, having any idea, it *judges* and concludes *it the ſame that is in other mens minds, ſignified by the ſame name*, or that it is conformable to the ordinary received ſignification or definition of that word, when indeed it is not, which is the moſt uſual miſtake in mixed modes, though other *ideas* alſo are liable to it.

§ 22. 2. *When judged to agree to real Exiſtence, when they do not.*

SECONDLY, When it having a complex *idea* made up of ſuch a collection of ſimple ones, as nature never puts together, *it judges it to agree to a ſpecies of creatures really exiſting*, as when it joins the weight of tin, to the colour, fuſibility, and fixedneſs of gold.

§ 23. 3. *When judged adequate, without being ſo.*

THIRDLY, When in its complex *idea* it has united a certain number of ſimple *ideas* that do really exiſt together in ſome ſort of creatures, but has alſo left out others as much inſeparable, *it judges this to be a perfect complete* idea *of a ſort of things which really it is not; v. g.* having joined the *ideas* of ſubſtance, yellow, malleable, moſt heavy and fuſible, it takes that complex *idea* to be the complete *idea* of gold, when yet its peculiar fixedneſs and ſolubility in *aqua regia* are as inſeparable from thoſe other *ideas* or qualities of that body, as they are one from another.

§ 24. 4. *When judged to repreſent the real Eſſence.*

FOURTHLY, The miſtake is yet greater, *when I judge that this complex* idea *contains in it the real eſſence of any body exiſting*, when at leaſt it contains but ſome few of thoſe properties which flow from its real eſſence and conſtitution; I ſay, only ſome few of thoſe properties; for thoſe properties conſiſting moſtly in the active and paſſive powers it has, in reference to other things, all that are vulgarly known of any one body, and of which the complex *idea* of that kind of things is uſually made, are but a very few, in compariſon of what a man, that has ſeveral ways tried and examined it, knows of that one ſort of things; and all that the moſt expert man knows, are but few, in compariſon of what are really in that body, and depend on its internal or eſſential conſtitution. The eſſence of a triangle lies in a very little compaſs, conſiſts in a very few *ideas*; three lines including a ſpace make up that eſſence; but the properties that flow from this eſſence, are more than can be eaſily known or enumerated: So I imagine it is in ſubſtances; their real eſſences lie in a little compaſs, though the properties flowing from that internal conſtitution are endleſs.

§ 25. Ideas *when falſe.*

To conclude; a man having no notion of any thing without him, but by the *idea* he has of it in his mind (which *idea* he has a power to call by what name he pleaſes), he may indeed make an *idea* neither anſwering the reality of things, nor agreeing to the *ideas* commonly ſignified by other peoples words, but cannot make a wrong or *falſe idea* of a thing, which is no otherwiſe known to him but by the *idea* he has of it: *v. g.* When I frame an *idea* of the legs, arms, and body of a man, and join to this a horſe's head and neck, I do not make a *falſe idea* of any thing, becauſe it repreſents nothing without me: But when I call it a *Man* or *Tartar*, and imagine it either to repreſent ſome real being without me, or to be the ſame *idea* that others call by the ſame name; in either of theſe caſes I may err; and upon this account it is, that it comes to be termed a *falſe idea*; though indeed the *falſehood* lies not in the *idea*, but in that tacit mental propoſition, wherein a conformity and reſemblance is attributed to it, which it has not: But yet, if having framed ſuch an *idea* in my mind, without thinking either that exiſtence, or the name *Man* or *Tar-*

tar belongs to it, I will call it *Man* or *Tartar*, I may be justly thought fantastical in the naming, but not erroneous in my judgment, nor the *idea* any way *false*.

§ 26. *More properly to be called Right or Wrong.* Upon the whole matter, I think that our *ideas*, as they are considered by the mind, either in reference to the proper signification of their names, or in reference to the reality of things, *may* very fitly *be called right or wrong* ideas, according as they agree or disagree to those patterns to which they are referred: But if any one had rather call them *true* or *false*, it is fit he use a liberty, which every one has, to call things by those names he thinks best; though in propriety of speech, *truth* or *falsehood*, will, I think, scarce agree to them, but as they, some way or other, virtually contain in them some mental proposition. The *ideas* that are in a man's mind, simply considered, cannot be wrong, unless complex ones, wherein inconsistent parts are jumbled together: All other *ideas* are in themselves right, and the knowledge about them right and true knowledge; but when we come to refer them to any thing, as to their patterns and archetypes, then they are capable of being wrong, as far as they disagree with such archetypes.

CHAP. XXXIII.

OF THE ASSOCIATION OF IDEAS.

§ 1. *Something unreasonable in most Men.*

THERE is scarce any one that does not observe something that seems odd to him, and is in itself really extravagant in the opinions, reasonings and actions of other men. The least flaw of this kind, if at all different from his own, every one is quick-sighted enough to espy in another, and will by the authority of reason forwardly condemn, though he be guilty of much greater unreasonableness in his own tenets and conduct, which he never perceives and will very hardly, if at all, be convinced of.

§ 2. *Not wholly from Self-love.*

THIS proceeds not wholly from ſelf-love, though that has often a great hand in it. Men of fair minds, and not given up to the over-weening of ſelf-flattery, are frequently guilty of it; and in many caſes one with amazement hears the arguings, and is aſtoniſhed at the obſtinacy of a worthy man, who yields not to the evidence of reaſon, though laid before him as clear as day-light.

§ 3. *Nor from Education.*

THIS ſort of unreaſonableneſs is uſually imputed to education and prejudice, and for the moſt part truly enough, though that reaches not the bottom of the diſeaſe, nor ſhows diſtinctly enough where it riſes, or wherein it lies. Education is often rightly aſſigned for the cauſe, and prejudice is a good general name for the thing itſelf; but yet I think he ought to look a little farther, who would trace this ſort of madneſs to the root it ſprings from, and ſo explain it, as to ſhow whence this flaw has its original in very ſober and rational minds, and wherein it conſiſts.

§ 4. *A degree of Madneſs.*

I SHALL be pardoned for calling it by ſo harſh a name as *madneſs*, when it is conſidered, that oppoſition to reaſon deſerves that name, and is really madneſs; and there is ſcarce a man ſo free from it, but that if he ſhould always, on all occaſions, argue or do as in ſome caſes he conſtantly does, would not be thought fitter for *Bedlam* than civil converſation. I do not here mean when he is under the power of an unruly paſſion, but in the ſteady calm courſe of his life. That which will yet more apologiſe for this harſh name, and ungrateful imputation on the greateſt part of mankind, is, that inquiring a little by the by into the nature of madneſs, B. II. C. 11. § 13. I found it to ſpring from the very ſame root, and to depend on the very ſame cauſe we are here ſpeaking of. This conſideration of the thing itſelf, at a time when I thought not the leaſt on the ſubject which I am now treating of, ſuggeſted it to me. And if this be a weakneſs to which all men are ſo liable, if this be a taint which ſo univerſally infects mankind, the greater care ſhould be taken to lay it open under its due name, thereby to excite the greater care in its prevention and cure.

§ 5. *From a wrong Connection of* Ideas.

SOME of our *ideas* have a natural correſpondence and connection one with another: It is the office and excellency of our reaſon to trace theſe, and hold them together in that union and correſpondence which is founded in their peculiar beings. Beſides this, there is another connection of *ideas* wholly owing to chance or cuſtom: *Ideas* that in themſelves are not at all of kin, come to be ſo united in ſome mens minds, that it is very hard to ſeparate them; they always keep in company, and the one no ſooner at any time comes into the underſtanding, but its aſſociates appear with it, and if they are more than two, which are thus united, the whole gang, always inſeparable, ſhow themſelves together.

§ 6. *This Connection how made.*

THIS ſtrong combination of *ideas*, not allied by nature, the mind makes in itſelf either voluntarily or by chance; and hence it comes in different men to be very different, according to their different inclinations, education, intereſts, &c. Cuſtom ſettles habits of thinking in the underſtanding, as well as of determining in the will, and of motions in the body; all which ſeems to be but trains of motion in the animal ſpirits, which once ſet a-going, continue in the ſame ſteps they have been uſed to, which, by often treading, are worn into a ſmooth path, and the motion in it becomes eaſy, and as it were natural. As far as we can comprehend thinking, thus *ideas* ſeem to be produced in our minds; or if they are not, this may ſerve to explain their following one another in an habitual train, when once they are put into that track, as well as it does to explain ſuch motions of the body. A muſician uſed to any tune, will find, that let it but once begin in his head, the *ideas* of the ſeveral notes of it will follow one another orderly in his underſtanding, without any care or attention, as regularly as his fingers move orderly over the keys of the organ to play out the tune he has begun, though his inattentive thoughts be elsewhere a-wandering. Whether the natural cause of these *ideas*, as well as of that regular dancing of his fingers, be the motion of his animal spirits, I will not determine, how probable soever, by this instance, it appears to be so; but this may help us a little to conceive of intellectual habits, and of the tying together of *ideas*.

§ 7. *Some Antipathies an Effect of it.*

THAT there are such associations of them made by custom in the minds of most men, I think nobody will question, who has well considered himself or others; and to this, perhaps, might be justly attributed most of the sympathies and antipathies observable in men, which work as strongly, and produce as regular effects as if they were natural, and are therefore called so, though they at first had no other original but the accidental connection of two *ideas*, which either the strength of the first impression, or future indulgence, so united, that they always afterwards kept company together in that man's mind, as if they were but one *idea*. I say most of the antipathies, I do not say all, for some of them are truly natural, depend upon our original constitution, and are born with us; but a great part of those which are counted natural, would have been known to be from unheeded, though, perhaps, early impressions, or wanton fancies at first, which would have been acknowledged the original of them, if they had been warily observed. A grown person surfeiting with honey, no sooner hears the name of it, but his fancy immediately carries sickness and qualms to his stomach, and he cannot bear the very *idea* of it; other *ideas* of dislike, and sickness, and vomiting, presently accompany it, and he is disturbed, but he knows from whence to date this weakness, and can tell how he got this indisposition: Had this happened to him by an over-dose of honey, when a child, all the same effects would have followed, but the cause would have been mistaken, and the antipathy counted natural.

§ 8.

I MENTION this not out of any great necessity there is in this present argument, to distinguish nicely between natural and acquired antipathies; but I take notice of it for another purpoſe, *viz.* that thoſe who have children, or the charge of their education, would think it worth their while diligently to watch, and carefully to prevent the undue connection of *ideas* in the minds of young people: This is the time moſt ſuſceptible of laſting impreſſions; and though thoſe relating to the health of the body, are by diſcreet people minded and fenced againſt, yet I am apt to doubt, that thoſe which relate more peculiarly to the mind, and terminate in the underſtanding or paſſions, have been much leſs heeded than the thing deſerves; nay, thoſe relating purely to the underſtanding, have, as I ſuſpect, been by moſt men wholly overlooked.

§ 9. *A great Cauſe of Errors.*

THIS wrong connection in our minds, of *ideas*, in themſelves looſe and independent one of another, has ſuch an influence, and is of ſo great force to ſet us awry in our actions, as well moral as natural, paſſions, reaſonings, and notions themſelves, that perhaps there is not any one thing that deſerves more to be looked after.

§ 10. *Inſtances.*

THE *ideas* of *goblins* and *ſprights*, have really no more to do with darkneſs than light; yet let but a fooliſh maid inculcate theſe often on the mind of a child, and raiſe them there together, poſſibly he ſhall never be able to ſeparate them again ſo long as he lives; but darkneſs ſhall for ever afterwards bring with it thoſe frightful *ideas*, and they ſhall be ſo joined that he can no more bear the one than the other.

§ 11.

A MAN receives a ſenſible injury from another, thinks on the man and that action over and over, and by ruminating on them ſtrongly, or much in his mind, ſo cements thoſe two *ideas* together, that he makes them almoſt one; never thinks on the man, but the pain and diſpleaſure he ſuffered comes into his mind with it, ſo that he ſcarce diſtinguiſhes them, but has as much an averſion for the one as the other: Thus hatreds are often begotten from ſlight and almoſt innocent occaſions, and quarrels propagated and continued in the world.

§ 12.

A MAN has ſuffered pain or ſickneſs in any place; he ſaw his friend die in ſuch a room; though theſe have in nature nothing to do one with another, yet when the *idea* of the place occurs to his mind, it brings (the impreſſion being once made) that of the pain and diſpleaſure with it; he confounds them in his mind, and can as little bear the one as the other.

§ 13. *Why Time cures ſome Diſorders in the Mind which Reaſon cannot.*

WHEN this combination is ſettled, and whilſt it laſts, it is not in the power of reaſon to help us, and relieve us from the effects of it. *Ideas* in our minds, when they are there, will operate according to their natures and circumſtances; and here we ſee the cauſe why time cures certain affections, which reaſon, though in the right, and allowed to be ſo, has not power over, nor is able againſt them to prevail with thoſe who are apt to hearken to it in other caſes. The death of a child, that was the daily delight of his mother's eyes, and joy of her ſoul, rends from her heart the whole comfort of her life, and gives her all the torment imaginable; uſe the conſolations of reaſon in this caſe, and you were as good preach eaſe to one on the rack, and hope to allay, by rational diſcourſes, the pain of his joints tearing aſunder. Till time has by diſuſe ſeparated the ſenſe of that enjoyment, and its loſs from the *idea* of the child returning to her memory, all repreſentations, though ever ſo reaſonable, are in vain; and therefore ſome in whom the union between theſe *ideas* is never diſſolved, ſpend their lives in mourning, and carry an incurable ſorrow to their graves.

§ 14. *Farther Inſtances of the Effect of the Aſſociation of* Ideas.

A FRIEND of mine knew one perfectly cured of madneſs, by a very harſh and offenſive operation: The gentleman, who was thus recovered, with great ſenſe of gratitude and acknowledgment, owned the cure all his life after, as the greateſt obligation he could have received;

but whatever gratitude and reason suggested to him, he could never bear the sight of the operator; that image brought back with it the *idea* of that agony which he suffered from his hands, which was too mighty and intolerable for him to endure.

§ 15.

MANY children, imputing the pain they endured at school to their books they were corrected for, so join those *ideas* together, that a book becomes their aversion, and they are never reconciled to the study and use of them all their lives after; and thus reading becomes a torment to them, which otherwise possibly they might have made the greatest pleasure of their lives. There are rooms convenient enough, that some men cannot study in, and fashions of vessels, which though ever so clean and commodious, they cannot drink out of, and that by reason of some accidental *ideas* which are annexed to them, and make them offensive; and who is there that hath not observed some man to flag at the appearance, or in the company of some certain person not otherwise superior to him, but because having once on some occasion got the ascendant, the *idea* of authority and distance goes along with that of the person, and he that has been thus subjected, is not able to separate them?

§ 16.

INSTANCES of this kind are so plentiful every where, that if I add one more, it is only for the pleasant oddness of it: It is of a young gentleman, who having learned to dance, and that to great perfection, there happened to stand an old trunk in the room where he learned. The *idea* of this remarkable piece of household-stuff, had so mixed itself with the turns and steps of all his dances, that though in that chamber he could dance excellently well, yet it was only whilst that trunk was there; nor could he perform well in any other place, unless that or some such other trunk had its due position in the room. If this story shall be suspected to be dressed up with some comical circumstances, a little beyond precise nature, I answer for myself, that I had it some years since from a very sober and worthy man, upon his own knowledge, as I report it, and I dare ſay, there are very few inquiſitive perſons, who read this, who have not met with accounts, if not examples of this nature, that may parallel, or at leaſt juſtify this.

§ 17. *Its Influence on intellectual Habits.*

INTELLECTUAL habits and defects this way contracted, are not leſs frequent and powerful, though leſs obſerved. Let the *ideas* of being and matter be ſtrongly joined, either by education or much thought, whilſt theſe are ſtill combined in the mind, what notions, what reaſonings will there be about ſeparate ſpirits? Let cuſtom from the very childhood have joined figure and ſhape to the *ideas* of God, and what abſurdities will that mind be liable to about the Deity?

Let the *idea* of infallibility be inſeparably joined to any perſon, and theſe two conſtantly together poſſeſs the mind, and then one body in two places at once, ſhall, unexamined, be ſwallowed for a certain truth, by an implicit faith, whenever that imagined infallible perſon dictates and demands aſſent without inquiry.

§ 18. *Obſervable in different Sects.*

SOME ſuch wrong and unnatural combinations of *ideas* will be found to eſtabliſh the irreconcileable oppoſition between different ſects of philoſophy and religion; for we cannot imagine every one of their followers to impoſe wilfully on himſelf, and knowingly refuſe truth offered by plain reaſon. Intereſt, though it does a great deal in the caſe, yet cannot be thought to work whole ſocieties of men to ſo univerſal a perverſeneſs, as that every one of them, to a man, ſhould knowingly maintain falſehood; ſome at leaſt muſt be allowed to do what all pretend to, *i. e.* to purſue truth ſincerely; and therefore there muſt be ſomething that blinds their underſtandings, and makes them not ſee the falſehood of what they embrace for real truth. That which thus captivates their reaſons, and leads men of ſincerity blindfold from common ſenſe, will, when examined, be found to be what we are ſpeaking of. Some independent *ideas*, of no alliance to one another, are by education, cuſtom, and the conſtant din of their party, ſo coupled in their minds, that they always appear there together, and they can no more ſeparate them in their thoughts, than if they were but one *idea*, and they operate as if they were ſo. This gives ſenſe to *jargon*, demonſtration to abſurdities, and conſiſtency to nonſenſe, and is the foundation of the greateſt, I had almoſt ſaid of all the errors in the world; or if it does not reach ſo far, it is at leaſt the moſt dangerous one, ſince ſo far as it obtains, it hinders men from ſeeing and examining. When two things in themſelves disjoined, appear to the ſight conſtantly united, if the eye ſees theſe things rivetted which are looſe, where will you begin to rectify the miſtakes that follow in two *ideas*, that they have been accuſtomed ſo to join in their minds, as to ſubſtitute one for the other, and, as I am apt to think, often without perceiving it themſelves? This, whilſt they are under the deceit of it, makes them incapable of conviction, and they applaud themſelves as zealous champions for truth, when indeed they are contending for error; and the confuſion of two different *ideas*, which a cuſtomary connection of them in their minds hath to them made in effect but one, fills their heads with falſe views, and their reaſonings with falſe conſequences.

§ 19. *Concluſion.*

HAVING thus given an account of the original, ſorts and extent of our *ideas*, with ſeveral other conſiderations about theſe (I know not whether I may ſay) inſtruments or materials of our knowledge, the method I at firſt propoſed to myſelf, would now require that I ſhould immediately proceed to ſhow what uſe the underſtanding makes of them, and what knowledge we have by them. This was that which, in the firſt general view I had of this ſubject, was all that I thought I ſhould have to do; but upon a nearer approach, I find that there is ſo cloſe a connection between *ideas* and words, and our abſtract *ideas*, and general words have ſo conſtant a relation one to another, that it is impoſſible to ſpeak clearly and diſtinctly of our knowledge, which all conſiſts in propoſitions, without conſidering firſt the nature, uſe and ſignification of language; which therefore muſt be the buſineſs of the next book.

BOOK III.—CHAP. I.

OF WORDS OR LANGUAGE IN GENERAL.

§ 1. *Man fitted to form articulate Sounds.*

GOD having deſigned man for a ſociable creature, made him not only with an inclination, and under a neceſſity to have fellowſhip with thoſe of his own kind, but furniſhed him alſo with language, which was to be the great inſtrument and common tie of ſociety. *Man* therefore had by nature his organs ſo faſhioned, as to be *fit to frame articulate ſounds*, which we call words: But this was not enough to produce language; for parrots, and ſeveral other birds, will be taught to make articulate ſounds diſtinct enough, which yet by no means are capable of language.

§ 2. *To make them Signs of* Ideas.

BESIDES articulate ſounds therefore, it was farther neceſſary, that he ſhould be *able to uſe theſe ſounds as ſigns of internal conceptions*, and to make them ſtand as marks for the *ideas* within his own mind, whereby they might be made known to others, and the thoughts of mens minds be conveyed from one to another.

§ 3. *To make general Signs.*

BUT neither was this ſufficient to make words ſo uſeful as they ought to be. It is not enough for the perfection of language, that ſounds can be made ſigns of *ideas*, unleſs thoſe *ſigns* can be ſo made uſe of, as *to comprehend ſeveral particular things*; for the multiplication of words would have perplexed their uſe, had every particular thing need of a diſtinct name to be ſignified by. To remedy this inconvenience, language had yet a farther improvement in the uſe of general terms, whereby one word was made to mark a multitude of particular exiſtences; which advantageous uſe of ſounds was obtained only by the difference of the *ideas* they were made ſigns of; thoſe names becoming general, which are made to ſtand for general *ideas*, and thoſe remaining particular, where the *ideas* they are uſed for are particular.

§ 4. *To make general Signs.*

Besides theſe names which ſtand for *ideas*, there be other words which men make uſe of, not to ſignify any *idea*, but the want or abſence of ſome *ideas* ſimple or complex, or all *ideas* together; ſuch as are *nihil* in Latin, and in Engliſh, *ignorance* and *barrenneſs*; all which negative or privative words, cannot be ſaid properly to belong to, or ſignify no *ideas*, for then they would be perfectly inſignificant ſounds; but they relate to poſitive *ideas*, and ſignify their abſence.

§ 5. *Words ultimately derived from ſuch as ſignify ſenſible* Ideas.

It may alſo lead us a little towards the original of all our notions and knowledge, if we remark how great a dependence our *words* have on common ſenſible *ideas*, and how thoſe, which are made uſe of to ſtand for actions and notions quite removed from ſenſe, *have their riſe from thence, and from obvious ſenſible* ideas *are tranſferred to more abſtruſe ſignifications*, and made to ſtand for *ideas* that come not under the cognizance of our ſenſes; *v. g.* to *imagine, apprehend, comprehend, adhere, conceive, inſtil, diſguſt, diſturbance, tranquillity*, &c. are all words taken from the operations of ſenſible things, and applied to certain modes of thinking. *Spirit*, in its primary ſignification, is breath; *angel*, a meſſenger; and I doubt not, but if we could trace them to their ſources, we ſhould find, in all languages, the names which ſtand for things that fall not under our ſenſes, to have had their firſt riſe from ſenſible *ideas*, by which we may give ſome kind of gueſs, what kind of notions they were, and whence derived, which filled their minds who were the firſt beginners of languages; and how nature, even in the naming of things, unawares ſuggeſted to men the originals and principles of all their knowledge; whilſt to give names that might make known to others any operations they felt in themſelves, or any other *ideas* that came not under their ſenſes, they were fain to borrow words from ordinary known *ideas* of ſenſation, by that means to make others the more eaſily to conceive thoſe operations they experimented in themſelves, which made no outward ſenſible appearances; and then when they had got known and agreed names, to ſignify thoſe internal operations of their own minds, they were ſufficiently furniſhed to make known by words all their other *ideas*, ſince they could conſiſt of nothing, but either of outward ſenſible perceptions, or of the inward operations of their minds about them; we having, as has been proved, no *ideas* at all, but what originally come either from ſenſible objects without, or what we feel within ourſelves, from the inward workings of our own ſpirits, of which we are conſcious to ourſelves within.

§ 6. *Diſtribution.*

But to underſtand better the uſe and force of language, as ſubſervient to inſtruction and knowledge, it will be convenient to conſider,

Firſt, To what it is that names, in the uſe of language, are immediately applied.

Secondly, Since all (except proper) names are general, and ſo ſtand not particularly for this or that ſingle thing, but for ſorts and ranks of things, it will be neceſſary to conſider, in the next place, what the ſorts and kinds, or, if you rather like the Latin names, *what the* ſpecies *and* genera *of things* are, wherein they conſiſt, and how they come to be made. Theſe being (as they ought) well looked into, we ſhall the better come to find the right uſe of words, the natural advantages and defects of language, and the remedies that ought to be uſed, to avoid the inconveniencies of obſcurity or uncertainty in the ſignification of words, without which it is impoſſible to diſcourſe with any clearneſs or order concerning knowledge; which being converſant about propoſitions, and thoſe moſt commonly univerſal ones, has greater connection with words than perhaps is ſuſpected.

Theſe conſiderations, therefore, ſhall be the matter of the following chapters.

CHAP. II.

OF THE SIGNIFICATION OF WORDS.

§ 1. *Words are ſenſible Signs neceſſary for Communication.* MAN, though he has great variety of thoughts, and ſuch from which others, as well as himſelf, might receive profit and delight, yet they are all within his own breaſt, inviſible, and hidden from others, nor can of themſelves be made appear. The comfort and advantage of ſociety not being to be had without communication of thoughts, it was neceſſary that man ſhould find out ſome external ſenſible ſigns, whereby thoſe inviſible *ideas*, which his thoughts are made up of, might be made known to others; for this purpoſe nothing was ſo fit, either for plenty or quickneſs, as thoſe articulate ſounds, which, with ſo much eaſe and variety, he found himſelf able to make. Thus we may conceive how *words*, which were by nature ſo well adapted to that purpoſe, came to be made uſe of by men, as the *ſigns* of their *ideas*, not by any natural connection that there is between particular articulate ſounds, and certain *ideas*, for then there would be but one language amongſt all men; but by a voluntary impoſition, whereby ſuch a word is made arbitrarily the mark of ſuch an *idea*. The uſe then of words is to be ſenſible marks of *ideas*, and the *ideas* they ſtand for are their proper and immediate ſignification.

§ 2. *Words are the ſenſible Signs of his* Ideas *who uſes them.* THE uſe men have of theſe marks, being either to record their own thoughts for the aſſiſtance of their own memory, or as it were to bring out their *ideas*, and lay them before the view of others; *words in their primary or immediate ſignification ſtand for nothing but the* ideas *in the mind of him that uſes them*, how imperfectly ſoever or careleſsly thoſe *ideas* are collected from the things which they are ſuppoſed to repreſent. When a man ſpeaks to another, it is that he may be underſtood; and the end of ſpeech is, that thoſe ſounds, as marks, may make known his *ideas* to the hearer: That then which words are the marks of, are the *ideas* of the ſpeaker; nor can any one apply them, as marks, immediately to any thing elſe, but the *ideas* that he himſelf hath; for this would be to make them ſigns of his own conceptions, and yet apply them to other *ideas*; which would be to make them ſigns and not ſigns of his *ideas* at the ſame time, and ſo in effect to have no ſignification at all. Words being voluntary ſigns, they cannot be voluntary ſigns impoſed by him on things he knows not; that would be to make them ſigns of nothing, ſounds without ſignification. A man cannot make his words the ſigns either of qualities in things, or of conceptions in the mind of another, whereof he has none in his own. Till he has ſome *ideas* of his own, he cannot ſuppoſe them to correſpond with the conceptions of another man, nor can he uſe any ſigns for them; for thus they would be the ſigns of he knows not what, which is in truth to be the ſigns of nothing: But when he repreſents to himſelf other mens *ideas* by ſome of his own, if he conſent to give them the ſame names that other men do, it is ſtill to his own *ideas*; to *ideas* that he has, and not to *ideas* that he has not.

§ 3. *Words are the ſenſible Signs of his* Ideas *who uſes them.*

THIS is ſo neceſſary in the uſe of language, that in this reſpect the knowing and the ignorant, the learned and unlearned, uſe the *words* they ſpeak (with any meaning) all alike. They, *in every man's mouth ſtand for the* Ideas *he has*, and which he would expreſs by them. A child having taken notice of nothing in the metal he hears called gold, but the bright ſhining yellow colour, he applies the word gold only to his own *idea* of that colour, and nothing elſe; and therefore calls the ſame colour in a peacock's tail, gold. Another that hath better obſerved, adds to ſhining yellow, great weight; and then the ſound gold, when he uſes it, ſtands for a complex *idea* of a ſhining yellow and very weighty ſubſtance. Another adds to thoſe qualities fuſibility; and then the word gold to him ſignifies a body, bright, yellow, fuſible, and very heavy. Another adds malleability. Each of theſe uſes equally the word gold, when they have occaſion to expreſs the *idea* which they have applied it to; but it is evident, that each can apply it only to his own *idea*, nor can he make it ſtand as a ſign of ſuch a complex *idea* as he has not.

§ 4. *Words often ſecretly referred, Firſt, to the* Ideas *in other mens minds.*

BUT though words, as they are uſed by men, can properly and immediately ſignify nothing but the *ideas* that are in the mind of the ſpeaker, yet they in their thoughts give them a ſecret reference to two other things.

Firſt, They ſuppoſe their words to be marks of the ideas *in the minds alſo of other men with whom they communicate;* for elſe they ſhould talk in vain, and could not be underſtood, if the ſounds they applied to one *idea* were ſuch as by the hearer were applied to another, which is to ſpeak two languages. But in this men ſtand not uſually to examine whether the *idea* they and thoſe they diſcourſe with have in their minds, be the ſame, but think it enough that they uſe the word, as they imagine, in the common acceptation of that language, in which they ſuppoſe, that the *idea* they make it a ſign of, is preciſely the ſame to which the underſtanding men of that country apply that name.

§ 5. *Secondly, to the Reality of things.*

SECONDLY, Becauſe *men* would not be thought to talk *barely* of their own imaginations, but of things as really they are, therefore they *often ſuppoſe their words to ſtand alſo for the reality of things.* But this relating more particularly to ſubſtances, and their names, as perhaps the former does to ſimple *ideas* and modes, we ſhall ſpeak of theſe two different ways of applying words more at large, when we come to treat of the names of mixed modes, and ſubſtances in particular; though, give me leave here to ſay, that it is a perverting the uſe of words, and brings unavoidable obſcurity and confuſion into their ſignification, whenever we make them ſtand for any thing but thoſe *ideas* we have in our own minds.

§ 6. *Words by uſe readily excite* Ideas.

CONCERNING words alſo, it is farther to be conſidered,

First, That they being immediately the figns of mens *ideas*, and by that means the inftruments whereby men communicate their conceptions, and exprefs to one another thofe thoughts and imaginations they have within their own breafts, *there comes by conftant ufe* to be fuch *a connection between certain founds, and the* ideas *they ftand for*, that the names heard, almoft as readily excite certain *ideas*, as if the objects themfelves, which are apt to produce them, did actually affect the fenfes; which is manifeftly fo in all obvious fenfible qualities, and in all fubftances that frequently and familiarly occur to us.

§ 7. *Words often ufed without Signification.*

SECONDLY, That though the proper and immediate fignification of words are *ideas* in the mind of the fpeaker, yet becaufe by familiar ufe from our cradles we come to learn certain articulate founds very perfectly, and have them readily on our tongues, and always at hand in our memories, but yet are not always careful to examine, or fettle their fignifications perfectly; it *often* happens that *men*, even when they would apply themfelves to an attentive confideration, *do fet their thoughts more on words than things*. Nay, becaufe words are many of them learned before the *ideas* are known for which they ftand, therefore fome, not only children, but men, fpeak feveral words no otherwife than parrots do, only becaufe they have learned them, and have been accuftomed to thofe founds. But fo far as words are of ufe and fignification, fo far is there a conftant connection between the found and the *idea*, and a defignation that the one ftand for the other; without which application of them they are nothing but fo much infignificant noife.

§ 8. *Their Signification perfectly arbitrary.*

WORDS by long and familiar ufe, as has been faid, come to excite in men certain *ideas* fo conftantly and readily, that they are apt to fuppofe a natural connection between them. But that they *fignify* only mens peculiar *ideas*, and that *by a perfectly arbitrary impofition*, is evident, in that they often fail to excite in others (even that ufe the fame language) the fame *ideas* we take them to be the ſigns of: and every man has ſo inviolable a liberty to make words ſtand for what *ideas* he pleaſes, that no one hath the power to make others have the ſame *ideas* in their minds that he has, when they uſe the ſame words that he does; and therefore the great *Auguſtus* himſelf, in the poſſeſſion of that power which ruled the world, acknowledged he could not make a new Latin word; which was as much as to ſay, that he could not arbitrarily appoint what *idea* any ſound ſhould be a ſign of, in the mouths and common language of his ſubjects. It is true, common uſe by a tacit conſent appropriates certain ſounds to certain *ideas* in all languages, which ſo far limits the ſignification of that ſound, that unleſs a man applies it to the ſame *idea*, he does not ſpeak properly: and let me add, that unleſs a man's words excite the ſame *ideas* in the hearer which he makes them ſtand for in ſpeaking, he does not ſpeak intelligibly. But whatever be the conſequence of any man's uſing of words differently, either from their general meaning, or the particular ſenſe of the perſon to whom he addreſſes them, this is certain, their ſignification, in his uſe of them, is limited to his *ideas*, and they can be ſigns of nothing elſe.

CHAP. III.

OF GENERAL TERMS.

§ 1. *The greateſt part of Words general.*

ALL things that exiſt being particulars, it may perhaps be thought reaſonable that words, which ought to be conformed to things, ſhould be ſo too; I mean, in their ſignification; but yet we find the quite contrary. The far *greateſt part of words*, that make all languages, *are general terms;* which has not been the effect of neglect or chance, but of reaſon and neceſſity.

§ 2. *For every particular thing to have a Name is impoſſible.*

FIRST, It is impoſſible that every particular thing ſhould have a diſtinct peculiar name. For the ſignification and ufe of words, depending on that connection which the mind makes between its *ideas*, and the founds it ufes as figns of them, it is neceffary, in the application of names to things, that the mind fhould have diftinct *ideas* of the things, and retain alfo the particular name that belongs to every one, with its peculiar appropriation to that *idea*. But it is beyond the power of human capacity to frame and retain diftinct *ideas* of all the particular things we meet with; every bird and beaft men faw, every tree and plant that affected the fenfes, could not find a place in the moft capacious underftanding. If it be looked on as an inftance of a prodigious memory, that fome generals have been able to call every foldier in their army by his proper name, we may eafily find a reafon, why men have never attempted to give names to each fheep in their flock, or crow that flies over their heads; much lefs to call every leaf of plants, or grain of fand that came in their way, by a peculiar name.

§ 3. *And ufelefs.*

SECONDLY, If it were poffible, *it would yet be ufelefs*, becaufe it would not ferve to the chief end of language. Men would in vain heap up names of particular things, that would not ferve them to communicate their thoughts. Men learn names and ufe them in talk with others, only that they may be underftood, which is then only done, when by ufe or confent, the found I make by the organs of fpeech, excites in another man's mind, who hears it, the *idea* I apply it to in mine, when I fpeak it. This cannot be done by names applied to particular things, whereof I alone having the *ideas* in my mind, the names of them could not be fignificant or intelligible to another, who was not acquainted with all thofe very particular things which had fallen under my notice.

§ 4.

THIRDLY, But yet granting this alfo feafible (which I think is not), yet *a diftinct name for every particular thing would not be of any great ufe for the improvement of knowledge*, which though founded in particular things, enlarges itfelf by general views, to which things reduced into ſorts under general names are properly ſubſervient: Theſe, with the names belonging to them, come within ſome compaſs, and do not multiply every moment, beyond what either the mind can contain; or uſe requires; and therefore in theſe, men have for the moſt part ſtopped, but yet not ſo as to hinder themſelves from diſtinguiſhing particular things, by appropriated names, where convenience demands it; and therefore in their own ſpecies, which they have moſt to do with, and wherein they have often occaſion to mention particular perſons, they make uſe of proper names, and their diſtinct individuals have diſtinct denominations.

§ 5. *What things have proper Names.*

BESIDES perſons, countries, alſo cities, rivers, mountains, and other the like diſtinctions of place, have uſually found peculiar names, and that for the ſame reaſon, they being ſuch as men have often an occaſion to mark particularly, and as it were ſet before others in their diſcourſes with them; and I doubt not, but if we had reaſon to mention particular horſes, as often as we have to mention particular men, we ſhould have *proper names* for the one as familiar as for the other, and *Bucephalus* would be a word as much in uſe as *Alexander.* And therefore we ſee that amongſt jockeys, horſes have their proper names to be known and diſtinguiſhed by, as commonly as their ſervants, because, amongſt them, there is often occaſion to mention this or that particular horſe, when he is out of ſight.

§ 6. *How general Words are made.*

THE next thing to be conſidered, is, *How general words come to be made:* For ſince all things that exiſt are only particulars, how come we by general terms, or where find we thoſe general natures they are ſuppoſed to ſtand for? Words become general, by being made the ſigns of general *ideas,* and *ideas* become general, by ſeparating from them the circumſtances of time and place, and any other *ideas,* that may determine them to this or that particular exiſtence. By this way of abſtraction they are made capable of repreſenting more individuals than one;

each of which having in it a conformity to that abſtract *idea*, is (as we call it) of that ſort.

§ 7.

But to deduce this a little more diſtinctly, it will not perhaps be amiſs to trace our notions and names from their beginning, and obſerve by what degrees we proceed, and by what ſteps we enlarge our *ideas* from our firſt infancy. There is nothing more evident, than that the *ideas* of the perſons children converſe with (to inſtance in them alone), are like the perſons themſelves, only particular. The *ideas* of the nurſe and the mother are well framed in their minds, and, like pictures of them there, repreſent only thoſe individuals. The names they firſt gave to them are confined to theſe individuals, and the names of *nurſe* and *mamma*, the child uſes, determine themſelves to thoſe perſons. Afterwards, when time and a larger acquaintance has made them obſerve, that there are a great many other things in the world that in ſome common agreements of ſhape, and ſeveral other qualities, reſemble their father and mother, and thoſe perſons they have been uſed to, they frame an *idea*, which they find thoſe many particulars do partake in, and to that they give, with others, the name *man*, for example; and *thus they come to have a general name* and a general *idea*, wherein they make nothing new, but only leave out of the complex *idea* they had of *Peter* and *James*, *Mary* and *Jane*, that which is peculiar to each, and retain only what is common to them all.

§ 8.

By the ſame way that they come by the general name and *idea* of *man*, they eaſily *advance to more general names* and notions; for obſerving, that ſeveral things that differ from their *idea* of *man*, and cannot therefore be comprehended under that name, have yet certain qualities wherein they agree with *man*, by retaining only thoſe qualities, and uniting them into one *idea*, they have again another and a more general *idea*, to which having given a name, they make a term of a more comprehenſive extenſion; which new *idea* is made, not by any new addition, but only, as before, by leaving out the ſhape, and ſome other properties ſignified by the name *man*, and retaining only a body, with life, ſenſe, and ſpontaneous motion, comprehended under the name *animal*.

§ 9. *General Natures are nothing but abſtract* Ideas. THAT this is the *way whereby men firſt formed general* ideas, *and general names to them*, I think is ſo evident, that there needs no other proof of it, but the conſidering of a man's ſelf or others, and the ordinary proceedings of their minds in knowledge. And he that thinks general natures or notions are any thing elſe but ſuch abſtract and partial *ideas* of more complex ones, taken at firſt from particular exiſtences, will, I fear, be at a loſs where to find them; for let any one reflect, and then tell me, wherein does his *idea* of *man* differ from that of *Peter* and *Paul*, or his *idea* of *horſe* from that of *Bucephalus*, but in the leaving out ſomething that is peculiar to each individual, and retaining ſo much of thoſe particular complex *ideas* of ſeveral particular exiſtences, as they are found to agree in? Of the complex *ideas* ſignified by the names *man* and *horſe*, leaving out but thoſe particulars wherein they differ, and retaining only thoſe wherein they agree, and of thoſe making a new diſtinct complex *idea*, and giving the name *animal* to it, one has a more general term, that comprehends with man ſeveral other creatures. Leave out of the *idea* of *animal*, ſenſe and ſpontaneous motion, and the remaining complex *idea*, made up of the remaining ſimple ones of body, life, and nouriſhment, becomes a more general one, under the more comprehenſive term *vivens*. And not to dwell longer on this particular, ſo evident in itſelf, by the ſame way the mind proceeds to *body*, *ſubſtance*, and at laſt to *being*, *thing*, and ſuch univerſal terms, which ſtand for any of our *ideas* whatſoever. To conclude, this whole *myſtery* of *genera* and *ſpecies*, which make ſuch a noiſe in the ſchools, and are with juſtice ſo little regarded out of them, is nothing elſe but abſtract *ideas*, more or leſs comprehenſive, with names annexed to them; in all which this is conſtant and unvariable, that every more general term ſtands for ſuch an *idea*, as is but a part of any of thoſe contained under it.

§ 10. *Why the* Genus *is ordinarily made uſe of in Definitions.*

THIS may ſhow us the reaſon, *why, in the defining of words,* which is nothing but declaring their ſignification, *we make uſe of the genus,* or next general word that comprehends it, which is not out of neceſſity, but only to ſave the labour of enumerating the ſeveral ſimple *ideas* which the next general word or *genus* ſtands for; or, perhaps, ſometimes the ſhame of not being able to do it. But though defining by *genus* and *differentia* (I crave leave to uſe theſe terms of art, though originally Latin, ſince they moſt properly ſuit thoſe notions they are applied to), I ſay, though defining by the *genus* be the ſhorteſt way, yet I think it may be doubted whether it be the beſt. This I am ſure, it is not the only, and ſo not abſolutely neceſſary; for definition being nothing but making another underſtand by words, what *idea* the term defined ſtands for, a definition is beſt made by enumerating thoſe ſimple *ideas* that are combined in the ſignification of the term defined; and if inſtead of ſuch an enumeration, men have accuſtomed themſelves to uſe the next general term, it has not been out of neceſſity, or for greater clearneſs, but for quickneſs and diſpatch ſake; for, I think, that to one who deſired to know what *ideas* the word *man* ſtood for, if it ſhould be ſaid, that man was a ſolid extended ſubſtance, having life, ſenſe, ſpontaneous motion, and the faculty of reaſoning; I doubt not but the meaning of the term *man* would be as well underſtood, and the *idea* it ſtands for be at leaſt as clearly made known, as when it is defined to be a *rational animal,* which by the ſeveral definitions of *animal, vivens,* and *corpus,* reſolves itſelf into thoſe enumerated *ideas.* I have, in explaining the term *man,* followed here the ordinary definition of the ſchools, which though, perhaps, not the moſt exact, yet ſerves well enough to my preſent purpoſe: And one may, in this inſtance, ſee what gave occaſion to the rule, that a definition muſt conſiſt of *genus* and *differentia;* and it ſuffices to ſhow us the little neceſſity there is of ſuch a rule, or advantage in the ſtrict obſerving of it: For definitions, as has been ſaid, being only the explaining of one word by ſeveral others, ſo that the meaning or *idea* it ſtands for may be certainly known, languages are not always ſo made according to the rules of logic, that every term can have its ſignification exactly and clearly expreſſed by two others. Experience ſufficiently ſatisfies us to the contrary, or elſe thoſe who have made this rule have done ill, that they have given us ſo few definitions conformable to it. But of definitions, more in the next chapter.

§ 11. *General and Univerſal are Creatures of the Underſtanding.*

To return to general words, it is plain, by what has been ſaid, that *general* and *univerſal* belong not to the real exiſtence of things, but *are the inventions and creatures of the underſtanding*, made by it for its own uſe, and concern only ſigns, whether words or *ideas*. Words are general, as has been ſaid, when uſed for ſigns of general *ideas*, and ſo are applicable indifferently to many particular things; and *ideas* are general, when they are ſet up as the repreſentatives of many particular things; but univerſality belongs not to things themſelves, which are all of them particular in their exiſtence; even thoſe words and *ideas*, which in their ſignification are general. When, therefore, we quit particulars, the generals that reſt are only creatures of our own making, their general nature being nothing but the capacity they are put into by the underſtanding, of ſignifying or repreſenting many particulars; for the ſignification they have, is nothing but a relation that by the mind of man is added to them.

§ 12. *Abſtract* Ideas *are the Eſſences of the* Genera *and* Species.

THE next thing therefore to be conſidered, is, *What kind of ſignification it is, that general words have.* For as it is evident that they do not ſignify barely one particular thing, (for then they would not be general terms, but proper names) ſo on the other ſide it is as evident they do not ſignify a plurality; for man and men would then ſignify the ſame, and the diſtinction of numbers (as the grammarians call them) would be ſuperfluous and uſeleſs. That then which general words ſignify, is a ſort of things; and each of them does that, by being a ſign of an abſtract *idea* in the mind; to which *idea*, as things exiſting are found to agree, ſo they come to be ranked under that name, or, which is all one, be of that ſort; whereby it is evident, that the *eſſences* of the ſorts, or (if the Latin word pleaſes better) *ſpecies* of things, are nothing elſe but theſe abſtract *ideas*. For the having the eſſence of any ſpecies, being that which makes any thing to be of that ſpecies, and the conformity to the *idea* to which the name is annexed, being that which gives a right to that name, the having the eſſence, and the having that conformity, muſt needs be the ſame thing; ſince to be of any ſpecies, and to have a right to the name of that ſpecies, is all one. As for example, to be a *man*, or of the ſpecies *man*, and to have right to the name *man*, is the ſame thing. Again, to be a *man*, or of the ſpecies *man*, and have the eſſence of a *man*, is the ſame thing. Now ſince nothing can be a *man*, or have a right to the name *man*, but what has a conformity to the abſtract *idea* the name *man* ſtands for; nor any thing be a man, or have a right to the ſpecies *man*, but what has the eſſence of that ſpecies; it follows, that the abſtract *idea* for which the name ſtands, and the eſſence of the ſpecies, is one and the ſame; from whence it is eaſy to obſerve, that the eſſences of the ſorts of things, and conſequently the ſorting of this, is the workmanſhip of the underſtanding, that abſtracts and makes thoſe general *ideas*.

§ 13. *They are the workmanſhip of the Underſtanding, but have their foundation in the Similitude of things.*

I WOULD not here be thought to forget, much leſs to deny, that nature in the production of things makes ſeveral of them alike: There is nothing more obvious, eſpecially in the races of animals, and all things propagated by ſeed. But yet, I think, we may ſay the *ſorting* of them under names *is the workmanſhip of the underſtanding, taking occaſion from the ſimilitude* it obſerves amongſt them to make abſtract general *ideas*, and ſet them up in the mind, with names annexed to them, as patterns or forms (for in that ſenſe the word form has a very proper ſignification), to which as particular things exiſting are found to agree, ſo they come to be of that ſpecies, have that denomination, or are put into that *claſſis.* For when we ſay, this is a *man*, that a *horſe*; this *juſtice*, that *cruelty*; this a *watch*, that a *jack*; what do we elſe but rank things under different ſpecific names, as agreeing to thoſe abſtract *ideas*, of which we have made thoſe names the ſigns? and what are the eſſences of thoſe ſpecies ſet out and marked by names, but thoſe abſtract *ideas* in the mind, which are as it were the bonds between particular things that exiſt, and the names they are to be ranked under? And when general names have any connection with particular beings, theſe abſtract *ideas* are the *medium* that unites them; ſo that the eſſences of ſpecies, as diſtinguiſhed and denominated by us, neither are nor can be any thing but thoſe preciſe abſtract *ideas* we have in our minds; and therefore the ſuppoſed real eſſences of ſubſtances, if different from our abſtract *ideas*, cannot be the eſſences of the ſpecies we rank things into; for two ſpecies may be one as rationally, as two different eſſences be the eſſence of one ſpecies: and I demand what are the alterations may or may not be in a *horſe* or *lead*, without making either of them to be of another ſpecies? In determining the ſpecies of things by our abſtract *ideas*, this is eaſy to reſolve: but if any one will regulate himſelf herein by ſuppoſed real eſſences, he will, I ſuppoſe, be at a loſs; and he will never be able to know when any thing preciſely ceaſes to be of the ſpecies of a *horſe* or *lead*.

§ 14. *Each diſtinct abſtract* Idea *is a diſtinct Eſſence.* Nor will any one wonder, that I ſay theſe *eſſences*, or abſtract *ideas* (which are meaſures of name, and the boundaries of ſpecies), are *the workmanſhip of the underſtanding*, who conſiders, that at leaſt the complex ones are often, in ſeveral men, different collections of ſimple *ideas*; and therefore that is *covetouſneſs* to one man, which is not ſo to another. Nay, even in ſubſtances, where their abſtract *ideas* ſeem to be taken from the things themſelves, they are not conſtantly the ſame, no, not in that ſpecies which is moſt familiar to us, and with which we have the moſt intimate acquaintance; it having been more than once doubted, whether the *fœtus* born of a woman were a *man*, even ſo far as that it hath been debated, whether it were or were not to be nouriſhed and baptized; which could not be, if the abſtract *idea* of eſſence, to which the name man belonged, were of nature's making, and were not the uncertain and various collection of ſimple *ideas* which the underſtanding puts together, and then abſtracting it, affixed a name to it; ſo that in truth *every diſtinct abſtract* idea *is a diſtinct eſſence*, and the names that ſtand for ſuch diſtinct *ideas*, are the names of things eſſentially different. Thus, a circle is as eſſentially different from an oval as a ſheep from a goat, and rain is as eſſentially different from ſnow as water from earth; that abſtract *idea* which is the eſſence of one being impoſſible to be communicated to the other. And thus any two abſtract *ideas*, that in any part vary one from another, with two diſtinct names annexed to them, conſtitute two diſtinct ſorts, or, if you pleaſe, *ſpecies*, as eſſentially different as any two the moſt remote or oppoſite in the world.

§ 15. *Real and Nominal Eſſence.*

BUT ſince the *eſſences* of things are thought by ſome (and not without reaſon) to be wholly unknown, it may not be amiſs to conſider the *ſeveral ſignifications of the word eſſence.*

Firſt, *Eſſence* may be taken for the being of any thing, whereby it is what it is; and thus the real internal, but generally in ſubſtances unknown, conſtitution of things, whereon their diſcoverable qualities depend, may be called their *eſſence*. This is the proper original ſignification of the word, as is evident from the formation of it; *eſſentia*, in its primary notation, ſignifying properly *being*: And in this ſenſe it is ſtill uſed, when we ſpeak of the *eſſence* of particular things, without giving them any name.

Secondly, The learning and difputes of the fchools having been much bufied about *genus* and *fpecies*, the word *effence* has almoft loft its primary fignification; and inftead of the real conftitution of things, has been almoft wholly applied to the artificial conftitution of *genus* and *fpecies*. It is true, there is ordinarily fuppofed a real conftitution of the forts of things, and it is paft doubt there muft be fome real conftitution on which any collection of fimple *ideas* co-exifting muft depend. But it being evident, that things are ranked under names into forts or *fpecies*, only as they agree to certain abftract *ideas*, to which we have annexed thofe names, the *effence* of each *genus* or fort comes to be nothing but that abftract *idea*, which the general or *fortal* (if I may have leave fo to call it from *fort*, as I do *general* from *genus*) name ftands for; and this we fhall find to be that which the word *effence* imports in its moft familiar ufe. Thefe two forts of *effences*, I fuppofe, may not unfitly be termed, the one the *real*, the other the *nominal effence*.

§ 16. *Conftant Connection between the name and nominal Effence.*

BETWEEN *the nominal effence and the name*, there is fo *near a connection*, that the name of any fort of things cannot be attributed to any particular being but what has this *effence*, whereby it anfwers that abftract *idea*, whereof that name is the fign.

§ 17. *Suppofition that Species are diftinguifhed by their real Effences, ufelefs.*

CONCERNING the real effences of corporeal fubftances (to mention thofe only), there are, if I miftake not, two opinions. The one is of thofe, who, ufing the word *effence* for they know not what, fuppofe a certain number of thofe *effences*, according to which all natural things are made, and wherein they do exactly every one of them partake, and fo become of this or that *fpecies*. The other and more rational opinion, is of thofe who look on all natural things to have a real but unknown conftitution of their infenfible parts, from which flow thofe fenfible qualities which ferve us to diftinguifh them one from another, according as we have occaſion to rank them into ſorts under common denominations. The former of theſe opinions, which ſuppoſes theſe *eſſences* as a certain number of forms or moulds, wherein all natural things that exiſt are caſt, and do equally partake, has, I imagine, very much perplexed the knowledge of natural things. The frequent productions of monſters, in all the ſpecies of animals, and of changelings, and other ſtrange iſſues of human birth, carry with them difficulties not poſſible to conſiſt with this *hypotheſis;* ſince it is as impoſſible that two things, partaking exactly of the ſame real *eſſence*, ſhould have different properties, as that the two figures partaking in the ſame real eſſence of a circle ſhould have different properties. But were there no other reaſon againſt it, yet the *ſuppoſition of eſſences that cannot be known*, and the making them nevertheleſs to be that which diſtinguiſhes the ſpecies of things, is ſo *wholly uſeleſs* and unſerviceable to any part of our knowledge, that that alone were ſufficient to make us lay it by, and content ourſelves with ſuch *eſſences* of the ſorts or ſpecies of things as come within the reach of our knowledge, which, when ſeriouſly conſidered, will be found, as I have ſaid, to be nothing elſe but thoſe abſtract complex *ideas*, to which we have annexed diſtinct general names.

§ 18. *Real and nominal Eſſence the ſame in ſimple* Ideas *and Modes, different in Subſtances.*

Essences being thus diſtinguiſhed into *nominal* and *real*, we may farther obſerve, that *in* the ſpecies of *ſimple* ideas *and modes* they *are always the ſame*, but *in ſubſtances always quite different.* Thus, a figure including a ſpace between three lines, is the real as well as nominal *eſſence* of a triangle, it being not only the abſtract *idea* to which the general name is annexed, but the very *eſſentia* or being of the thing itſelf, that foundation from which all its properties flow, and to which they are all inſeparably annexed. But it is far otherwiſe concerning that parcel of matter which makes the ring on my finger, wherein theſe two *eſſences* are apparently different; for it is the real conſtitution of its inſenſible parts on which depend all thoſe properties of colour, weight, fuſibility, fixedneſs, *&c.* which makes it to be *gold*, or gives it a right to that name, which is therefore its nominal *eſſence*; ſince nothing can be called *gold* but what has a conformity of qualities to that abſtract complex *idea* to which that name is annexed. But this diſtinction of *eſſences*, belonging particularly to ſubſtances, we ſhall, when we come to conſider their names, have an occaſion to treat of more fully.

§ 19. *Eſſences ingenerable and incorruptible.*

THAT ſuch *abſtract* ideas, *with names to them*, as we have been ſpeaking of, *are eſſences*, may farther appear by what we are told concerning *eſſences*, *viz.* that they are all ingenerable and incorruptible; which cannot be true of the real conſtitutions of things which begin and periſh with them. All things that exiſt, beſides their author, are all liable to change; eſpecially thoſe things we are acquainted with, and have ranked into bands under diſtinct names or enſigns. Thus that which was graſs to-day, is to-morrow the fleſh of a ſheep, and within few days after becomes part of a man: In all which, and the like changes, it is evident their real *eſſence*, *i. e.* that conſtitution whereon the properties of theſe ſeveral things depended, is deſtroyed, and periſhes with them. But *eſſences* being taken for *ideas* eſtabliſhed in the mind, with names annexed to them, they are ſuppoſed to remain ſteadily the ſame, whatever mutations the particular ſubſtances are liable to; for whatever becomes of *Alexander* and *Bucephalus*, the *ideas* to which *man* and *horſe* are annexed, are ſuppoſed nevertheleſs to remain in the ſame; and ſo the *eſſences* of thoſe ſpecies are preſerved whole and undeſtroyed, whatever changes happen to any, or all of the individuals of thoſe *ſpecies*. By this means, the *eſſence* of a *ſpecies* reſts ſafe and entire, without the exiſtence of ſo much as one individual of that kind: For were there now no circle exiſting any where in the world (as perhaps that figure exiſts not any where exactly marked out), yet the *idea* annexed to that name would not ceaſe to be what it is, nor ceaſe to be as a pattern to determine which of the particular figures we meet with have or have not a right to the name *circle*, and so to show which of them, by having that essence, was of that *species*. And though there neither were nor had been in nature such a beast as an *unicorn*, or such a fish as a *mermaid*; yet supposing those names to stand for complex abstract *ideas* that contained no inconsistency in them, the *essence* of a *mermaid* is as intelligible as that of a *man*, and the *idea* of an *unicorn* as certain, steady and permanent as that of a horse. From what has been said, it is evident, that the doctrine of the immutability of *essences* proves them to be only abstract *ideas*; and is founded on the relation established between them and certain sounds as signs of them, and will always be true as long as the same name can have the same signification.

§ 20. *Recapitulation.*

To conclude, this is that which in short I would say, *viz.* That all the great business of *genera* and *species*, and their *essences*, amounts to no more but this; that men making abstract *ideas*, and settling them in their minds with names annexed to them, do thereby enable themselves to consider things, and discourse of them, as it were in bundles, for the easier and readier improvement and communication of their knowledge; which would advance but slowly, were their words and thoughts confined only to particulars.

CHAP. IV.

OF THE NAMES OF SIMPLE IDEAS.

§ 1. *Names of simple* Ideas, *Modes and Substances, have each something peculiar.*

THOUGH all words, as I have shown, signify nothing immediately but the *ideas* in the mind of the speaker; yet upon a nearer survey we shall find that the *names of simple* ideas, *mixed modes* (under which I comprise relations too), *and natural substances, and each of them, have something peculiar* and different from the other. For example:

§ 2. 1. *Names of ſimple* Ideas *and Subſtances intimate real Exiſtence.*

FIRST, The *names of ſimple* ideas *and ſubſtances*, with the abſtract *ideas* in the mind, which they immediately ſignify, *intimate* alſo *ſome real exiſtence*, from which was derived their original pattern. But the *names of mixed modes terminate in the* idea that is in the mind, and lead not the thoughts any farther; as we ſhall ſee more at large in the following chapter.

§ 3. 2. *Names of ſimple* Ideas, *and Modes ſignify always both real and nominal Eſſence.*

SECONDLY, The *names of ſimple* ideas *and modes, ſignify always the real as well as nominal eſſence of their ſpecies.* But *the names of natural ſubſtances ſignify rarely*, if ever, any thing but *barely the nominal eſſences* of thoſe ſpecies, we ſhall ſhow in the chapter that treats of the names of ſubſtances in particular.

§ 4. 3. *Names of ſimple* Ideas *undefinable.*

THIRDLY, The *names of ſimple* ideas *are not capable of any definitions;* the names of all complex *ideas* are. It has not, that I know, been yet obſerved by any body, what words are, and what are not capable of being defined; the want whereof is (as I am apt to think) not ſeldom the occaſion of great wrangling and obſcurity in mens diſcourſes; whilſt ſome demand definitions of terms that cannot be defined, and others think they ought to reſt ſatisfied in an explication made by a more general word, and its reſtriction (or to ſpeak in terms of art, by a genus and difference); when even after ſuch definition made according to rule, thoſe who hear it, have often no more a clear conception of the meaning of the word than they had before. This at leaſt I think, that the ſhowing what words are, and what are not capable of definitions, and wherein conſiſts a good definition, is not wholly beſides our preſent purpoſe; and perhaps will afford ſo much light to the nature of theſe ſigns, and our *ideas*, as to deſerve a more particular conſideration.

§ 5. *If all were definable, it would be a proceſs* in infinitum.

I WILL not here trouble myſelf, to prove that all terms

are not definable from that progreſs, *in infinitum*, which it will viſibly lead us into, if we ſhould allow that all names could be defined; for if the terms of one definition were ſtill to be defined by another, where at laſt ſhould we ſtop? But I ſhall, from the nature of our *ideas*, and the ſignification of our words, ſhow, *why ſome names can, and others cannot be defined*, and which they are.

§ 6. *What a Definition is.*

I THINK it is agreed, that *a definition* is nothing elſe, but *the ſhowing the meaning of one word by ſeveral other not ſynonymous terms;* the meaning of words being only the *ideas* they are made to ſtand for by him that uſes them. The meaning of any term is then ſhowed, or the word is defined, when by other words, the *idea* it is made the ſign of, and annexed to in the mind of the ſpeaker, is as it were repreſented or ſet before the view of another, and thus its ſignification aſcertained. This is the only uſe and end of definitions, and therefore the only meaſure of what is or is not a good definition.

§ 7. *Simple* Ideas *why undefinable.*

THIS being premiſed, I ſay, that *the names of ſimple* Ideas, and thoſe only, *are incapable of being defined*; the reaſon whereof is this, that the ſeveral terms of a definition, ſignifying ſeveral *ideas*, they can altogether by no means repreſent an *idea* which has no compoſition at all; and therefore a definition, which is properly nothing but the ſhowing the meaning of one word by ſeveral others not ſignifying each the ſame thing, can in the names of ſimple *idea* have no place.

§ 8. *Inſtances—Motion.*

THE not obſerving this difference in our *ideas*, and their names, has produced that eminent trifling in the ſchools, which is ſo eaſy to be obſerved in the definitions they give us of ſome few of theſe ſimple *ideas;* for as to the greateſt part of them, even thoſe maſters of definitions were fain to leave them untouched, merely by the impoſſibility they found in it. What more exquiſite *jargon* could the wit of man invent, than this definition, *the act of a being in power, as far forth as in power?* which would puzzle any rational man, to whom it was not already known by its famous absurdity, to guess what word it could ever be supposed to be the explication of. If *Tully* asking a *Dutchman* what *beweeginge* was, should have received this explication in his own language, that it was *actus entis in potentia quatenus in potentia;* I ask, whether any one can imagine he could thereby have understood what the word *beweeginge* signified, or have guessed what *idea* a *Dutchman* ordinarily had in his mind, and would signify to another, when he used that sound?

§ 9.

NOR have the modern philosophers, who have endeavoured to throw off the *jargon* of the schools, and speak intelligibly, much better succeeded in defining simple *ideas*, whether by explaining their causes, or any otherwise. The *atomists*, who define motion to be a *passage from one place to another*, what do they more than put one synonymous word for another? For what is *passage*, other than *motion?* And if they were asked what passage was, how would they better define it than by *motion?* For is it not at least as proper and significant to say, *passage is a motion from one place to another*, as to say, *motion is a passage*, &c.? This is to translate and not to define, when we change two words of the same signification one for another; which when one is better understood than the other, may serve to discover what *idea* the unknown stands for, but is very far from a *definition;* unless we will say every *English* word in the dictionary is the definition of the *Latin* word it answers, and the motion is a definition of *motus*. *Nor will the successive application of the parts of the* superficies *of one body to those of another*, which the *Cartesians* give us, prove a much better definition of motion, when well examined.

§ 10. *Light.*

THE act of perspicuous, as far forth as perspicuous, is another peripatetic definition of a simple *idea;* which, though not more absurd than the former of *motion*, yet betrays its uselessness and insignificancy more plainly, because experience will easily convince any one, that it cannot make the meaning of the word *light* (which it pretends to define) at all underſtood by a blind man. But the definition of *motion* appears not at firſt ſight ſo uſeleſs, becauſe it eſcapes this way of trial; for this ſimple *idea*, entering by the touch as well as ſight, it is impoſſible to ſhow an example of any one, who has no other way to get the *idea* of *motion*, but barely by the definition of that name. Thoſe who tell us, that *light* is a great number of little globules, ſtriking briſkly on the bottom of the eye, ſpeak more intelligibly than the ſchools; but yet theſe words ever ſo well underſtood would make the *idea* the word *light* ſtands for, no more known to a man that underſtands it not before, than if one ſhould tell him, that light was nothing but a company of little tennis balls, which fairies all day long ſtruck with rackets againſt ſome mens foreheads, whilſt they paſſed by others. For granting this explication of the thing to be true, yet the *idea* of the cauſe of *light*, if we had it ever ſo exact, would no more give us the *idea* of *light* itſelf, as it is ſuch a particular perception in us, than the *idea* of the figure and motion of a ſharp piece of ſteel would give us the *idea* of that pain which it is able to cauſe in us: for the cauſe of any ſenſation, and the ſenſation itſelf, in all the ſimple *ideas* of one ſenſe, are two *ideas*; and two *ideas* ſo different and diſtant one from another, that no two can be more ſo. And therefore ſhould *Des Cartes's* globules ſtrike ever ſo long on the *retina* of a man who was blind by a *gutta ſerena*, he would thereby never have any *idea* of *light*, or any thing approaching it, though he underſtood what little globules were, and what ſtriking on another body was, ever ſo well; and therefore the *Carteſians* very well diſtinguiſh between that light which is the cauſe of that ſenſation in us, and the *idea* which is produced in us by it, and is that which is properly light.

§ 11. *Simple* Ideas *why undefinable, farther explained.* *SIMPLE ideas*, as has been ſhown, *are only* to be *got* by thoſe *impreſſions* objects themſelves make on our minds, by the proper inlets appointed to each ſort. If they are not received this way, all the *words* in the world, *made use of to explain or define any of their names, will never be able to produce in us the* idea *it stands for;* for words being sounds, can produce in us no other simple *ideas* than of those very sounds, nor excite any in us, but by that voluntary connection which is known to be between them and those simple *ideas* which common use has made them signs of. He that thinks otherwise, let him try if any words can give him the taste of a pine apple, and make him have the true *idea* of the relish of that celebrated delicious fruit. So far as he is told it has a resemblance with any tastes, whereof he has the *ideas* already in his memory, imprinted there by sensible objects, not strangers to his palate, so far may he approach that resemblance in his mind. But this is not giving us that *idea* by *definition*, but exciting in us other simple *ideas*, by their known names, which will be still very different from the true taste of that fruit itself. In light and colours, and all other simple *ideas*, it is the same thing; for the signification of sounds is not natural, but only imposed and arbitrary. And no definition of *light* or *redness* is more fitted, or able to produce either of those *ideas* in us, than the sound *light* or *red* by itself; for to hope to produce an *idea* of light or colour by a sound, however formed, is to expect that sounds should be visible, or colours audible, and to make the ears do the office of all the other senses; which is all one as to say, that we might taste, smell and see by the ears; a sort of philosophy worthy only of *Sancho Pancha*, who had the faculty to see *Dulcinea* by hearsay. And therefore he that has not before received into his mind, by the proper inlet, the simple *idea* which any word stands for, can never come to know the signification of that word by any other words or sounds whatsoever put together, according to any rules of definition. The only way is, by applying to his senses the proper object, and so producing that *idea* in him for which he has learned the name already. A studious blind man, who had mightily beat his head about visible objects, and made use of the explication of his books and friends, to understand those names of light and colours which often came in his way, bragged one day that he now underſtood what *ſcarlet* ſignified. Upon which his friend demanding, what *ſcarlet* was? the blind man anſwered, it was like the ſound of a trumpet. Juſt ſuch an underſtanding of the name of any other ſimple *idea* will he have, who hopes to get it only from a definition, or other words made uſe of to explain it.'

§ 12. *The contrary ſhowed in complex* Ideas *by Inſtances of a Statue and Rainbow.*

THE caſe is quite otherwiſe *in complex ideas;* which conſiſting of ſeveral ſimple ones, it is in the power of words ſtanding for the ſeveral *ideas* that make that compoſition, to imprint complex *ideas* in the mind which were never there before, and ſo make their names be underſtood. In ſuch collections of *ideas*, paſſing under one name, *definition*, or the teaching the ſignification of one word by ſeveral others, has place, and *may make us underſtand the names* of things, which never came within the reach of our ſenſes, and frame *ideas* ſuitable to thoſe in other mens minds, when they uſe thoſe names, provided that none of the terms of the definition ſtand for any ſuch ſimple *ideas*, which he to whom the explication is made has never yet had in his thought. Thus the word *ſtatue* may be explained to a blind man by other words, when *picture* cannot; his ſenſes having given him the *idea* of figure, but not of colours, which therefore words cannot excite in him. This gained the prize to the painter againſt the ſtatuary; each of which contending for the excellency of his art, and the ſtatuary bragging that his was to be preferred, becauſe it reached farther, and even thoſe who had loſt their eyes could yet perceive the excellency of it; the painter agreed to refer himſelf to the judgment of a blind man; who being brought where there was a ſtatue made by the one, and a picture drawn by the other, he was firſt led to the ſtatue, in which he traced with his hands all the lineaments of the face and body, and with great admiration applauded the ſkill of the workman. But being led to the picture, and having his hands laid upon it, was told, that now he touched the head, and then the forehead, eyes, noſe, &c. as his hand moved over the parts of the picture on the cloth, without finding any the leaſt diſtinction; whereupon he cried out, that certainly that muſt needs be a very admirable and divine piece of workmanſhip, which could repreſent to them all thoſe parts, where he could neither feel nor perceive any thing.

§ 13.

He that ſhould uſe the word *rainbow* to one who knew all thoſe colours, but yet had never ſeen that *phenomenon*, would, by enumerating the figure, largeneſs, poſition and order of the colours, ſo well define that word that it might be perfectly underſtood; but yet that *definition*, how exact and perfect ſoever, would never make a blind man underſtand it; becauſe ſeveral of the ſimple *ideas* that make that complex one, being ſuch as he never received by ſenſation and experience, no words are able to excite them in his mind.

§ 14. *The names of complex* Ideas *when to be made intelligible by words.*

Simple *ideas* as has been ſhowed, can only be got by experience, from thoſe objects which are proper to produce in us thoſe perceptions. *When* by this means we have our minds ſtored with them, and know the names for them, then *we are in a condition to define*, and by *definition* to underſtand the names of complex *ideas* that are made up of them. But when any term ſtands for a ſimple *idea* that a man has never yet had in his mind, it is impoſſible by any words to make known its meaning to him. When any term ſtands for an *idea* a man is acquainted with, but is ignorant that that term is the ſign of it, there another name, of the ſame *idea* which he has been accuſtomed to, may make him underſtand its meaning. But in no caſe whatſoever is any name of any ſimple *idea* capable of a *definition*.

§ 15. 4. *Names of Simple* Ideas *leaſt doubtful.*

Fourthly, But though the names of *ſimple ideas* have not the help of *definition* to determine their ſignification, yet that hinders not but that they *are generally leſs doubtful and uncertain, than thoſe of mixed modes and ſubſtances*; becauſe they ſtanding only for one ſimple perception, men for the moſt part eaſily and perfectly agree in their ſignification; and there is little room for miſtake and wrangling about their meaning. He that knows once that whiteneſs is the name of that colour he has obſerved in ſnow or milk, will not be apt to miſapply that word as long as he retains that *idea*; which when he has quite loſt, he is not apt to miſtake the meaning of it, but perceives he underſtands it not. There is neither a multiplicity of ſimple *ideas* to be put together, which makes the doubtfulneſs in the names of mixed modes, nor a ſuppoſed, but an unknown real eſſence, with properties depending thereon, the preciſe number whereof are alſo unknown, which makes the difficulty in the names of ſubſtances; but, on the contrary, in ſimple *ideas*, the whole ſignification of the name is known at once, and conſiſts not of parts, whereof more or leſs being put in, the *idea* may be varied, and ſo the ſignification of its name be obſcure or uncertain.

§ 16. 5. *Simple* Ideas *have few Aſcents* in linea predicamentali.

FIFTHLY, This farther may be obſerved concerning *ſimple* ideas, and their names, that they *have but few aſcents* in linea predicamentali (as they call it) *from the loweſt ſpecies to the* ſummum genus: The reaſon whereof is, that the loweſt ſpecies being but one ſimple *idea*, nothing can be left out of it; that ſo the difference being taken away, it may agree with ſome other thing in one *idea* common to them both; which having one name, is the *genus* of the other two: *v. g.* There is nothing can be left out of the *idea* of white and red, to make them agree in one common appearance, and ſo have one general name; as *rationality* being left out of the complex *idea* of *man*, makes it agree with brute, in the more general *idea* and name of *animal*. And therefore when to avoid unpleaſant enumerations, men would comprehend both *white* and *red*, and ſeveral other ſuch ſimple *ideas*, under one general name, they have been fain to do it by a word, which denotes only the way they get into the mind; for when *white*, *red* and *yellow* are all comprehended under the *genus* or name *colour*, it ſignifies no more but ſuch *ideas* as are produced in the mind only by the ſight, and have entrance only through the eyes. And when they would frame yet a more general term, to comprehend both *colours* and *ſounds*, and the like ſimple *ideas*, they do it by a word that ſignifies all ſuch as come into the mind only by one ſenſe; and ſo the general term *quality*, in its ordinary acceptation, comprehends colours, ſounds, taſtes, ſmells and tangible qualities, with diſtinction from extenſion, number, motion, pleaſure and pain, which make impreſſions on the mind, and introduce their *ideas* by more ſenſes than one.

§ 17. 6. *Names of ſimple* Ideas *ſtand for* Ideas *not at all arbitrary.*

SIXTHLY, The names of ſimple *ideas*, ſubſtances, and mixed modes, have alſo this difference, that thoſe *of mixed modes* ſtand for *ideas* perfectly *arbitrary;* thoſe *of ſubſtances* are not perfectly ſo, but *refer to a pattern, though with ſome latitude; and thoſe of ſimple* ideas *are* perfectly taken from the exiſtence of things, and are *not arbitrary at all.* Which what difference it makes in the ſignifications of their names, we ſhall ſee in the following chapters.

The names of ſimple modes differ little from thoſe of ſimple *ideas*.

CHAP. V.

OF THE NAMES OF MIXED MODES AND RELATIONS.

§ 1. *They ſtand for abſtract* Ideas, *as other general Names.*

THE names of mixed modes being general, they ſtand, as has been ſhown, for ſorts or ſpecies of things, each of which has its peculiar eſſence. The eſſences of theſe ſpecies alſo, as has been ſhowed, are nothing but the abſtract *ideas* in the mind, to which the name is annexed. Thus far the names and eſſences of mixed modes have nothing but what is common to them with other *ideas*, but if we take a little nearer ſurvey of them, we ſhall find that they have ſomething peculiar, which perhaps may deſerve our attention.

§ 2. 1. *The* Ideas *they ſtand for are made by the Underſtanding.*

THE firſt particularity I ſhall obſerve in them, is, that the abſtract *ideas*, or, if you pleaſe, the eſſences of the ſeveral ſpecies of *mixed modes, are made by the underſtanding*, wherein they differ from thoſe of ſimple *ideas*; in which ſort the mind has no power to make any one, but only receives ſuch as are preſented to it, by the real exiſtence of things operating upon it.

§ 3. 2. *Made arbitrarily and without Patterns.*

IN the next place, theſe *eſſences of the ſpecies of mixed modes, are* not only *made* by the mind, but made *very arbitrarily*, made without patterns, or reference to any real exiſtence; wherein they differ from thoſe of ſubſtances, which carry with them the ſuppoſition of ſome real being, from which they are taken, and to which they are conformable. But in its complex *ideas* of mixed modes, the mind takes a liberty not to follow the exiſtence of things exactly: It unites and retains certain collections, as ſo many diſtinct ſpecific *ideas*; whilſt others, that as often occur in nature, and are as plainly ſuggeſted by outward things, paſs neglected, without particular names or ſpecifications. Nor does the mind, in theſe of mixed modes, as in the complex *ideas* of ſubſtances, examine them by the real exiſtence of things, or verify them by patterns, containing ſuch peculiar compoſitions in nature. To know whether his *idea* of *adultery* or *inceſt* be right, will a man ſeek it any where amongſt things exiſting? Or is it true, becauſe any one has been witneſs to ſuch an action? No: but it ſuffices here, that men having put together ſuch a collection into one complex *idea*, that makes the *archetype* and ſpecific *idea*, whether ever any ſuch action were committed *in rerum natura* or no.

§ 4. *How this is done.*

To underſtand this aright, we muſt conſider *wherein this making of theſe complex* ideas *conſiſts*: and that is not in the making any new *idea*, but putting together thoſe which the mind had before; wherein the mind does these three things: First, it chooses a certain number: Secondly, it gives them connection, and makes them into one *idea*: Thirdly, it ties them together by a name. If we examine how the mind proceeds in these, and what liberty it takes in them, we shall easily observe how these essences of the species of mixed modes are the workmanship of the mind, and consequently, that the species themselves are of mens making.

§ 5. *Evidently arbitrary, that the* Idea *is often before the Existence.*

NOBODY can doubt, but that these *ideas* of mixed modes are made by a voluntary collection of *ideas*, put together in the mind, independent from any original patterns in nature, who will but reflect that this sort of complex *ideas* may be made, abstracted, and have names given them, and so a species be constituted, before any one individual of that species ever existed. Who can doubt but the *ideas of sacrilege* or *adultery* might be framed in the mind of men, and have names given them; and so these species of mixed modes be constituted, before either of them was ever committed; and might be as well discoursed of and reasoned about, and as certain truths discovered of them, whilst yet they had no being but in the understanding, as well as now, that they have but too frequently a real existence? Whereby it is plain, how much *the sorts of mixed modes are the creatures of the understanding*, where they have a being as subservient to all the ends of real truth and knowledge, as when they really exist: and we cannot doubt but law-makers have often made laws about species of actions, which were only the creatures of their own understandings; beings that had no other existence, but in their own minds. And I think nobody can deny, but that the *resurrection* was a species of mixed modes in the mind, before it really existed.

§ 6. *Instances—Murder, Incest, Stabbing.*

To see *how arbitrarily these essences of mixed modes are made* by the mind, we need but take a view of almost any of them. A little looking into them will satisfy us, that it is the mind that combines ſeveral ſcattered independent *ideas* into one complex one, and by the common name it gives them, makes them the eſſence of a certain ſpecies, without regulating itſelf by any connection they have in nature: For what greater connection in nature has the *idea* of a man, than the *idea* of a ſheep, with killing; that this is made a particular ſpecies of action, ſignified by the word *murder*, and the other not? Or what union is there in nature between the *idea* of the relation of a father, with killing, than that of a ſon or neighbour; that thoſe are combined into one complex *idea*, and thereby made the eſſence of the diſtinct ſpecies *parricide*, whilſt the other make no diſtinct ſpecies at all? But though they have made killing a man's father, or mother, a diſtinct ſpecies from killing his ſon and daughter; yet in ſome other caſes, ſon and daughter are taken in too, as well as father and mother; and they are all equally comprehended in the ſame ſpecies, as in that of inceſt. Thus the mind in mixed modes arbitrarily unites into complex *ideas* ſuch as it finds convenient; whilſt others that have altogether as much union in nature, are left looſe, and never combined into one *idea*, becauſe they have no need of one name. It is evident then, that the mind by its free choice gives a connection to a certain number of *ideas*, which in nature have no more union with one another, than others that it leaves out: why elſe is the part of the weapon the beginning of the wound is made with, taken notice of, to make the diſtinct ſpecies called *ſtabbing*, and the figure and matter of the weapon left out? I do not ſay this is done without reaſon, as we ſhall ſee more by and by; but this I ſay, that it is done by the free choice of the mind, purſuing its own ends; and that therefore theſe ſpecies of mixed modes are the workmanſhip of the underſtanding: and there is nothing more evident than that for the moſt part, in the framing theſe *ideas*, the mind ſearches not its patterns in nature, nor refers the *ideas* it makes to the real exiſtence of things, but puts ſuch together as may beſt ſerve its own purpoſes, without tying itſelf to a preciſe imitation of any thing that really exiſts.

§ 7. *But still subservient to the end of Language.*

But though these complex *ideas*, or *essences of mixed modes*, depend on the mind, and are made by it with great liberty, yet they *are not made at random*, and jumbled together without any reason at all. Though these complex *ideas* be not always copied from nature, yet they are always suited to the end for which abstract *ideas* are made: and though they be combinations made of *ideas* that are loose enough, and have as little union in themselves, as several others to which the mind never gives a connection that combines them into one *idea*, yet they are always made for the convenience of communication, which is the chief end of language. The use of language is, by short sounds to signify with ease and dispatch general conceptions; wherein not only abundance of particulars may be contained, but also a great variety of independent *ideas* collected into one complex one. In the making, therefore, of the species of mixed modes, men have had regard only to such combinations as they had occasion to mention one to another. Those they have combined into distinct complex *ideas*, and given names to; whilst others that in nature have as near an union are left loose and unregarded: For to go no farther than human actions themselves, if they would make distinct abstract *ideas* of all the varieties might be observed in them, the number must be infinite, and the memory confounded with the plenty, as well as overcharged to little purpose. It suffices, that men make and name so many complex *ideas* of these mixed modes, as they find they have occasion to have names for, in the ordinary occurrence of their affairs. If they join to the *idea* of killing, the *idea* of father or mother, and so make a distinct species from killing a man's son or neighbour, it is because of the different heinousness of the crime, and the distinct punishment is due to the murdering a man's father and mother, different from what ought to be inflicted on the murder of a son or neighbour; and therefore they find it necessary to mention it by a distinct name, which is the end of making that distinct combination. But though the *ideas* of mother and daughter are so differently treated, in reference to the *idea* of killing, that the one is joined with it, to make a distinct abstract *idea* with a name, and so a distinct species, and the other not; yet in respect of carnal knowledge, they are both taken in under *incest*; and that still for the same convenience of expressing under one name, and reckoning of one species, such unclean mixtures as have a peculiar turpitude beyond others; and this to avoid circumlocutions and tedious descriptions.

§ 8. *Whereof the intranslatable Words of divers Languages are a proof.*

A MODERATE skill in *different languages* will easily satisfy one of the truth of this; it being so obvious to observe great store of *words in one* language, *which have not any that answer them in another*; which plainly shows, that those of one country, by their customs and manner of life, have found occasion to make several complex *ideas*, and give names to them, which others never collected into specific *ideas*. This could not have happened, if these species were the steady workmanship of nature, and not collections made and abstracted by the mind, in order to naming, and for the convenience of communication. The terms of our law, which are not empty sounds, will hardly find words that answer them in the *Spanish* or *Italian*, no scanty languages; much less, I think, could any one translate them into the *Caribees* or *Westoe* tongues: and the *Versura* of the *Romans*, or *Corban* of the *Jews*, have no words in other languages to answer them; the reason whereof is plain, from what has been said. Nay, if we will look a little more nearly into this matter, and exactly compare different languages, we shall find, that though they have words which in translations and dictionaries are supposed to answer one another, yet there is scarce one of ten amongst the names of complex *ideas*, especially of mixed modes, that stands for the same precise *idea*, which the word does that in dictionaries it is rendered by. There are no *ideas* more common, and less compounded, than the measures of time, extension, and weight; and the *Latin* names, *hora*, *pes*, *libra*, are without difficulty rendered by the

English names *hour*, *foot*, and *pound;* but yet there is nothing more evident, than that the *ideas* a *Roman* annexed to theſe *Latin* names, were very far different from thoſe which an *Engliſhman* expreſſes by thoſe *Engliſh* ones. And if either of theſe ſhould make uſe of the meaſures that thoſe of the other language deſigned by their names, he would be quite out in his account. Theſe are too ſenſible proofs to be doubted; and we ſhall find this much more ſo in the names of more abſtract and compounded *ideas*, ſuch as are the greateſt part of thoſe which make up moral diſcourſes; whoſe names, when men come curiouſly to compare with thoſe they are tranſlated into, in other languages, they will find very few of them exactly to correſpond in the whole extent of their ſignifications.

§ 9. *This ſhows Species to be made for Communication.* THE reaſon why I take ſo particular notice of this, is; that we may not be miſtaken about *genera* and *ſpecies*, and their *eſſences*, as if they were things regularly and conſtantly made by nature, and had a real exiſtence in things, when they appear, upon a more wary ſurvey, to be nothing elſe but an artifice of the underſtanding, for the eaſier ſignifying ſuch collections of *ideas*, as it ſhould often have occaſion to communicate by one general term, under which divers particulars, as far forth as they agreed to that abſtract *idea*, might be comprehended. And if the doubtful ſignification of the word *ſpecies*, may make it ſound harſh to ſome, that I ſay that the ſpecies of mixed modes are made by the underſtanding; yet, I think, it can by nobody be denied, that it is the mind makes thoſe abſtract complex *ideas*, to which ſpecific names are given. And if it be true, as it is, that the mind makes the patterns for ſorting and naming of things, I leave it to be conſidered who makes the boundaries of the ſort of *ſpecies;* ſince with me, *ſpecies* and *ſort* have no other difference, than that of a *Latin* and *Engliſh idiom*.

§ 10. *In mixed Modes it is the Name that ties the Combination together, and makes it a Species.*

THE near relation that there is *between ſpecies*, *eſſences*, and their *general name*, at leaſt *in mixed modes*, will farther appear, when we conſider that it is the name that ſeems to preſerve thoſe *eſſences*, and give them their laſting duration; for the connection between the looſe parts of thoſe complex *ideas* being made by the mind, this union, which has no particular foundation in nature, would ceaſe again, were there not ſomething that did as it were hold it together, and keep the parts from ſcattering. Though therefore it be the mind that makes the collection, it is the name which is as it were the knot that ties them faſt together. What a vaſt variety of different *ideas* does the word *triumphus* hold together, and deliver to us as one *ſpecies!* Had this name been never made or quite loſt, we might no doubt, have had deſcriptions of what paſſed in that ſolemnity: but yet, I think, that which holds thoſe different parts together, in the unity of one complex *idea*, is that very word annexed to it; without which, the ſeveral parts of that would no more be thought to make one thing, than any other ſhow, which having never been made but once, had never been united into one complex *idea*, under one denomination. How much therefore in mixed modes, the unity neceſſary to any eſſence depends on the mind, and how much the continuation and fixing of that unity depends on the name in common uſe annexed to it, I leave to be conſidered by thoſe, who look upon *eſſences* and *ſpecies* as real eſtabliſhed things in nature.

§ 11.

SUITABLE to this, we find, that *men ſpeaking of mixed modes, ſeldom* imagine or *take any other for ſpecies of them but ſuch as are ſet out by name:* becauſe they being of man's making only, in order to naming, no ſuch *ſpecies* are taken notice of, or ſuppoſed to be, unleſs a *name* be joined to it, as the ſign of man's having combined into one *idea* ſeveral looſe ones; and by that *name* giving a laſting union to the parts, which would otherwiſe ceaſe to have any, as ſoon as the mind laid by that abſtract *idea*, and ceaſed actually to think on it. But when a name is once annexed to it, wherein the parts of that complex *idea* have a ſettled and permanent union, then is the eſſence as it were eſtabliſhed, and the *ſpecies* looked on as complete. For to what purpoſe ſhould the memory charge itſelf with ſuch compoſitions, unleſs it were by abſtraction to make them general? And to what purpoſe make them general, unleſs it were that they might have general *names*, for the convenience of diſcourſe and communication? Thus we ſee, that killing a man with a ſword or a hatchet, are looked on as no diſtinct ſpecies of action: but if the point of the ſword firſt enter the body, it paſſes for a diſtinct *ſpecies*, where it has a diſtinct *name*; as in *England*, in whoſe language it is called *ſtabbing*; but in another country, where it has not happened to be ſpecified under a peculiar *name*, it paſſes not for a diſtinct *ſpecies*. But in the *ſpecies* of corporeal ſubſtances, though it be the mind that makes the nominal eſſence, yet ſince thoſe *ideas* which are combined in it are ſuppoſed to have an union in nature, whether the mind joins them or no, therefore thoſe are looked on as diſtinct *ſpecies*, without any operation of the mind, either abſtracting or giving a *name* to that complex *idea*.

§ 12. *For the Originals of mixed Modes, we look no farther than the Mind, which alſo ſhows them to be the workmanſhip of the Underſtanding.*

Conformably alſo to what has been ſaid, concerning the *eſſences* of the *ſpecies* of *mixed modes*, that they are the creatures of the underſtanding rather than the works of nature; conformable, I ſay, to this, we find that *their names lead our thoughts to the mind, and no farther.* When we ſpeak of *juſtice* or *gratitude*, we frame to ourſelves no imagination of any thing exiſting, which we would conceive; but our thoughts terminate in the abſtract *ideas* of thoſe virtues, and look not farther; as they do, when we ſpeak of a *horſe* or *iron*, whoſe ſpecific *ideas* we conſider not as barely in the mind, but as in things themſelves, which afford the original patterns of thoſe *ideas*. But in mixed modes, at leaſt the moſt conſiderable parts of them, which are moral beings, we conſider the original patterns as being in the mind; and to thoſe we refer for the diſtinguiſhing of particular beings under names. And hence I think it is, that theſe *eſſences* of the *ſpecies* of mixed modes, are by a more particular name called *notions*; as by a peculiar right, appertaining to the underſtanding.

§ 13. *Their being made by the Underſtanding without Patterns, ſhows the reaſon why they are ſo compounded.*

Hence likewiſe we may learn, *Why the complex* ideas *of mixed modes are commonly more compounded and decompounded than thoſe of natural ſubſtances*; becauſe they being the workmanſhip of the underſtanding, purſuing only its own ends, and the conveniency of expreſſing in ſhort thoſe *ideas* it would make known to another, does with great liberty unite often into one abſtract *idea* things that in their nature have no coherence; and ſo, under one term, bundle together a great variety of compounded and decompounded *ideas*. Thus the name of *proceſſion*, what a great mixture of independent *ideas* of perſons, habits, tapers, orders, motions, ſounds, does it contain in that complex one, which the mind of man has arbitrarily put together, to expreſs by that one name? Whereas the complex *ideas* of the ſorts of ſubſtances are uſually made up of only a ſmall number of ſimple ones; and in the ſpecies of animals, theſe two, *viz.* ſhape and voice, commonly make the whole nominal eſſence.

§ 14. *Names of mixed Modes ſtand always for their real Eſſences.*

Another thing we may obſerve from what has been ſaid, is, that *the names of mixed modes always ſignify* (when they have any determined ſignification) *the real eſſences of their ſpecies*; for theſe abſtract *ideas*, being the workmanſhip of the mind, and not referred to the real exiſtence of things, there is no ſuppoſition of any thing more ſignified by that name, but barely that complex *idea* the mind itſelf has formed, which is all it would have expreſſed by it, and is that on which all the properties of the *ſpecies* depend, and from which alone they all flow, and ſo in theſe the *real* and *nominal eſſence* is the ſame; which of what concernment it is to the certain knowledge of general truth we ſhall ſee hereafter.

§ 15. *Why their Names are usually got before their* Ideas.

THIS also may show us the reason, *Why for the most part the names of mixed modes are got, before the* Ideas *they stand for are perfectly known;* because there being no *species* of these ordinarily taken notice of, but what have names, and those *species*, or rather their essences, being abstract complex *ideas* made arbitrarily by the mind, it is convenient, if not necessary, to know the names, before one endeavour to frame these complex *ideas*, unless a man will fill his head with a company of abstract complex *ideas*, which others having no names for, he has nothing to do with, but to lay by and forget again. I confess, that in the beginning of languages, it was necessary to have the *idea* before one gave it the name; and so it is still, where making a new complex *idea*, one also, by giving it a new name, makes a new word; but this concerns not languages made, which have generally pretty well provided for *ideas*, which men have frequent occasion to have and communicate; and in such, I ask, whether it be not the ordinary method, that children learn the names of mixed modes before they have their *ideas*? What one of a thousand ever frames the abstract *idea* of *glory* and *ambition*, before he has heard the name of them? In simple *ideas* and substances, I grant it is otherwise; which being such *ideas* as have a real existence and union in nature, the *ideas* or names are got one before the other, as it happens.

§ 16. *Reason of my being so large on this Subject.*

WHAT has been said here of mixed modes, is with very little difference applicable also to relations; which, since every man himself may observe, I may spare myself the pains to enlarge on; especially, since what I have here said concerning words in this third book, will possibly be thought by some to be much more than what so slight a subject required. I allow it might be brought into a narrower compass; but I was willing to stay my reader on an argument that appears to me new, and a little out of the way (I am sure it is one I thought not of when I began to write), That by searching it to the bottom, and turning it on every ſide, ſome part or other might meet with every one's thoughts, and give occaſion to the moſt averſe or negligent to reflect on a general miſcarriage; which, though of great conſequence, is little taken notice of. When it is conſidered what a pudder is made about *eſſences*, and how much all ſorts of knowledge, diſcourſe, and converſation are peſtered and diſordered by the careleſs and confuſed uſe and application of words, it will perhaps be thought worth while thoroughly to lay it open. And I ſhall be pardoned if I have dwelt long on an argument which I think, therefore, needs to be inculcated; becauſe the faults men are uſually guilty of this kind, are not only the greateſt hinderances of true knowledge, but are ſo well thought of, as to paſs for it. Men would often ſee what a ſmall pittance of reaſon and truth, or poſſibly none at all, is mixed with thoſe huffing opinions they are ſwelled with, if they would but look beyond faſhionable ſounds, and obſerve what *ideas* are or are not comprehended under thoſe words with which they are ſo armed at all points, and with which they ſo confidently lay about them. I ſhall imagine I have done ſome ſervice to truth, peace and learning, if by any enlargement on this ſubject, I can make men reflect on their own uſe of language; and give them reaſon to ſuſpect, that ſince it is frequent for others, it may alſo be poſſible for them, to have ſometimes very good and approved words in their mouths and writings, with very uncertain, little, or no ſignification; and therefore it is not unreaſonable for them to be wary herein themſelves, and not to be unwilling to have them examined by others. With this deſign, therefore, I ſhall go on with what I have farther to ſay concerning this matter.

CHAP. VI.

OF THE NAMES OF SUBSTANCES.

§ 1. *The common Names of Subſtances ſtand for Sorts.*

THE *common names of ſubſtances*, as well as other general terms, *ſtand for ſorts;* which is nothing elſe but the being made ſigns of ſuch complex *ideas*, wherein several particular substances do or might agree, by virtue of which they are capable of being comprehended in one common conception, and signified by one name: I say, do or might agree; for though there be but one sun existing in the world, yet the *idea* of it being abstracted, so that more substances (if there were several) might each agree in it, it is as much a sort, as if there were as many suns as there are stars. They want not their reasons who think there are, and that each fixed star would answer the *idea* the *name* sun stands for, to one who were placed in a due distance; which, by the way, may show us how much the sorts, or, if you please, *genera* and *species* of things (for those *Latin* terms signify to me no more than the *English* word *sort*) depend on such collections of *ideas* as men have made, and not on the real nature of things, since it is not impossible, but that in propriety of speech, that might be a sun to one, which is a star to another.

§ 2. *The Essence of each sort is the abstract* Ideas.

THE measure and boundary of each sort, or *species*, whereby it is constituted that particular sort, and distinguished from others, is that we call its *essence*, which *is* nothing but that *abstract* idea *to which the name is annexed;* so that every thing contained in that *idea* is essential to that sort. This, though it be all the *essence* of natural substances that we know, or by which we distinguish them into sorts, yet I call it by a peculiar name, the *nominal essence*, to distinguish it from that real constitution of substances, upon which depends this *nominal essence*, and all the properties of that sort; which therefore, as has been said, may be called the *real essence:* *v. g.* the *nominal essence* of *gold* is that complex *idea* the word *gold* stands for, let it be, for instance, a body yellow, of a certain weight, malleable, fusible, and fixed: But the *real essence* is the constitution of the insensible parts of that body, on which those qualities, and all the other properties of gold depend. How far these two are different, though they are both called *essence*, is obvious at first sight to discover.

§ 3. *The nominal and real Essence different.*

For though perhaps voluntary motion, with sense and reason, joined to a body of a certain shape, be the complex *idea* to which I, and others, annex the name *man*, and so be the *nominal essence* of the *species* so called; yet nobody will say that that complex *idea* is the *real essence* and source of all those operations which are to be found in any individual of that sort. The foundation of all those qualities, which are the ingredients of our complex *idea*, is something quite different; and had we such a knowledge of that constitution of *man*, from which his faculties of moving, sensation, and reasoning, and other powers flow, and on which his so regular shape depends, as it is possible angels have, and it is certain his Maker has; we should have a quite other *idea* of his *essence* than what now is contained in our definition of that *species*, be it what it will; and our *idea* of any individual *man* would be as far different from what it now is, as is his who knows all the springs and wheels, and other contrivances within, of the famous clock at *Strasburg*, from that which a gazing countryman has of it, who barely sees the motion of the hand, and hears the clock strike, and observes only some of the outward appearances.

§ 4. *Nothing essential to Individuals.*

That *essence*, in the ordinary use of the word, relates to *sorts*, and that it is considered in particular beings no farther than as they are ranked into *sorts*, appears from hence; that take but away the abstract *ideas*, by which we sort individuals, and rank them under common names, and then the thought of any thing *essential* to any of them instantly vanishes; we have no notion of the one without the other; which plainly shows their relation. It is necessary for me to be as I am; GOD and nature has made me so; but there is nothing I have is essential to me: An accident, or disease, may very much alter my colour or shape; a fever, or fall, may take away my reason or memory, or both; and an apoplexy leave neither sense nor understanding, no, nor life. Other creatures of my shape may be made with more and better, or fewer and worſe faculties than I have; and others may have reaſon and ſenſe in a ſhape and body very different from mine. None of theſe are eſſential to the one or the other, or to any individual whatſoever, till the mind refers it to ſome ſort or *ſpecies* of things; and then preſently, according to the abſtract *idea* of that ſort, ſomething is found *eſſential.* Let any one examine his own thoughts, and he will find that as ſoon as he ſuppoſes or ſpeaks of *eſſential,* the conſideration of ſome *ſpecies,* or the complex *idea,* ſignified by ſome general name, comes into his mind; and it is in reference to that, that this or that quality is ſaid to be *eſſential:* So that if he be aſked, whether it be *eſſential* to me or any other particular corporeal being to have reaſon? I ſay no; no more than it is *eſſential* to this white thing I write on, to have words in it; but if that particular being be to be counted of the ſort *man,* and to have the name *man* given it, then reaſon is *eſſential* to it, ſuppoſing reaſon to be a part of the complex *idea* the name *man* ſtands for; as it is *eſſential* to this thing I write on to contain words, if I will give it the name *treatiſe,* and rank it under that *ſpecies.* So that *eſſential, and not eſſential, relate only to our abſtract* ideas, *and the names annexed to them,* which amounts to more but this; that whatever particular thing has not in it thoſe qualities which are contained in the abſtract *idea* which any general term ſtands for, cannot be ranked under that *ſpecies,* nor be called by that name, ſince that abſtract *idea* is the very *eſſence* of that *ſpecies.*

§ 5.

THUS if the *idea* of *body,* with ſome people, be bare extenſion or ſpace, then ſolidity is not *eſſential* to body: if others make the *idea,* to which they give the name *body,* to be ſolidity and extenſion, then ſolidity is eſſential to *body.* That, therefore, and *that alone is* conſidered as *eſſential, which makes a part of the complex* idea *the name of a ſort ſtands for,* without which no particular thing can be reckoned of that ſort, nor be entitled to that name. Should there be found a parcel of matter that had all the other qualities that are in *iron,* but wanted obedience to the loadſtone, and would neither be drawn by it, nor receive direction from it, would any one queſtion whether it wanted any thing *eſſential?* It would be abſurd to aſk, whether a thing really exiſting wanted any thing *eſſential* to it. Or could it be demanded, whether this made an *eſſential* or *ſpecific* difference or no; ſince we have no other meaſure of *eſſential* or *ſpecific*, but our abſtract *ideas?* And to talk of ſpecific differences in nature, without reference to general *ideas* and names, is to talk unintelligibly: For I would aſk any one, what is ſufficient to make an *eſſential* difference in nature, between any two particular beings, without any regard had to ſome abſtract *idea*, which is looked upon as the eſſence and ſtandard of a *ſpecies?* All ſuch patterns and ſtandards, being quite laid aſide, particular beings, conſidered barely in themſelves, will be found to have all their qualities equally *eſſential;* and every thing in each individual will be *eſſential* to it, or, which is more, nothing at all: For though it may be reaſonable to aſk, whether obeying the magnet be *eſſential* to *iron?* yet, I think, it is very improper and inſignificant to aſk, whether it be *eſſential* to the particular parcel of matter I cut my pen with, without conſidering it under the name *iron*, or as being of a certain *ſpecies*. And if, as has been ſaid, our abſtract *ideas*, which have names annexed to them, are the boundaries of *ſpecies*, nothing can be *eſſential* but what is contained in thoſe *ideas*.

§ 6.

IT is true I have often mentioned a *real eſſence*, diſtinct in ſubſtances from thoſe abſtract *ideas* of them, which I call their *nominal eſſence*. By this *real eſſence* I mean that real conſtitution of any thing, which is the foundation of all thoſe properties that are combined in, and are conſtantly found to co-exiſt with the *nominal eſſence;* that particular conſtitution which every thing has within itſelf, without any relation to any thing without it. But *eſſence*, even in this ſenſe, *relates to a ſort*, and ſuppoſes a *ſpecies;* for being that real conſtitution on which the properties depend, it neceſſarily ſuppoſes a ſort of things, properties belonging only to *ſpecies*, and not to individuals; *v. g.* Suppoſing the nominal eſſence of *gold* to be body of ſuch a peculiar colour and weight, with malleability and fuſibility, the real eſſence is that conſtitution of the parts of matter on which theſe qualities, and their union, depend; and is alſo the foundation of its ſolubility in *aq. regia*, and other properties accompanying that complex *idea*. Here are *eſſences* and *properties*, but all upon ſuppoſition of a ſort, or general abſtract *idea*, which is conſidered as immutable; but there is no individual parcel of matter, to which any of theſe qualities are ſo annexed, as to be *eſſential* to it, or inſeparable from it. That which is *eſſential* belongs to it as a condition, whereby it is of this or that ſort; but take away the conſideration of its being ranked under the name of ſome abſtract *idea*, and then there is nothing neceſſary to it, nothing inſeparable from it. Indeed, as to the *real eſſences* of ſubſtances, we only ſuppoſe their being, without preciſely knowing what they are: But that which annexes them ſtill to the *ſpecies*, is the nominal eſſence, of which they are the ſuppoſed foundation and cauſe.

§ 7. *The nominal Eſſence bounds the Species.*

THE next thing to be conſidered is, by which of thoſe eſſences it is that *ſubſtances are determined into* ſorts, or *ſpecies*; and that, it is evident, is *by the nominal eſſence*; for it is that alone that the name, which is the mark of the ſort, ſignifies. It is impoſſible, therefore, that any thing ſhould determine the ſorts of things, which we rank under general names, but that *idea* which that name is deſigned as a mark for; which is that, as has been ſhown, which we call the *nominal eſſence*. Why do we ſay, this is a *horſe*, and that a *mule*; this is an *animal*, that an *herb*? How comes any particular thing to be of this or that *ſort*, but becauſe it has that nominal eſſence, or, which is all one, agrees to that abſtract *idea* that name is annexed to? And I deſire any one but to reflect on his own thoughts when he hears or ſpeaks any of thoſe or other names of ſubſtances, to know what ſort of *eſſences* they ſtand for.

§ 8.

AND that the *ſpecies of things to us are nothing but the*

ranking them under diſtinct names, according to the complex ideas *in us*, and not according to preciſe, diſtinct, real *eſſences* in them, is plain from hence, that we find many of the individuals that are ranked into one ſort, called by one common name, and ſo received as being of one *ſpecies*, have yet qualities depending on their real conſtitutions, as far different one from another, as from others from which they are accounted to differ *ſpecifically*. This, as it is eaſy to be obſerved by all who have to do with natural bodies, ſo chemiſts eſpecially, are often, by ſad experience, convinced of it, when they, ſometimes in vain, ſeek for the ſame qualities in one parcel of ſulphur, antimony, or vitriol, which they have found in others; for though they are bodies of the ſame *ſpecies*, having the ſame nominal *eſſence* under the ſame name, yet do they often, upon ſevere ways of examination, betray qualities ſo different one from another, as to fruſtrate the expectation and labour of very wary chemiſts. But if things were diſtinguiſhed into *ſpecies*, according to their real eſſences, it would be as impoſſible to find different properties in any two individual ſubſtances of the ſame *ſpecies*, as it is to find different properties in two circles, or two equilateral triangles. That is properly the *eſſence* to us, which determines every particular to this or that *claſſis*, or, which is the ſame thing, to this or that general name; and what can that be elſe, but that abſtract *idea* to which that name is annexed, and ſo has, in truth, a reference, not ſo much to the being of particular things, as to their general denominations?

§ 9. *Not the real Eſſence, which we know not.*

NOR indeed *can we* rank and *ſort things*, and conſequently (which is the end of ſorting) denominate them *by their real eſſences*, becauſe we know them not. Our faculties carry us no farther towards the knowledge and diſtinction of ſubſtances, than a collection of thoſe ſenſible *ideas* which we obſerve in them, which, however made with the greateſt diligence and exactneſs we are capable of, yet is more remote from the true internal conſtitution from which thoſe qualities flow, than, as I ſaid, a countryman's *idea* is from the inward contrivance of that famous clock at *Straſburg*, whereof he only ſees the outward figure and motions. There is not ſo contemptible a plant or animal, that does not confound the moſt enlarged underſtanding. Though the familiar uſe of things about us take off our wonder, yet it cures not our ignorance. When we come to examine the ſtones we tread on, or the iron we daily handle, we preſently find we know not their make, and can give no reaſon of the different qualities we find in them. It is evident the internal conſtitution, whereon their properties depend, is unknown to us; for, to go no farther than the groſſeſt and moſt obvious we can imagine amongſt them, What is that texture of parts, that real *eſſence*, that makes lead and antimony fuſible, wood and ſtones not? What makes lead and iron malleable, antimony and ſtones not? And yet how infinitely theſe come ſhort of the fine contrivances and unconceivable *real eſſences* of plants or animals, every one knows. The workmanſhip of the all-wiſe and powerful God, in the great fabric of the univerſe, and every part thereof, farther exceeds the capacity and comprehenſion of the moſt inquiſitive and intelligent man, than the beſt contrivance of the moſt ingenious man doth the conceptions of the moſt ignorant of rational creatures: Therefore we in vain pretend to range things into ſorts, and diſpoſe them into certain claſſes, under names, by their *real eſſences*, that are ſo far from our diſcovery or comprehenſion. A blind man may as ſoon ſort things by their colours, and he that has loſt his ſmell as well diſtinguiſh a lily and a roſe by their odours, as by thoſe internal conſtitutions which he knows not. He that thinks he can diſtinguiſh ſheep and goats by their real eſſences that are unknown to him, may be pleaſed to try his ſkill in thoſe *ſpecies* called *caſſiowary* and *querechinchio*, and by their internal real eſſences determine the boundaries of thoſe *ſpecies*, without knowing the complex *idea* of ſenſible qualities that each of thoſe ſtand for, in the countries where thoſe animals are to be found.

§ 10. *Not ſubſtantial Forms, which we know leſs.* THOSE, therefore, who have been taught, that the ſeveral *species* of substances had their distinct internal *substantial forms*, and that it was those *forms* which made the distinction of substances into their true *species* and *genera*, were led yet farther out of the way, by having their minds set upon fruitless inquiries after *substantial forms*, wholly unintelligible, and whereof we have scarce so much as any obscure or confused conception in general.

§ 11. *That the nominal Essence is that whereby we distinguish Species, farther evident from Spirits.*

THAT our *ranking* and distinguishing natural *substances into species*, *consists in the nominal essences* the mind makes, and not in the real essences to be found in the things themselves, is farther evident from our *ideas* of *spirits*; for the mind getting, only by reflecting on its own operations, those simple *ideas* which it attributes to *spirits*, it hath, or can have no other notion of *spirit*, but by attributing all those operations it finds in itself, to a sort of beings, without consideration of matter. And even the most advanced notion we have of God, is but attributing the same simple *ideas* which we have got from reflection on what we find in ourselves, and which we conceive to have more perfection in them, than would be in their absence; attributing, I say, those simple *ideas* to him in an unlimited degree. Thus having got, from reflecting on ourselves, the *idea* of existence, knowledge, power, and pleasure, each of which we find it better to have than to want, and the more we have of each, the better; joining all these together, with infinity to each of them, we have the complex *idea* of an eternal omniscient, omnipotent, infinitely-wise and happy Being. And though we are told that there are different *species of angels*, yet we know not how to frame distinct specific *ideas* of them; not out of any conceit that the existence of more *species* than one of *spirits* is impossible, but because having no more simple *ideas* (nor being able to frame more) applicable to such beings, but only those few taken from ourselves, and from the actions of our own minds in thinking, and being delighted, and moving several parts of our bodies, we can no otherwise distinguish in our conceptions the several *species* of *spirits*, one from another, but by attributing these operations and powers, we find in ourselves, to them in a higher or lower degree; and so have no very distinct specific *ideas* of *spirits*, except only of GOD, to whom we attribute both duration, and all those other *ideas*, with infinity; to the other *spirits*, with limitation. Nor as I humbly conceive do we, between GOD and them in our *ideas*, put any difference by any number of simple *ideas*, which we have of one, and not of the other, but only that of infinity. All the particular *ideas* of existence, knowledge, will, power, and motion, &c. being *ideas* derived from the operations of our minds, we attribute all of them to all sorts of *spirits*, with the difference only of degrees, to the utmost we can imagine, even infinity, when we would frame, as well as we can, an *idea* of the first Being; who yet, it is certain, is infinitely more remote in the real excellency of his nature, from the highest and perfectest of all created beings, than the greatest man, nay, purest seraphim, is from the most contemptible part of matter, and consequently must infinitely exceed what our narrow understandings can conceive of him.

§ 12. *Whereof there are probably numberless Species.*
It is not impossible to conceive, nor repugnant to reason, that there may be many *species of spirits*, as much separated and diversified one from another, by distinct properties, whereof we have no *ideas*, as the *species* of sensible things are distinguished one from another by qualities which we know and observe in them. That there should be more *species* of intelligent creatures above us, than there are of sensible and material below us, is probable to me from hence, that in all the visible corporeal world, we see no chasms or gaps. All quite down from us, the descent is by easy steps, and a continued series of things, that in each remove differ very little one from the other. There are fishes that have wings, that are not strangers to the airy region; and there are some birds, that are inhabitants of the water whose blood is cold as fishes, and their flesh is so like in taste, that the scrupulous are allowed them on fish days

There are animals so near of kin both to birds and beasts, that they are in the middle between both: Amphibious animals link the terrestrial and aquatic together; seals live at land and at sea, and porpoises have the warm blood and entrails of a hog, not to mention what is confidently reported of mermaids or sea-men. There are some brutes, that seem to have as much knowledge and reason, as some that are called men; and the animal and vegetable kingdoms are so nearly joined, that if you will take the lowest of one, and the highest of the other, there will scarce be perceived any great difference between them; and so on, till we come to the lowest and the most inorganical parts of matter, we shall find every where, that the several *species* are linked together, and differ but in almost insensible degrees. And when we consider the infinite power and wisdom of the Maker, we have reason to think, that it is suitable to the magnificent harmony of the universe, and the great design and infinite goodness of the Architect, that the *species* of creatures should also, by gentle degrees, ascend upward from us toward his infinite perfection, as we see they gradually descend from us downwards: Which if it be probable, we have reason then to be persuaded, that there are far more *species* of creatures above us, than there are beneath; we being, in degrees of perfection, much more remote from the infinite being of GOD, than we are from the lowest state of being, and that which approaches nearest to nothing. And yet of all those distinct *species*, for the reasons above said, we have no clear distinct *ideas*.

§ 13. *The nominal Essence, that of the Species, proved from Water and Ice.*

But to return to the *species* of corporeal substances. If I should ask any one, whether *ice* and *water* were two distinct *species* of things, I doubt not but I should be answered in the affirmative; and it cannot be denied, but he that says they are two distinct *species*, is in the right. But if an *Englishman*, bred in *Jamaica*, who perhaps had never seen nor heard of *ice*, coming into *England* in the winter, find the water he puts in his bason at night, in a great part frozen in the morning, and not knowing any peculiar name it had, ſhould call it hardened water; I aſk, whether this would be a new *ſpecies* to him different from water? And I think, it would be anſwered here, It would not be to him a new *ſpecies*, no more than congealed jelly, when it is cold, is a diſtinct *ſpecies* from the ſame jelly fluid and warm; or than liquid gold, in the furnace, is a diſtinct *ſpecies* from hard gold in the hands of a workman. And if this be ſo, it is plain, that our *diſtinct ſpecies are nothing but diſtinct complex* ideas, *with diſtinct names annexed to them.* It is true, every ſubſtance that exiſts has its peculiar conſtitution, whereon depend thoſe ſenſible qualities and powers we obſerve in it; but the ranking of things into *ſpecies*, which is nothing but ſorting them under ſeveral titles, is done by us according to the *ideas* that we have of them; which, though ſufficient to diſtinguiſh them by names, ſo that we may be able to diſcourſe of them, when we have them not preſent before us, yet if we ſuppoſe it to be done by their real internal conſtitutions, and that things exiſting are diſtinguiſhed by nature into ſpecies, by real eſſences, according as we diſtinguiſh them into *ſpecies* by names, we ſhall be liable to great miſtakes.

§ 14. *Difficulties againſt a certain number of real Eſſences.*

To diſtinguiſh ſubſtantial beings into *ſpecies*, according to the uſual ſuppoſition, that there are certain preciſe *eſſences* or *forms* of things, whereby all the individuals exiſting are by nature diſtinguiſhed into *ſpecies*, theſe things are neceſſary:

§ 15.

FIRST, To be aſſured that nature, in the production of things, always deſigns them to partake of certain regulated eſtabliſhed *eſſences*, which are to be the models of all things to be produced. This, in that crude ſenſe it is uſually propoſed, would need ſome better explication before it can fully be aſſented to.

§ 16.

SECONDLY, It would be neceſſary to know whether nature always attains that *essence* it designs in the production of things. The irregular and monstrous births, that in divers sorts of animals have been observed, will always give us reason to doubt of one or both of these.

§ 17.

THIRDLY, It ought to be determined whether those we call *monsters* be really a distinct *species*, according to the scholastic notion of the word *species*; since it is certain, that every thing that exists has its particular constitution: And yet we find that some of these monstrous productions have few or none of those qualities, which are supposed to result from, and accompany the *essence* of that *species*, from whence they derive their originals, and to which, by their descent, they seem to belong.

§ 18. *Our nominal Essences of Substances, not perfect Collections of properties.*

FOURTHLY, The *real essences* of those things, which we distinguish into *species*, and as so distinguished we name, ought to be known; *i. e.* we ought to have *ideas* of them. But since we are ignorant in these four points, *the supposed real essences of things stand us not in stead for the distinguishing substances into species.*

§ 19.

FIFTHLY, The only imaginable help in this case would be, that having framed perfect complex *ideas* of the *properties* of things, flowing from their different real essences, we should thereby distinguish them into *species*. But neither can this be done; for being ignorant of the real essence itself, it is impossible to know all these properties that flow from it, and are so annexed to it, that any one of them being away, we may certainly conclude, that that essence is not there, and so the thing is not of that *species*. We can never know what are the precise number of properties depending on the real essence of *gold*, any one of which failing, the real essence of gold, and consequently gold, would not be there, unless we knew the real essence of gold itself, and by that determined that *species*. By the word *gold* here, I must be understood to design a particular piece of matter; *v. g.* the last guinea that was coined; for if it should stand here in its ordinary signification for that complex *idea* which I or any one else calls *gold*, *i. e.* for the nominal essence of gold, it would be *jargon*: so hard is it to show the various meaning and imperfection of words, when we have nothing else but words to do it by.

§ 20.

By all which it is clear, that our *distinguishing substances into species* by names, *is not* at all *founded on their real essences*; nor can we pretend to range and determine them exactly into species, according to the internal essential differences.

§ 21. *But such a Collection as our Name stands for.* But since, as has been remarked, we have need of general words, though we know not the real essences of things; all we can do is to collect such a number of simple *ideas*, as by examination we find to be united together in things existing, and thereof to make one complex *idea*; which, though it be not the real essence of any substance that exists, is yet *the specific essence* to which our name belongs, and is convertible with it; by which we may at least try the truth of these nominal essences. For example, there be that say, that the essence of *body* is extension; if it be so, we can never mistake in putting the essence of any thing for the thing itself. Let us then in discourse put *extension* for *body*; and when we would say that body moves, let us say that extension moves, and see how it will look. He that should say that one extension by impulse moves another extension, would by the bare expression sufficiently show the absurdity of such a notion. The *essence* of any thing, in respect of us, is the whole complex *idea*, comprehended and marked by that name; and in substances, besides the several distinct simple *ideas* that make them up, the confused one of substance, or of an unknown support and cause of their union, is always a part; and therefore the essence of body is not bare extension, but an extended solid thing; and so to say an extended solid thing moves, or impels another, is all one, and as intelligible as to say, *body* moves or impels. Likewise to say, that a rational animal is capable of conversation, is all one as to ſay a *man*: But no one will ſay, that rationality is capable of converſation, becauſe it makes not the whole eſſence to which we give the name man.

§ 22. *Our abſtract* Ideas *are to us the Meaſures of ſpecies—Inſtance in that of Man.*

THERE are creatures in the world that have ſhapes like ours, but are hairy, and want language and reaſon. There are naturals amongſt us that have perfectly our ſhape, but want reaſon, and ſome of them language too. There are creatures, as it is ſaid, (*ſit fides penes authorem*, but there appears no contradiction that there ſhould be ſuch) that, with language, and reaſon, and a ſhape in other things agreeing with ours, have hairy tails; others, where the males have no beards, and others where the females have. If it be aſked, Whether theſe be all *men* or no, all of human *ſpecies*? it is plain, the queſtion refers only to the nominal eſſence; for thoſe of them to whom the definition of the word *man*, or the complex *idea* ſignified by that name, agrees, are *men*, and the other not. But if the inquiry be made concerning the ſuppoſed real eſſence, and whether the internal conſtitution and frame of theſe ſeveral creatures be ſpecifically different, it is wholly impoſſible for us to anſwer, no part of that going into our ſpecific *idea*; only, we have reaſon to think, that where the faculties or outward frame ſo much differs, the internal conſtitution is not exactly the ſame. But what difference in the internal real conſtitution makes a ſpecific difference, it is in vain to inquire, whilſt *our meaſures of ſpecies* be, as they *are*, *only our abſtract ideas*, which we know, and not that internal conſtitution, which makes no part of them. Shall the difference of hair only on the ſkin, be a mark of a different internal ſpecific conſtitution between a changeling and a drill, when they agree in ſhape, and want of reaſon and ſpeech? and ſhall not the want of reaſon and ſpeech be a ſign to us of different real conſtitutions and *ſpecies* between a changeling and a reaſonable man? And ſo of the reſt, if we pretend that the diſtinction of *ſpecies* or ſorts is fixedly eſtabliſhed by the real frame and ſecret conſtitutions of things.

§ 23. *Species not distinguished by Generation.*

Nor let any one say, that the power of propagation in animals by the mixture of male and female, and in plants by seeds, keeps the supposed real *species* distinct and entire; for granting this to be true, it would help us in the distinction of the *species* of things no farther than the tribes of animals and vegetables. What must we do for the rest? But in those two it is not sufficient; for, if history lie not, women have conceived by drills; and what real *species*, by that measure, such a production will be in nature, will be a new question. And we have reason to think this is not impossible, since mules and jumarts, the one from the mixture of an ass and a mare, the other from the mixture of a bull and a mare, are so frequent in the world. I once saw a creature that was the issue of a cat and a rat, and had the plain marks of both about it, wherein nature appeared to have followed the pattern of neither sort alone, but to have jumbled them both together; to which, he that shall add the monstrous productions that are so frequently to be met with in nature, will find it hard, even in the race of animals, to determine by the pedigree of what *species* every animal's issue is, and be at a loss about the real essence, which he thinks certainly conveyed by generation, and has alone a right to the specific name. But farther, if the *species* of animals and plants are to be distinguished only by propagation, must I go to the *Indies* to see the sire and dam of the one, and the plant from which the seed was gathered that produced the other, to know whether this be a tyger, or that tea?

§ 24. *Not by substantial Forms.*

Upon the whole matter, it is evident, that it is their own collections of sensible qualities, that men make the essences of their several sorts of substances, and that their real internal structures are not considered by the greatest part of men in the sorting them; much less were any *substantial forms* ever thought on by any, but those who have in this one part of the world learned the language of the schools; and yet those ignorant men, who pretend not any insight into the real essences, nor trouble themſelves about ſubſtantial forms, but are content with knowing things one from another by their ſenſible qualities, are often better acquainted with their differences, can more nicely diſtinguiſh them from their uſes, and better know what they may expect from each, than theſe learned quick-ſighted men, who look ſo deep into them, and talk ſo confidently of ſomething more hidden and eſſential.

§ 25. *The ſpecific Eſſences are made by the Mind.* BUT ſuppoſing that the *real eſſences* of ſubſtances were diſcoverable by thoſe that would ſeverely apply themſelves to that inquiry, yet we could not reaſonably think that the *ranking of things under general names was regulated by* thoſe internal real conſtitutions, or any thing elſe but *their obvious appearances*; ſince languages in all countries, have been eſtabliſhed long before ſciences; ſo that they have not been philoſophers, or logicians, or ſuch who have troubled themſelves about *forms* and *eſſences*, that have made the general names that are in uſe amongſt the ſeveral nations of men; but thoſe more or leſs comprehenſive terms have for the moſt part, in all languages, received their birth and ſignification from ignorant and illiterate people, who ſorted and denominated things by thoſe ſenſible qualities they found in them; thereby to ſignify them, when abſent, to others, whether they had an occaſion to mention a ſort or a particular thing.

§ 26. *Therefore very various and uncertain.* SINCE then it is evident, that we ſort and name ſubſtances by their *nominal*, and not by their real *eſſences*, the next thing to be conſidered is, how and by whom theſe *eſſences* come to be made. As to the latter, it is evident they *are made by the mind*, and not by nature; for were they nature's workmanſhip, they could not be ſo various and different in ſeveral men, as experience tells us they are. For if we will examine it, we ſhall not find the nominal eſſence of any one *ſpecies* of ſubſtances in all men the ſame; no, not of that which of all others we are the moſt intimately acquainted with. It could not poſſibly be, that the abſtract *idea* to which the name *man* is given, ſhould be different in ſeveral men, if it were of nature's making; and that to one it ſhould be *animal rationale*, and to another *animal implume bipes latis unguibus*. He that annexes the name *man*, to a complex *idea* made up of ſenſe and ſpontaneous motion, joined to a body of ſuch a ſhape, as thereby one eſſence of the *ſpecies man*; and he that, upon farther examination, adds rationality, has another eſſence of the *ſpecies* he calls *man*; by which means, the ſame individual will be a true *man* to the one, which is not ſo to the other. I think, there is ſcarce any one will allow this upright figure, ſo well known, to be the eſſential difference of the *ſpecies man*; and yet how far men determine of the ſorts of animals rather by their ſhape than deſcent, is very viſible, ſince it has been more than once debated, whether ſeveral human *fœtus's* ſhould be preſerved or received to baptiſm or no, only becauſe of the difference of their outward configuration from the ordinary make of children, without knowing whether they were not as capable of reaſon, as infants caſt in another mould; ſome whereof, though of an approved ſhape, are never capable of as much appearance of reaſon, all their lives, as is to be found in an ape or an elephant, and never give any ſigns of being acted by a rational ſoul; whereby it is evident, that the outward figure, which only was found wanting, and not the faculty of reaſon, which nobody could know would be wanting in its due ſeaſon, was made eſſential to the human *ſpecies*. The learned divine and lawyer, muſt, on ſuch occaſions, renounce his ſacred definition of *animal rationale*, and ſubſtitute ſome other eſſence of the human *ſpecies*. Monſieur Menage furniſhes us with an example worth the taking notice of on this occaſion. *When the Abbot of St Martin*, ſays he, *was born, he had ſo little of the figure of a man, that it beſpoke him rather a monſter. It was for ſome time under deliberation, whether he ſhould be baptized or no. However, he was baptized and declared a man proviſionally* [till time ſhould ſhow what he would prove.] *Nature had moulded him ſo untowardly, that he was called all his life the Abbot Malotrue*, *i. e.* Ill-ſhaped. *He was of* Caen. Menagiana, 278-430. This child, we ſee, was very near being excluded out of the *ſpecies* of *man* barely by his ſhape. He eſcaped very narrowly as he was; and it is certain, a figure a little more oddly turned had caſt him, and he had been executed as a thing not to be allowed to paſs for a man; and yet there can be no reaſon given, why, if the lineaments of his face had been a little altered, a rational ſoul could not have been lodged in him; why a viſage ſomewhat longer, or a noſe flatter, or a wider mouth, could not have conſiſted, as well as the reſt of his ill figure, with ſuch a ſoul, ſuch parts, as made him, disfigured as he was, capable to be a dignitary in the church.

§ 27.

WHEREIN, then, would I gladly know, conſiſts the preciſe and *unmoveable boundaries* of that *ſpecies*? It is plain, if we examine, there is *no* ſuch thing *made by nature* eſtabliſhed by her amongſt men. The real eſſence of that, or any other ſort of ſubſtances, it is evident, we know not, and therefore are ſo undetermined in our nominal eſſences, which we make ourſelves, that if ſeveral men were to be aſked concerning ſome oddly ſhaped *fœtus*, as ſoon as born, whether it were *man* or no, it is paſt doubt one ſhould meet with different anſwers; which could not happen, if the nominal eſſences, whereby we limit and diſtinguiſh the *ſpecies* of ſubſtances, were not made by man with ſome liberty, but were exactly copied from preciſe boundaries ſet by nature, whereby it diſtinguiſhed all ſubſtances into certain ſpecies. Who would undertake to reſolve what ſpecies that monſter was of, which is mentioned by Licetus, *lib.* 1. *c.* 3. with a man's head and hog's body? Or thoſe other, which to the bodies of men had the heads of beaſts, as dogs, horſes, *&c.*? If any of theſe creatures had lived, and could have ſpoke, it would have increaſed the difficulty. Had the upper part to the middle been of human ſhape, and all below ſwine, had it been murder to deſtroy it? or, muſt the biſhop have been conſulted, whether it were man enough to be admitted to the font or no? as, I have been told, it happened in France ſome years ſince, in ſomewhat a like caſe. So uncertain are the boundaries of ſpecies of animals to us who have no other meaſures than the complex *ideas* of our own collecting; and ſo far are we from certainly knowing what a *man* is, though, perhaps, it will be judged great ignorance to make any doubt about it. And yet, I think, I may ſay, that the certain boundaries of that ſpecies are ſo far from being determined, and the preciſe number of ſimple *ideas*, which make the nominal eſſence, ſo far from being ſettled and perfectly known, that very material doubts may ſtill ariſe about it; and I imagine, none of the definitions of the word *man*, which we yet have, nor deſcriptions of that ſort of animal, are ſo perfect and exact, as to ſatisfy a conſiderate inquiſitive perſon, much leſs to obtain a general conſent, and to be that which men would every where ſtick by in the deciſion of caſes, and determining of life and death, baptiſm or no baptiſm, in productions that might happen.

§ 28. *But not ſo arbitrary as Mixed Modes.*

BUT though theſe *nominal eſſences of ſubſtances* are made by the mind, they are *not* yet *made ſo arbitrarily as thoſe of mixed modes.* To the making of any nominal eſſence, it is neceſſary, *Firſt*, That the *ideas* whereof it conſiſts, have ſuch an union as to make but one *idea*, how compounded ſoever: *Secondly*, That the particular *ideas* ſo united be exactly the ſame, neither more nor leſs; for if two abſtract complex *ideas* differ either in number or ſorts of their component parts, they make two different, and not one and the ſame eſſence. In the firſt of theſe, the mind, in making its complex *ideas* of ſubſtances, only follows nature, and puts none together which are not ſuppoſed to have an union in nature. Nobody joins the voice of a ſheep with the ſhape of a horſe, nor the colour of lead with the weight and fixedneſs of gold, to be the complex *ideas* of any real ſubſtances, unleſs he has a mind to fill his head with *chimeras*, and his diſcourſe with unintelligible words. Men obſerving certain qualities always joined and exiſting together, therein copied nature, and of *ideas* ſo united, made their complex ones of ſubſtances.

For though men may make what complex *ideas* they pleaſe, and give what names to them they will, yet if they will be underſtood, when they ſpeak of things really exiſting, they muſt in ſome degree conform their *ideas* to the things they would ſpeak of, or elſe mens language will be like that of *Babel;* and every man's words being intelligible only to himſelf, would no longer ſerve to converſation, and the ordinary affairs of life, if the *ideas* they ſtand for be not ſome way anſwering the common appearances and agreement of ſubſtances as they really exiſt.

§ 29. *Though very imperfect.*

SECONDLY, Though the mind of man, *in making* its *complex ideas of ſubſtances*, never puts any together that do not really or are not ſuppoſed to co-exiſt, and ſo it truly borrows that union from nature, yet *the number* it combines *depends upon the various care, induſtry or fancy of him that makes it.* Men generally content themſelves with ſome few ſenſible obvious qualities, and often, if not always, leave out others as material, and as firmly united, as thoſe that they take. Of ſenſible ſubſtances, there are two ſorts; one of organized bodies which are propagated by ſeed; and in theſe, the ſhape is that which to us is the leading quality and moſt characteriſtical part that determines the ſpecies; and therefore in vegetables and animals, an extended ſolid ſubſtance of ſuch a certain figure uſually ſerves the turn. For however ſome men ſeem to prize their definition of *animal rationale*, yet ſhould there a creature be found that had language and reaſon, but partook not of the uſual ſhape of a man, I believe it would hardly paſs for a *man*, how much ſoever it were *animal rationale;* and if *Balaam's* aſs had, all his life, diſcourſed as rational as he did once with his maſter, I doubt yet whether any one would have thought him worthy the name *man*, or allowed him to be of the ſame ſpecies with himſelf. As in vegetables and animals it is the ſhape, ſo in moſt other bodies, not propagated by ſeed, it is the colour we muſt fix on, and are moſt led by. Thus, where we find the colour of gold, we are apt to imagine all the other qualities, comprehended in our complex *idea*, to be there alſo; and we commonly take theſe two obvious qualities, *viz.* ſhape and colour, for ſo preſumptive *ideas* of ſeveral *ſpecies*, that in a good picture we readily ſay this is a lion, and that a roſe; this is a gold, and that a ſilver goblet, only by the different figures and colours repreſented to the eye by the pencil.

§ 30. *Which yet ſerve for common converſe.*

But though this ſerves well enough for groſs and confuſed conceptions, and inaccurate ways of talking and thinking; yet *men are far enough from having agreed on the preciſe number of ſimple* ideas, *or* qualities *belonging to any ſort of things ſignified by its name:* Nor is it a wonder, ſince it requires much time, pains, and ſkill, ſtrict inquiry, and long examination, to find out what and how many thoſe ſimple *ideas* are, which are conſtantly and inſeparably united in nature, and are always to be found together in the ſame ſubject. Moſt men wanting either time, inclination, or induſtry enough for this, even to ſome tolerable degree, content themſelves with ſome few obvious and outward appearances of things, thereby readily to diſtinguiſh and ſort them for the common affairs of life; and ſo without farther examination give them names, or take up the names already in uſe; which, though in common converſation they paſs well enough for the ſigns of ſome few obvious qualities coexiſting, are yet far enough from comprehending, in a ſettled ſignification, a preciſe number of ſimple *ideas*, much leſs all thoſe which are united in nature. He that ſhall conſider, after ſo much ſtir about *genus* and *ſpecies*, and ſuch a deal of talk of ſpecific differences, how few words we have yet ſettled definitions of, may with reaſon imagine that thoſe *forms*, which there hath been ſo much noiſe made about, are only *chimeras*, which give us no light into the ſpecific natures of things; and he that ſhall conſider, how far the names of ſubſtances are from having ſignifications, wherein all who uſe them do agree, will have reaſon to conclude, that though the nominal eſſences of ſubſtances are all ſuppoſed to be copied from nature, yet they are all, or moſt of them, very imperfect, ſince the compoſition of thoſe complex *ideas* are, in ſeveral men, very different; and therefore that theſe boundaries of *ſpecies* are as men, and not as nature makes them, if at leaſt there are in nature any ſuch prefixed bounds. It is true, that many particular ſubſtances are ſo made by nature, that they have agreement and likeneſs one with another, and ſo afford a foundation of being ranked into ſorts. But the ſorting of things by us, or the making of determinate *ſpecies*, being in order to naming and comprehending them under general terms, I cannot ſee how it can be properly ſaid, that nature ſets the boundaries of the *ſpecies* of things; or if it be ſo, our boundaries of *ſpecies* are not exactly conformable to thoſe in nature; for we having need of general names for preſent uſe, ſtay not for a perfect diſcovery of all thoſe qualities which would beſt ſhow us their moſt material differences and agreements; but we ourſelves divide them, by certain obvious appearances, into *ſpecies*, that we may the eaſier under general names communicate our thoughts about them. For having no other knowledge of any ſubſtance, but of the ſimple *ideas* that are united in it, and obſerving ſeveral particular things to agree with others in ſeveral of thoſe ſimple *ideas*, we make that collection our ſpecific *idea*, and give it a general name, that in recording our own thoughts, and in our diſcourſe with others, we may in one ſhort word deſign all the individuals that agree in that complex *idea*, without enumerating the ſimple *ideas* that make it up, and ſo not waſte our time and breath in tedious deſcriptions; which we ſee they are fain to do, who would diſcourſe of any new ſort of things they have not yet a name for.

§ 31. *Eſſences of Species under the ſame name very different.*

But however theſe ſpecies of ſubſtances paſs well enough in ordinary converſation, it is plain that this complex *idea*, wherein they obſerve ſeveral individuals to agree, is by different men made very differently; by ſome more, and others leſs accurately. In ſome, this complex *idea* contains a greater, and in others a ſmaller number of qualities; and so is apparently such as the mind makes it. The yellow shining colour makes *gold* to children; others add weight, malleableness, and fusibility; and others yet other qualities, which they find joined with that yellow colour, as constantly as its weight and fusibility; for in all these and the like qualities, one has as good a right to be put into the complex *idea* of that substance wherein they are all joined, as another; and therefore *different men* leaving out or putting in several simple *ideas*, which others do not, according to their various examination, skill or observation of that subject, *have different essences of gold;* which must therefore be of their own, and not of nature's making.

§ 32. *The more general our* Ideas *are, the more incomplete and partial they are.*

If the number of simple *ideas*, that make the nominal essence of the lowest species, or first sorting of individuals, depends on the mind of man variously collecting them, it is much more evident that they do so, in the more comprehensive *classis*, which by the masters of logic are called *genera*. These are complex *ideas* designedly imperfect; and it is visible at first sight, that several of those qualities, that are to be found in the things themselves, are purposely left out of *generical ideas*. For as the mind, to make general *ideas* comprehending several particulars, leaves out those of time, and place, and such other that make them incommunicable to more than one individual; so to make other yet more general *ideas*; that may comprehend different sorts, it leaves out those qualities that distinguish them, and puts into its new collection only such *ideas* as are common to several sorts. The same convenience that made men express several parcels of yellow matter coming from Guinea and Peru under one name, sets them also upon making of one name that may comprehend both gold and silver, and some other bodies of different sorts. This is done by leaving out those qualities which are peculiar to each sort, and retaining a complex *idea* made up of those that are common to them all, to which the name *metal* being annexed, there is a *genus* consti-

2

tuted, the essence whereof being that abstract *idea*, containing only malleableness and fusibility, with certain degrees of weight and fixedness, wherein some bodies of several kinds agree, leaves out the colour and other qualities peculiar to gold and silver, and the other sorts comprehended under the name *metal;* whereby it is plain, that men follow not exactly the patterns set them by nature, when they make their general *ideas* of substances, since there is no body to be found, which has barely malleableness and fusibility in it, without other qualities as inseparable as those. But men, in making their general *ideas*, seeing more the convenience of language and quick dispatch, by short and comprehensive signs, than the true and precise nature of things as they exist, have, in the framing their abstract *ideas*, chiefly pursued that end which was to be furnished with store of general and variously comprehensive names; so that in this whole business of *genera* and *species*, the *genus*, or more comprehensive, is but a partial conception of what is in the *species*, and the *species* but a partial *idea* of what is to be found in each individual. If, therefore, any one will think, that a *man*, and a *horse*, and an animal, and a plant, &c. are distinguished by real essences made by nature, he must think nature to be very liberal of these real essences, making one for body, another for an animal, and another for a horse, and all these essences liberally bestowed upon *Bucephalus*. But if we would rightly consider what is done in all these *genera* and *species*, or sorts, we should find that there is no new thing made, but only more or less comprehensive signs, whereby we may be enabled to express, in a few syllables, great numbers of particular things, as they agree in more or less general conceptions, which we have framed to that purpose: In all which we may observe, that the more general term is always the name of a less complex *idea*, and that each *genus* is but a partial conception of the *species* comprehended under it; so that if these abstract general *ideas* be thought to be complete, it can only be in respect of a certain established relation between them and certain names, which are made use of to signify them, and not in respect of any thing existing, as made by nature.

§ 33. *This all accommodated to the end of Speech.* THIS is *adjusted to the true end of speech*, which is to be the easiest and shortest way of communicating our notions: For thus, he that would discourse of things as they agreed in the complex *idea* of extension and solidity, needed but use the word *body* to denote all such; he that to these would join others signified by the words life, sense, and spontaneous motion, needed but use the word *animal*, to signify all which partook of those *ideas*; and he that had made a complex *idea* of a body, with life, sense, and motion, with the faculty of reasoning, and a certain shape joined to it, needed but use the short monosyllable *man*, to express all particulars that correspond to that complex *idea*. This is the proper business of *genus* and *species*; and this men do, without any consideration of *real essences* or *substantial forms*, which come not within the reach of our knowledge when we think of those things, nor within the signification of our words when we discourse with others.

§ 34. *Instance in Contraries.*

WERE I to talk with any one of a sort of birds I lately saw in St. James's Park, about three or four feet high, with a covering of something between feathers and hair, of a dark brown colour, without wings, but in the place thereof two or three little branches coming down like sprigs of Spanish broom, long great legs, with feet only of three claws, and without a tail, I must make this description of it, and so may make others understand me: But when I am told that the name of it is *Cassauris*, I may then use that word to stand in discourse for all my complex *idea* mentioned in that description, though by that word, which is now become a specific name, I know no more of the real essence or constitution of that sort of animals than I did before, and knew probably as much of the nature of that *species* of birds before I learned the name, as many *Englishmen* do of swans or herons, which are specific names very well known of sorts of birds common in *England*.

§ 35. *Men determine the Sorts.*

FROM what has been ſaid, it is evident, that *men make ſorts of things;* for it being different eſſences alone that make different *ſpecies*, it is plain, that they who make thoſe abſtract *ideas*, which are the nominal eſſences, do thereby make the *ſpecies* or ſort. Should there be a body found, having all the other qualities of gold, except malleableneſs, it would no doubt be made a queſtion whether it were gold or no, *i. e.* whether it were of that *ſpecies*. This could be determined only by that abſtract *idea* to which every one annexed the name *gold;* ſo that it would be true gold to him, and belong to that *ſpecies* who included not malleableneſs in his nominal eſſence, ſignified by the ſound *gold;* and, on the other ſide, it would not be true gold, or of that *ſpecies*, to him who included malleableneſs in his ſpecific *idea*. And who, I pray, is it that makes theſe diverſe *ſpecies* even under one and the ſame name, but men that make two different abſtract *ideas* conſiſting not exactly of the ſame collection of qualities? Nor is it a mere ſuppoſition to imagine, that a body may exiſt, wherein the other obvious qualities of gold may be without malleableneſs, ſince it is certain, that gold itſelf will be ſometimes ſo eager (as artiſts call it), that it will as little endure the hammer as glaſs itſelf. What we have ſaid, of the putting in or leaving malleableneſs out of the complex *idea*, the name *gold* is by any one annexed to, may be ſaid of its peculiar weight, fixedneſs, and ſeveral other the like qualities; for whatſoever is left out or put in, it is ſtill the complex *idea*, to which that name is annexed, that makes the *ſpecies;* and as any particular parcel of matter anſwers that *idea*, ſo the name of the ſort belongs truly to it, and it is of that *ſpecies;* and thus any thing is true *gold*, perfect *metal*. All which determination of the *ſpecies*, it is plain, depends on the underſtanding of man, making this or that complex *idea*.

§ 36. *Nature makes the Similitude.*

THIS, then, in ſhort, is the caſe: *Nature makes many particular things which do agree* one with another, in many ſenſible qualities, and probably too in their internal frame and conſtitution; but it is not this real eſſence that diſtinguiſhes them into *ſpecies;* it is *men*, who, taking occaſion from the qualities they find united in them, and wherein they obſerve often ſeveral individuals to agree, *range them into ſorts, in order to their naming*, for the convenience of comprehenſive ſigns, under which individuals, according to their conformity to this or that abſtract *idea*, come to be ranked as under enſigns: ſo that this is of the blue, that the red regiment; this is a man, that a drill: And in this, I think, conſiſts the whole buſineſs of *genus* and *ſpecies*.

§ 37.

I do not deny but nature, in the conſtant production of particular beings, makes them not always new and various, but very much alike, and of kin one to another. But I think it nevertheleſs true, that *the boundaries of the ſpecies whereby men ſort them, are made by men*, ſince the eſſences of the *ſpecies*, diſtinguiſhed by different names, are, as has been proved, of man's making, and ſeldom adequate to the internal nature of the things they are taken from; ſo that we may truly ſay, ſuch a manner of ſorting of things is the workmanſhip of men.

§ 38. *Each abſtract* Idea *is an Eſſence.*

One thing I doubt not but will ſeem very ſtrange in this doctrine, which is, that from what has been ſaid, it will follow, that *each abſtract* idea, *with a name to it, makes a diſtinct ſpecies*. But who can help it if truth will have it ſo? for ſo it muſt remain till ſomebody can ſhow us the *ſpecies* of things limited and diſtinguiſhed by ſomething elſe, and let us ſee that general terms ſignify not our abſtract *ideas*, but ſomething different from them. I would fain know why a ſhock and a hound are not as diſtinct *ſpecies* as a ſpaniel and an elephant. We have no other *idea* of the different eſſence of an elephant and a ſpaniel, than we have of the different eſſence of a ſhock and a hound; all the eſſential difference, whereby we know and diſtinguiſh them one from another, conſiſting only in the different collection of ſimple *ideas*, to which we have given thoſe different names.

§ 39. Genera *and* Species *are in order to naming.* How much *the making of* ſpecies *and* genera *is in order to general names,* and how much general names are neceſſary, if not to the being, yet at leaſt to the compleating of a *ſpecies,* and making it paſs for ſuch, will appear, beſides what has been ſaid above concerning ice and water, in a very familiar example. A ſilent and a ſtriking *watch* are but one *ſpecies* to thoſe who have but one name for them: but he that has the name *watch* for one, and *clock* for the other, and diſtinct complex *ideas,* to which thoſe names belong, to him they are different *ſpecies.* It will be ſaid, perhaps, that the inward contrivance and conſtitution is different between theſe two, which the watchmaker has a clear *idea* of; and yet it is plain they are but one *ſpecies* to him, when he has but one name for them. For what is ſufficient in the inward contrivance to make a new *ſpecies?* There are ſome *watches* that are made with four wheels, others with five: Is this a ſpecific difference to the workman? Some have ſtrings and fuſees, and others none; ſome have the balance looſe, and others regulated by a ſpiral ſpring, and others by hogs briſtles: Are any or all of theſe enough to make a ſpecific difference to the workman, that knows each of theſe, and ſeveral other different contrivances, in the internal conſtitutions of *watches?* It is certain each of theſe hath a real difference from the reſt; but whether it be an eſſential, a ſpecific difference or no, relates only to the complex *idea* to which the name *watch* is given: as long as they all agree in the *idea* which that name ſtands for, and that name does not as a generical name comprehend different *ſpecies* under it, they are not eſſentially nor ſpecifically different. But if any one will make minuter diviſions from differences that he knows in the internal frame of watches, and to ſuch preciſe complex *ideas,* gives names that ſhall prevail, they will then be new *ſpecies* to them, who have thoſe *ideas* with names to them, and can, by thoſe differences, diſtinguiſh watches into theſe ſeveral ſorts, and then *watch* will be a generical name. But yet they would be no diſtinct *ſpecies* to men ignorant of clockwork and the inward contrivances of watches, who had no other *idea* but the outward ſhape and bulk, with the marking of the hours by the hand; for to them all thoſe other names would be but ſynonymous terms for the ſame *idea*, and ſignify no more, nor no other thing but a *watch*. Juſt thus, I think, it is in natural things. Nobody will doubt that the wheels or ſprings (if I may ſo ſay) within, are different in a *rational man* and a *changeling*, no more than that there is a difference in the frame between a *drill* and a *changeling*. But whether one or both theſe differences be eſſential or ſpecifical, is only to be known to us, by their agreement or diſagreement with the complex *idea* that the name *man* ſtands for; for by that alone can it be determined, whether one, or both, or neither of thoſe be a man or no.

§ 40. *Species of artificial things leſs confuſed than natural.* FROM what has been before ſaid, we may ſee the reaſon *why, in the ſpecies of artificial things, there is generally leſs confuſion and uncertainty than in natural*; becauſe an *artificial* thing being a production of man, which the artificer deſigned, and therefore well knows the *idea* of, the name of it is ſuppoſed to ſtand for no other *idea*, nor to import any other eſſence than what is certainly to be known, and eaſy enough to be apprehended: For the *idea* or eſſence of the ſeveral ſorts of *artificial* things conſiſting, for the moſt part, in nothing but the determinate figure of ſenſible parts, and ſometimes motion depending thereon, which the artificer faſhions in matter, ſuch as he finds for his turn; it is not beyond the reach of our faculties to attain a certain *idea* thereof, and ſo ſettle the ſignification of the names, whereby the ſpecies of *artificial* things are diſtinguiſhed with leſs doubt, obſcurity, and equivocation, than we can in things natural, whoſe differences and operations depend upon contrivances beyond the reach of our diſcoveries.

§ 41. *Artificial things of diſtinct Species.*

I MUST be excuſed here if I think *artificial things are of diſtinct ſpecies*, as well as natural; ſince I find they are as plainly and orderly ranked into ſorts, by different abſtract *ideas*, with general names annexed to them, as diſtinct one from another as thoſe of natural ſubſtances: For why ſhould we not think a watch and piſtol, as diſtinct ſpecies one from another, as a horſe and a dog, they being expreſſed in our minds by diſtinct *ideas*, and to others by diſtinct appellations?

§ 42. *Subſtances alone have proper Names.*

THIS is farther to be obſerved concerning *ſubſtances*, that they alone of all our ſeveral ſorts of *ideas* have particular or proper names, whereby one only particular thing is ſignified; becauſe in ſimple *ideas*, modes, and relations, it ſeldom happens that men have occaſion to mention often this or that particular when it is abſent. Beſides, the greateſt part of mixed modes, being actions which periſh in their birth, are not capable of a laſting duration as ſubſtances, which are the actors, and wherein the ſimple *ideas* that make up the complex *ideas* deſigned by the name, have a laſting union.

§ 43. *Difficulty to treat of words.*

I MUST beg pardon of my reader, for having dwelt ſo long upon this ſubject, and perhaps with ſome obſcurity. But I deſire it may be conſidered how *difficult* it is *to lead another by words into the thoughts of things ſtripped of thoſe ſpecific differences* we give them; which things, if I name not, I ſay nothing; and if I do name them, I thereby rank them into ſome ſort or other, and ſuggeſt to the mind the uſual abſtract *idea* of that *ſpecies*, and ſo croſs my purpoſe. For to talk of a *man*, and to lay by, at the ſame time, the ordinary ſignification of the name man, which is our complex *idea* uſually annexed to it, and bid the reader conſider *man* as he is in himſelf, and as he is really diſtinguiſhed from others in his interna conſtitution, or real eſſence, that is, by ſomething he knows not what, looks like trifling; and yet thus one muſt do who would ſpeak of the ſuppoſed real eſſences and *ſpecies* of things, as thought to be made by nature, if it be but only to make it underſtood, that there is no ſuch thing ſignified by the general names which ſubſtances are called by, but becauſe it is difficult by known familiar names to do this. Give me leave to endeavour by an example to make the different conſideration the mind has of ſpecific names and *ideas* a little more clear, and to ſhow how the complex *ideas* of modes are referred ſometimes to archetypes in the minds of other intelligent beings, or, which is the ſame, to the ſignification annexed by others to their received names, and ſometimes to no archetypes at all. Give me leave alſo to ſhow how the mind always refers its *ideas* of ſubſtances, either to the ſubſtances themſelves, or to the ſignification of their names as to the *archetypes;* and alſo to make plain the nature of *ſpecies*, or ſorting of things, as apprehended, and made uſe of by us; and of the eſſences belonging to thoſe *ſpecies*, which is perhaps of more moment, to diſcover the extent and certainty of our knowledge than we at firſt imagine.

§ 44. *Inſtance of Mixed Modes in* Kinneah *and* Niouph.

Let us ſuppoſe *Adam* in the ſtate of a grown man, with a good underſtanding, but in a ſtrange country, with all things new and unknown about him, and no other faculties, to attain the knowledge of them, but what one of this age has now. He obſerves *Lamech* more melancholy than uſual, and imagines it to be from a ſuſpicion he has of his wife *Adah* (whom he moſt ardently loved), that ſhe had too much kindneſs for another man. *Adam* diſcourſes theſe his thoughts to *Eve*, and deſires her to take care that *Adah* commit not folly: and in theſe diſcourſes with *Eve* he makes uſe of theſe two new words, *Kinneah* and *Niouph*. In time *Adam's* miſtake appears, for he finds *Lamech's* trouble proceeded from having killed a man: but yet the two names, *Kinneah* and *Niouph*, the one ſtanding for ſuſpicion, in a huſband, of his wife's diſloyalty to him, and the other for the act of committing diſloyalty, loſt not their diſtinct ſignifications. It is plain then that here were two diſtinct complex *ideas* of mixed modes, with names to them, two diſtinct ſpecies of actions eſſentially different. I aſk wherein conſiſted the eſſences of theſe two diſtinct ſpecies of action? And it is plain it conſiſted in a preciſe combination of ſimple *ideas*, different in one from the other. I aſk, whether the complex *idea* in *Adam's* mind, which he called *Kinneah*, were adequate or no? And it is plain it was; for it being a combination of ſimple *ideas*, which he, without any regard to any archetype, without reſpect to any thing as a pattern, voluntarily put together, abſtracted and gave the name *Kinneah* to, to expreſs in ſhort to others, by that one ſound, all the ſimple *ideas* contained and united in that complex one, it muſt neceſſarily follow, that it was an adequate *idea*; his own choice having made that combination, it had all in it he intended it ſhould, and ſo could not but be perfect, could not but be adequate, it being referred to no other archetype which it was ſuppoſed to repreſent.

§ 45.

THESE words, *Kinneah* and *Niouph*, by degrees grew into common uſe, and then the caſe was ſomewhat altered. *Adam's* children had the ſame faculties, and thereby the ſame power that he had to make what complex *ideas* of mixed modes they pleaſed in their own minds, to abſtract them, and make what ſounds they pleaſed the ſigns of them. But the uſe of names being to make our *ideas* within us known to others, that cannot be done but when the ſame ſign ſtands for the ſame *idea* in two who would communicate their thoughts, and diſcourſe together. Thoſe, therefore, of *Adam's* children, that found theſe two words, *Kinneah* and *Niouph*, in familiar uſe, could not take them for inſignificant ſounds, but muſt needs conclude they ſtood for ſomething, for certain *ideas*, abſtract *ideas*, they being general names; which abſtract *ideas* were the eſſences of the ſpecies diſtinguiſhed by thoſe names. If, therefore, they would uſe theſe words as names of ſpecies already eſtabliſhed and agreed on, they were obliged to conform the *ideas* in their minds ſignified by theſe names, to the *ideas* that they ſtood for in other mens minds, as to their patterns and *archetypes*; and then indeed their *ideas* of theſe complex modes were liable to be inadequate, as being very apt (eſpecially thoſe that conſiſted of combinations of many ſimple *ideas*), not to be exactly conformable to the *ideas* in other mens minds, uſing the ſame names, though for this there be uſually a remedy at hand, which is to aſk the meaning of any word we underſtand not of him that uſes it, it being as impoſſible to know certainly what the words jealouſy and adultery (which I think anſwer קנאה and נאוב), ſtand for in another man's mind, with whom I would diſcourſe about them, as it was impoſſible, in the beginning of language, to know what *Kinneah* and *Niouph* ſtood for in another man's mind, without explication, they being voluntary ſigns in every one.

§ 46. *Inſtance of Subſtances in* Zahab.

LET us now alſo conſider, after the ſame manner, the names of ſubſtances in their firſt application. One of *Adam's* children roving in the mountains, lights on a glittering ſubſtance which pleaſes his eye; home he carries it to *Adam*, who, upon conſideration of it, finds it to be hard, to have a bright yellow colour, and an exceeding great weight. Theſe, perhaps, at firſt, are all the qualities he takes notice of in it, and, abſtracting this complex *idea*, conſiſting of a ſubſtance having that peculiar bright yellowneſs, and a weight very great in proportion to its bulk, he gives it the name *Zahab*, to denote and mark all ſubſtances that have theſe ſenſible qualities in them. It is evident now, that, in this caſe, *Adam* acts quite differently from what he did before in forming thoſe *ideas* of mixed modes, to which he gave the name *Kinneah* and *Niouph*; for there he puts *ideas* together only by his own imagination, not taken from the exiſtence of any thing, and to them he gave names, to denominate all things that ſhould happen to agree to thoſe his abſtract *ideas*, without conſidering whether any ſuch thing did exiſt or no; the ſtandard there was of his own making. But in the forming his *idea* of this new ſubſtance, he takes the quite contrary courſe: Here he has a ſtandard made by nature; and, therefore, being to repreſent that to himſelf, by the *idea* he has of it, even when it is abſent, he puts in no ſimple *idea* into his complex one, but what he has the perception of from the thing itſelf; he takes care that his *idea* be conformable to this *archetype*, and intends the name ſhould ſtand for an *idea* ſo conformable.

§ 47.

THIS piece of matter, thus denominated *Zahab* by *Adam*, being quite different from any he had seen before, nobody, I think, will deny to be a distinct species, and to have its peculiar essence; and that the name *Zahab* is the mark of the species, and a name belonging to all things partaking in that essence: But here it is plain, the essence *Adam* made the name *Zahab* stand for, was nothing but a body hard, shining, yellow, and very heavy. But in the inquisitive mind of man, not content with the knowledge of these, as I may say superficial qualities, puts *Adam* on farther examination of this matter; he therefore knocks and beats it with flints, to see what was discoverable in the inside; he finds it yield to blows, but not easily separate into pieces; he finds it will bend without breaking. Is not now ductility to to be added to his former *idea*, and made part of the essence of the species that name *Zahab* stands for? Farther trials discover fusibility and fixedness. Are not they also, by the same reason that any of the others were, to be put into the complex *idea* signified by the name *Zahab*? If not, what reason will there be shown more for the one than the other? If these must, then all the other properties, which any farther trials shall discover in this matter, ought by the same reason to make a part of the ingredients of the complex *idea*, which the name *Zahab* stands for, and so be the essences of the species marked by that name; which properties, because they are endless, it is plain, that the *idea* made after this fashion by this *archetype*, will be always inadequate.

§ 48. *Their* Ideas *imperfect, and therefore various.* BUT this is not all; it would also follow, that the *names of substances* would not only have (as in truth they have), but would also be supposed to *have different significations, as used by different men,* which would very much cumber the use of language; for if every distinct quality, that were discovered in any matter by any one, were supposed to make a necessary part of the complex *idea* signified by the common name given it, it must follow, that men must suppose the same word to signify different things,

I 6.

in different men; since they cannot doubt but different men may have discovered several qualities in substances of the same denomination, which others know nothing of.

§ 49. *Therefore to fix their Species, a real Essence is supposed.*

To avoid this, therefore, they have *supposed a real essence belonging to every species*, from which these properties all flow, and would have their name of the species stand for that. But they not having any *idea* of that real essence in substances, and their words signifying nothing but the *ideas* they have, that which is done by this attempt, is only to put the name or sound in the place and stead of the thing having that real essence, without knowing what the real essence is; and this is that which men do, when they speak of species of things, as supposing them made by nature, and distinguished by real essences.

§ 50. *Which Supposition is of no use.*

For let us consider, when we affirm, that all *gold* is fixed, either it means that fixedness is a part of the definition, part of the nominal essence the word *gold* stands for; and so this affirmation, *all gold is fixed*, contains nothing but the signification of the term *gold*; or else it means, that fixedness not being a part of the definition of the word *gold*, is a property of that substance itself; in which case, it is plain, that the word *gold* stands in the place of a substance, having the real essence of a species of things made by nature. In which way of substitution it has so confused and uncertain a signification, that though this proposition, *gold is fixed*, be in that sense an affirmation of something real, yet it is a truth will always fail us in its particular application, and so is of no real use nor certainty; for let it be never so true, that all *gold*, *i. e.* all that has the real essence of *gold*, is fixed, what serves this for, whilst we know not in this sense what is or is not *gold*? For if we know not the real essence of gold, it is impossible we should know what parcel of matter has that essence, and so whether it be true *gold* or no.

§ 51. *Conclusion.*

To conclude; what liberty *Adam* had at first to make

any complex *ideas* of mixed modes, by no other pattern but by his own thoughts, the ſame have all men ever ſince had. And the ſame neceſſity of conforming his *ideas* of ſubſtances to things without him, as to *archetypes* made by nature, that *Adam* was under, if he would not wilfully impoſe upon himſelf, the ſame are all men ever ſince under too. The ſame liberty alſo that *Adam* had of affixing any new name to any *idea*, the ſame has any one ſtill (eſpecially the beginners of languages, if we can imagine any ſuch), but only with this difference, that in places where men in ſociety have already eſtabliſhed a language amongſt them, the ſignification of words are very warily and ſparingly to be altered; becauſe men being furniſhed already with names for their *ideas*, and common uſe having appropriated known names to certain *ideas*, an affected miſapplication of them cannot but be very ridiculous. He that hath new notions, will, perhaps, venture ſometimes on the coining new terms to expreſs them; but men think it a boldneſs, and it is uncertain whether common uſe will ever make them paſs for current. But in communication with others, it is neceſſary that we conform the *ideas* we make the vulgar words of any language ſtand for, to their known proper ſignifications (which I have explained at large already), or elſe to make known that new ſignification we apply them to.

CHAP. VII.

OF PARTICLES.

§ 1. *Particles connect Parts, or whole Sentences together.*

BESIDES words, which are names of *ideas* in the mind, there are a great many others that are made uſe of, to ſignify the *connection* that the mind gives to *ideas, or propoſitions, one with another.* The mind, in communicating its thought to others, does not only need ſigns of the *ideas* it has then before it, but others alſo, to ſhow or intimate ſome particular action of its own, at that time, relating to thoſe *ideas.* This it does ſeveral ways; as *is,* and *is not,* are the general marks of the mind, affirming or denying. But besides affirmation or negation, without which there is in words no truth or falsehood, the mind does, in declaring its sentiments to others, connect not only the parts of propositions, but whole sentences one to another, with their several relations and dependencies, to make a coherent discourse.

§ 2. *In them consists the Art of well speaking.*

THE words, whereby it signifies what connection it gives to the several affirmations and negations, that it unites in one continued reasoning or narration, are generally called *particles;* and it is in the right use of these, that more particularly consists the clearness and beauty of a good style. To think well, it is not enough that a man has *ideas* clear and distinct in his thoughts, nor that he observes the agreement or disagreement of some of them; but he must think in train, and observe the dependence of his thoughts and reasonings one upon another; and to express well such methodical and rational thoughts, he must have words to *show* what *connection, restriction, distinction, opposition, emphasis,* &c. he gives to each respective *part of his discourse.* To mistake in any of these, is to puzzle, instead of informing his hearer; and therefore it is that those words, which are not truly by themselves the names of any *ideas,* are of such constant and indispensible use in language, and do much contribute to mens well expressing themselves.

§ 3. *They show what Relation the Mind gives to its own Thoughts.*

THIS part of grammar has been perhaps as much neglected, as some others over diligently cultivated. It is easy for men to write one after another, of *cases* and *genders, moods* and *tenses, gerunds* and *supines.* In these, and the like, there has been great diligence used; and particles themselves, in some languages, have been, with great show of exactness, ranked into their several orders. But though *prepositions* and *conjunctions,* &c. are names well known in grammar, and the particles contained under them carefully ranked into their distinct subdivisions; yet he who would show the right use of particles, and what significancy and force they have, muſt take a little more pains, enter into his own thoughts, and obſerve nicely the ſeveral poſtures of his mind in diſcourſing.

§ 4. *They ſhow what Relation the Mind gives to its own thoughts.*

NEITHER is it enough, for the explaining of theſe words, to render them, as it is uſually in dictionaries, by words of another tongue which come neareſt to their ſignification; for what is meant by them, is commonly as hard to be underſtood in one, as another language. They are all *marks of ſome action, or intimation of the mind;* and therefore to underſtand them rightly, the ſeveral views, poſtures, ſtands, turns, limitations and exceptions, and ſeveral other thoughts of the mind, for which we have either none, or very deficient names, are diligently to be ſtudied. Of theſe there are a great variety, much exceeding the number of particles, that moſt languages have to expreſs them by; and therefore it is not to be wondered that moſt of theſe particles have divers, and ſometimes almoſt oppoſite ſignifications. In the Hebrew tongue there is a particle conſiſting but of one ſingle letter, of which there are reckoned up, as I remember, ſeventy, I am ſure above fifty ſeveral ſignifications.

§ 5. *Inſtance in But.*

BUT is a particle, none more familiar in our language; and he that ſays it is a diſcretive conjunction, and that it anſwers *ſed* in *Latin*, or *mais* in *French*, thinks he has ſufficiently explained it; but it ſeems to me to intimate ſeveral relations the mind gives to the ſeveral propoſitions or parts of them, which it joins by this monoſyllable.

Firſt, *BUT to ſay no more;* here it intimates a ſtop of the mind in the courſe it was going, before it came to the end of it.

Secondly, *I ſaw BUT two plants;* here it ſhows, that the mind limits the ſenſe to what is expreſſed, with a negation of all other.

Thirdly, *You pray; BUT it is not that GOD would bring you to the true religion.*

Fourthly, *BUT that he would confirm you in your own.*

The firſt of theſe *BUTS* intimates a ſuppoſition in the mind of ſomething otherwiſe than it ſhould be; the latter ſhows, that the mind makes a direct oppoſition between that, and what goes before it.

Fifthly, *All animals have ſenſe; BUT a dog is an animal;* here it ſignifies little more, but that the latter propoſition is joined to the former, as the *minor* of a ſyllogiſm.

§ 6.

To theſe, I doubt not, might be added a great many other ſignifications of this particle, if it were my buſineſs to examine it in its full latitude, and conſider it in all the places it is to be found, which if one ſhould do, I doubt, whether in all thoſe manners it is made uſe of, it would deſerve the title of *diſcretive*, which grammarians give to it. But I intend not here a full explication of this ſort of ſigns. The inſtances I have given in this one, may give occaſion to reflect upon their uſe and force in language, and lead us into the contemplation of ſeveral actions of our minds in diſcourſing, which it has found a way to intimate to others by theſe particles; ſome whereof conſtantly, and others in certain conſtructions, have the ſenſe of a whole ſentence contained in them.

CHAP. VIII.

OF ABSTRACT AND CONCRETE TERMS.

§ 1. *Abſtract Terms not predicable one of another, and why.*

THE ordinary words of language, and our common uſe of them, would have given us light into the nature of our *ideas*, if they had been but conſidered with attention. The mind, as has been ſhown, has a power to abſtract its *ideas*, and ſo they become *eſſences*, general eſſences, whereby the ſorts of things are diſtinguiſhed. Now each abſtract *idea* being diſtinct, ſo that of any two the one can never be the other, the mind will, by its intuitive knowledge, perceive their difference; and therefore in propoſitions, no two whole *ideas* can ever be affirmed one of another. This we see in the common use of language, which permits *not any two abstract words, or names of abstract ideas, to be affirmed one of another.* For how near of kin soever they may seem to be, and how certain soever it is, that man is an animal, or rational, or white, yet every one at first hearing perceives the falsehood of these propositions, *humanity is animality,* or *rationality,* or *whiteness;* and this is as evident as any of the most allowed maxims. All our affirmations then are only inconcrete, which is the affirming, not one abstract *idea* to be another, but one abstract *idea* to be joined to another; which abstract *ideas,* in substances, may be of any sort; in all the rest, are little else but of relations; and in substances the most frequent are of powers: *v. g. a man is white,* signifies that the thing that has the essence of a man, has also in it the essence of whiteness, which is nothing but a power to produce the *idea* of whiteness in one, whose eyes can discover ordinary objects; or *a man is rational,* signifies that the same thing that hath the essence of a man, hath also in it the essence of rationality, *i. e.* a power of reasoning.

§ 2. *They show the difference of our* Ideas.

THIS distinction of names shows us also the difference of our *ideas;* for if we observe them, we shall find that our *simple ideas have all abstract, as well as concrete names;* the one whereof is (to speak the language of grammarians) a substantive, the other an adjective; as whiteness, white; sweetness, sweet. The like also holds in our *ideas* of modes and relations; as justice, just; equality, equal; only with this difference, that some of the concrete names of relations amongst men chiefly are substantives; as *paternitas, pater;* whereof it were easy to render a reason. But as to our *ideas* of *substances,* we have very few or *no abstract names* at all; for though the schools have introduced *animalitas, humanitas, corporietas,* and some others, yet they hold no proportion with that infinite number of names of substances, to which they never were ridiculous enough to attempt the coining of abstract ones; and those few that the schools forged, and put into the mouths of their scholars, could never yet get admittance into common uſe, or obtain the licence of public approbation; which ſeems to me at leaſt to intimate the confeſſion of all mankind, that they have no *ideas* of the real eſſences of ſubſtances, ſince they have not names for ſuch *ideas*: which no doubt they would have had, had not their conſciouſneſs to themſelves of their ignorance of them, kept them from ſo idle an attempt. And therefore, though they had *ideas* enough to diſtinguiſh gold from ſtone, and metal from wood, yet they but timorouſly ventured on ſuch terms, as *aurietas* and *ſaxietas*, *metallietas* and *lignietas*, or the like names, which ſhould pretend to ſignify the real eſſences of thoſe ſubſtances, whereof they knew they had no *ideas*. And indeed it was only the doctrine of *ſubſtantial forms*, and the confidence of miſtaken pretenders to a knowledge that they had not, which firſt coined, and then introduced *animalitas*, and *humanitas*, and the like; which yet went very little farther than their own ſchools, and could never get to be current amongſt underſtanding men. Indeed, *humanitas* was a word familiar amongſt the *Romans*, but in a far different ſenſe, and ſtood not for the abſtract eſſence of any ſubſtance, but was the abſtract name of a mode, and its concrete *humanus*, not *homo*.

CHAP. IX.

OF THE IMPERFECTION OF WORDS.

§ 1. *Words are uſed for recording and communicating our Thoughts.*

FROM what has been ſaid in the foregoing chapters, it is eaſy to perceive what imperfection there is in language, and how the very nature of words makes it almoſt unavoidable for many of them to be doubtful and uncertain in their ſignifications. To examine the perfection or imperfection of words, it is neceſſary firſt to conſider their uſe and end; for as they are more or leſs fitted to attain that, ſo are they more or leſs perfect. We have in the former part of this *diſcourſe*, often upon occaſion mentioned *a double uſe of words*.

First, One for the recording of our own thoughts.

Secondly, The other for the communicating of our thoughts to others.

§ 2. *Any Words will serve for recording.*

As to the first of these, *for the recording our own thoughts* for the help of our own memories, whereby, as it were, we talk to ourselves, any words will serve the turn; for since sounds are voluntary and indifferent signs of any *ideas*, a man may use what words he pleases, to signify his own *ideas* to himself; and there will be no imperfection in them, if he constantly use the same sign for the same *idea*, for then he cannot fail of having his meaning understood, wherein consists the right use and perfection of language.

§ 3. *Communication by words, Civil or Philosophical.*

SECONDLY, As to *communication of words*, that too *has a double use*.

I. *Civil.*

II. *Philosophical.*

First, By their *civil use*, I mean such a communication of thoughts and *ideas* by words, as may serve for the upholding common conversation and commerce, about the ordinary affairs and conveniencies of civil life, in the societies of men one amongst another.

Secondly, By the *philosophical use* of words, I mean such an use of them, as may serve to convey the precise notions of things, and to express, in general propositions, certain and undoubted truths, which the mind may rest upon and be satisfied with, in its search after true knowledge. These two uses are very distinct; and a great deal less exactness will serve in the one than in the other, as we shall see in what follows.

§ 4. *The Imperfection of Words is the Doubtfulness of their Signification.*

THE chief end of language in communication being to be understood, words serve not for that end, neither in civil nor philosophical discourse, when any word does not excite in the hearer the same *idea* which it stands for in the mind of the speaker. Now since sounds have no natural connection with our *ideas*, but have all their signification from the arbitrary imposition of men, the *doubtfulness* and uncertainty *of their signification*, which is the *imperfection* we here are speaking of, has its cause more in the *ideas* they stand for, than in any incapacity there is in one sound more than in another to signify any *idea*; for in that regard they are all equally perfect.

That then which makes doubtfulness and uncertainty in the signification of some more than other words, is the difference of *ideas* they stand for.

§ 5. *Causes of their Imperfection.*

WORDS having naturally no signification, the *idea* which each stands for must be learned and retained by those, who would exchange thoughts, and hold intelligible discourse with others in any language. But this is hardest to be done, where,

First, The *ideas* they stand for are very complex, and made up of a great number of *ideas* put together.

Secondly, Where the *ideas* they stand for have no certain connection in nature, and so no settled standard, any where in nature existing, to rectify and adjust them by.

Thirdly, Where the signification of the word is referred to a standard, which standard is not so easy to be known.

Fourthly, Where the signification of the word, and the real essence of the thing, are not exactly the same.

These are difficulties that attend the signification of several words that are intelligible: those which are not intelligible at all, such as names standing for any simple *ideas*, which another has not organs or faculties to attain, as the names of colours to a blind man, or sounds to a deaf man, need not here be mentioned.

In all these cases we shall find an imperfection in words, which I shall more at large explain, in their particular application to our several sorts of *ideas*: For if we examine them, we shall find that the *names of mixed modes are most liable to doubtfulness and imperfection, for the two first of these reasons; and the names of substances chiefly for the two latter.*

§ 6. *The Names of mixed Modes doubtful.*

FIRST, the names of *mixed modes* are many of them liable to great uncertainty and obscurity in their signification.

First, Because the Ideas *they stand for are so complex.*

I. Because of that *great composition* these complex *ideas* are often made up of. To make words serviceable to the end of communication, it is necessary (as has been said) that they excite in the hearer exactly the same *idea* they stand for in the mind of the speaker. Without this, men fill one another's heads with noise and sounds, but convey not thereby their thoughts, and lay not before one another their *ideas*, which is the end of discourse and language. But when a word stands for a very complex *idea* that is compounded and decompounded, it is not easy for men to form and retain that *idea* so exactly, as to make the name in common use stand for the same precise *idea* without any the least variation. Hence it comes to pass, that mens names of very compound *ideas*, such as for the most part are moral words, have seldom, in two different men, the same precise signification; since one man's complex *idea* seldom agrees with another's, and often differs from his own, from that which he had yesterday, or will have to-morrow.

§ 7. *Secondly, Because they have no Standards.*

II. *BECAUSE the names of mixed modes*, for the most part, *want standards* in nature, whereby men may rectify and adjust their significations; therefore they are very various and doubtful. They are assemblages of *ideas* put together at the pleasure of the mind, pursuing its own ends of discourse, and suited to its own notions; whereby it designs not to copy any thing really existing, but to denominate and rank things, as they come to agree, with those archetypes or forms it has made. He that first brought the word *sham*, *wheedle*, or *banter* in use, put together, as he thought fit, those *ideas* he made it stand for: And as it is with any new names of modes, that are now brought into any language, ſo was it with the old ones, when they were firſt made uſe of. Names therefore that ſtand for collections of *ideas* which the mind makes at pleaſure, muſt needs be of doubtful ſignification, when ſuch collections are no where to be found conſtantly united in nature, nor any patterns to be ſhown whereby men may adjuſt them. What the word *murder*, or *ſacrilege*, &c. ſignifies, can never be known from things themſelves: There be many of the parts of thoſe complex *ideas*, which are not viſible in the action itſelf; the intention of the mind, or the relation of holy things, which make a part of *murder* or *ſacrilege*, have no neceſſary connection with the outward and viſible action of him that commits either; and the pulling the trigger of the gun with which the murder is commited, and is all the action that perhaps is viſible, has no natural connection with thoſe other *ideas* that make up the complex one, named *murder*. They have their union and combination only from the underſtanding, which unites them under one name; but uniting them without any rule or pattern, it cannot be but that the ſignification of the name that ſtands for ſuch voluntary collections, ſhould be often various in the minds of different men, who have ſcarce any ſtanding rule to regulate themſelves and their notions by, in ſuch arbitrary *ideas*.

§ 8. *Propriety not a ſufficient Remedy.*

It is true, *common uſe*, that is the rule of propriety, may be ſuppoſed here to afford ſome aid, to ſettle the ſignification of language; and it cannot be denied but that in ſome meaſure it does. Common uſe *regulates the meaning of words* pretty well for common converſation, but nobody having an authority to eſtabliſh the preciſe ſignification of words, nor determine to what *ideas* any one ſhall annex them, common uſe is not ſufficient to adjuſt them to philoſophical diſcourſes; there being ſcarce any name of any very complex *idea* (to ſay nothing of others), which in common uſe has not a great latitude, and which, keeping within the bounds of propriety, may not be made the ſign of far different *ideas*. Beſides, the rule and meaſure of propriety itſelf being no where eſtabliſhed, it is often matter of diſpute whether this or that way of uſing a word be propriety of ſpeech or no. From all which it is evident, that the names of ſuch kind of very complex *ideas* are naturally liable to this imperfection, to be of doubtful and uncertain ſignification; and even in men that have a mind to underſtand one another, do not always ſtand for the ſame *idea* in ſpeaker and hearer. Though the names *glory* and *gratitude* be the ſame in every man's mouth through a whole country, yet the complex collective *idea*, which every one thinks on, or intends by that name, is apparently very different in men uſing the ſame language.

§ 9. *The way of learning theſe Names contributes alſo to their Doubtfulneſs.*

THE way alſo *wherein the names of mixed modes are ordinarily learned, does* not a little *contribute to the doubtfulneſs of their ſignification.* For if we will obſerve how children learn languages, we ſhall find that to make them underſtand what the names of ſimple *ideas*, or ſubſtances, ſtand for, people ordinarily ſhow them the thing whereof they would have them have the *idea*, and then repeat to them the name that ſtands for it, as *white, ſweet, milk, ſugar, cat, dog.* But as for mixed modes, eſpecially the moſt material of them, moral words, the ſounds are uſually learned firſt; and then to know what complex *ideas* they ſtand for, they are either beholden to the explication of others, or (which happens for the moſt part) are left to their own obſervation and induſtry; which being little laid out in the ſearch of the true and preciſe meaning of names, theſe moral words are in moſt mens mouths little more than bare ſounds; or when they have any, it is for the moſt part but a very looſe and undetermined, and conſequently obſcure and confuſed ſignification. And even thoſe themſelves, who have with more attention ſettled their notions, do yet hardly avoid the inconvenience, to have them ſtand for complex *ideas*, different from thoſe which other, even intelligent and ſtudious men, make them the ſigns of. Where ſhall one find any, either *controverſial debate*, or *familiar discourse*, concerning *honour*, *faith*, *grace*, *religion*, *church*, &c. wherein it is not easy to observe the different notions men have of them? which is nothing but this, that they are not agreed in the signification of those words, nor have in their minds the same complex *ideas* which they make them stand for; and so all the contests that follow thereupon are only about the meaning of a sound. And hence we see, that in the interpretation of laws, whether divine or human, there is no end; comments beget comments, and explications make new matter for explications: And of limiting, distinguishing, varying the signification of these moral words, there is no end. These *ideas* of mens making, are, by men still having the same power, multiplied *in infinitum*. Many a man, who was pretty well satisfied of the meaning of a text of scripture, or clause in the code, at first reading, has by consulting commentators quite lost the sense of it, and by those elucidations given rise or increase to his doubts, and drawn obscurity upon the place. I say not this, that I think commentaries needless, but to show how uncertain the names of mixed modes naturally are, even in the mouths of those who had both the intention and the faculty of speaking as clearly as language was capable to express their thoughts.

§ 10. *Hence unavoidable Obscurity in ancient Authors.* WHAT obscurity this has unavoidably brought upon the writings of men, who have lived in remote ages and different countries, it will be needless to take notice; since the numerous volumes of learned men, employing their thoughts that way, are proofs more than enough to show what attention, study, sagacity, and reasoning are required, to find out the true meaning of *ancient authors*. But there being no writings we have any great concernment to be very solicitous about the meaning of, but those that contain either truths we are required to believe, or laws we are to obey, and draw inconveniences on us when we mistake or transgress, we may be less anxious about the sense of other authors, who writing but their own opinions, we are under no greater necesfity to know them, than they to know ours. Our good or evil depending not on their decrees, we may fafely be ignorant of their notions; and therefore in the reading of them, if they do not ufe their words with a due clearnefs and perfpicuity, we may lay them afide, and without any injury done them, refolve thus with ourfelves,

Si non vis intelligi, debes negligi.

§ 11.

If the fignification of the names of mixed modes are uncertain, becaufe there be no real ftandards exifting in nature, to which thofe *ideas* are referred, and by which they may be adjufted, the *names of fubftances are of a doubtful fignification,* for a contrary reafon, *viz.* becaufe the *ideas* they ftand for are fuppofed conformable to the reality of things, and are *referred to ftandards* made by nature. In our *ideas* of fubftances we have not the liberty, as in mixed modes, to frame what combinations we think fit, to be the characteriftical notes to rank and denominate things by. In thefe we muft follow nature, fuit our complex *ideas* to real exiftences, and regulate the fignification of their names by the things themfelves, if we will have our names to be the figns of them, and ftand for them. Here, it is true, we have patterns to follow, but patterns that will make the fignification of their names very uncertain; for names muft be of a very unfteady and various meaning, if the *ideas* they ftand for be referred to ftandards without us, *that either cannot be known at all, or can be known but imperfectly and uncertainly.*

§ 12. *Names of Subftances referred,* 1. *To real Effences that cannot be known.*

The *names of fubftances have,* as has been fhowed, a double *reference* in their ordinary ufe.

Firft, Sometimes they are made to ftand for, and fo their fignification is fuppofed to agree to, *the real conftitution of things,* from which all their properties flow, and in which they all centre. But this real conftitution, or (as it is apt to be called) effence, being utterly unknown to us, any found that is put to ftand for it, muft be very uncertain in its application; and it will be impofſible to know what things are, or ought to be called an *horſe*, or *antimony*, when thoſe words are put for real eſſences, that we have no *ideas* of at all. And therefore in this ſuppoſition, the names of ſubſtances being referred to ſtandards that cannot be known, their ſignifications can never be adjuſted and eſtabliſhed by thoſe ſtandards.

§ 13. 2. *To co-exiſting Qualities, which are known but imperfectly.*

SECONDLY, The *ſimple ideas* that are found to *co-exiſt in ſubſtances* being that which their names immediatly ſignify, theſe, as united in the ſeveral ſorts of things, *are* the proper *ſtandards* to which their names are referred, and by which their ſignifications may beſt be rectified. But neither will theſe *archetypes* ſo well ſerve this purpoſe, as to leave theſe names without very various and uncertain ſignifications; becauſe theſe ſimple *ideas* that co-exiſt, and are united in the ſame ſubject, being very numerous, and having all an equal right to go into the complex ſpecific *idea*, which the ſpecific name is to ſtand for, men, though they propoſe to themſelves the very ſame ſubject to conſider, yet frame very different *ideas* about it; and ſo the name they uſe for it unavoidably comes to have, in ſeveral men, very different ſignifications. The ſimple qualities which make up the complex *ideas* being moſt of them powers, in relation to changes, which they are apt to make in, or receive from other bodies, are almoſt infinite. He that ſhall but obſerve what a great variety of alterations any one of the baſer metals is apt to receive from the different application only of fire, and how much a greater number of changes any of them will receive in the hands of a chemiſt, by the application of other bodies, will not think it ſtrange that I count the properties of any ſort of bodies not eaſy to be collected, and completely known by the ways of inquiry which our faculties are capable of. They being therefore at leaſt ſo many, that no man can know the preciſe and definite number, they are differently diſcovered by different men, according to their various ſkill, attention, and ways of handling; who therefore cannot choofe but have different *ideas* of the fame fubftance, and therefore make the fignification of its common name very various and uncertain; for the complex *ideas* of fubftances being made up of fuch fimple ones as are fuppofed to co-exift in nature, every one has a right to put into his complex *idea* thofe qualities he has found to be united together. For though in the fubftance *gold*, one fatisfies himfelf with colour and weight, yet another thinks folubility in *aqua regia* as neceffary to be joined with that colour in his *idea* of gold, as any one does its fufibility; folubility in *aqua regia* being a quality as conftantly joined with its colour and weight, as fufibility, or any other: Others put in its ductility or fixednefs, &c. as they have been taught by tradition or experience. Who of all thefe has eftablifhed the right fignification of the word *gold?* or who fhall be the judge to determine? Each has his ftandard in nature, which he appeals to, and with reafon thinks he has the fame right to put into his complex *idea* fignified by the word *gold*, thofe qualities which upon trial he has found united, as another, who has not fo well examined, has to leave them out, or a third, who has made other trials, has to put in others; for the union in nature of thefe qualities being the true ground of their union in one complex *idea*, who can fay one of them has more reafon to be put in or left out than another? From whence it will always unavoidably follow, that the complex *ideas* of fubftances, in men ufing the name for them, will be very various, and fo the fignifications of thofe names very uncertain.

§ 14. *To co-exifting Qualities, which are known but imperfectly.*

Besides, there is fcarce any particular thing exifting, which, in fome of its fimple *ideas*, does not communicate with a greater, and in others with a lefs number of particular beings: who fhall determine in this cafe which are thofe that are to make up the precife collection that is to be fignified by the fpecific name, or can with any juft authority prefcribe, which obvious or common qualities are to be left out, or which more fecret, or more particular, are to be put into the ſignification of the name of any ſubſtance? All *which* together ſeldom or never fail to *produce* that various and *doubtful ſignification in the names of ſubſtances*, which cauſes ſuch uncertainty, diſputes, or miſtakes, when we come to a philoſophical uſe of them.

§ 15. *With this Imperfection they may ſerve for civil, but not well for philoſophical Uſe.*

It is true, as *to civil and common converſation*, the general *names of ſubſtances*, regulated in their ordinary ſignification by ſome obvious qualities (as by the ſhape and figure in things of known ſeminal propagation, and in other ſubſtances, for the moſt part by colour, joined with ſome other ſenſible qualities), *do well enough* to deſign the things men would be underſtood to ſpeak of; and ſo they uſually conceive well enough the ſubſtances meant by the word *gold*, or *apple*, to diſtinguiſh the one from the other. *But in philoſophical inquiries and debates*, where general truths are to be eſtabliſhed, and conſequences drawn from poſitions laid down, there the preciſe ſignification of the names of ſubſtances will be found, not only *not* to be *well eſtabliſhed*, but alſo very hard to be ſo. For example, he that ſhall make malleableneſs, or a certain degree of fixedneſs, a part of his complex *idea* of *gold*, may make propoſitions concerning gold, and draw conſequences from them, that will truly and clearly follow from *gold* taken in ſuch a ſignification, but yet ſuch as another man can never be forced to admit, nor be convinced of their truth, who makes not malleableneſs, or the ſame degree of fixedneſs, part of that complex *idea* that the name *gold*, in his uſe of it, ſtands for.

§ 16. *Inſtance—Liquor.*

This is a natural, and almoſt unavoidable imperfection in almoſt all the names of ſubſtances, in all languages whatſoever, which men will eaſily find, when once paſſing from confuſed or looſe notions, they come to more ſtrict and cloſe inquiries; for then they will be convinced how doubtful and obſcure thoſe words are in their ſignification, which in ordinary uſe appeared very clear and determined. I was once in a meeting of very learned and ingenious phyſicians, where by chance there aroſe a queſtion, whether any liquor paſſed through the filaments of the nerves. The debate having been managed a good while by variety of arguments on both ſides, I (who had been uſed to ſuſpect that the greateſt part of diſputes were more about the ſignification of words, than a real difference in the conception of things) deſired, that before they went any farther on in this diſpute, they would firſt examine, and eſtabliſh among them, what the word *liquor* ſignified. They at firſt were a little ſurpriſed at the propoſal; and had they been perſons leſs ingenious, they might perhaps have taken it for a very frivolous or extravagant one, ſince there was no one there that thought not himſelf to underſtand very perfectly what the word liquor ſtood for, which I think too none of the moſt perplexed names of ſubſtances. However, they were pleaſed to comply with my motion, and upon examination, found, that the ſignification of that word was not ſo ſettled and certain as they had all imagined, but that each of them made it a ſign of a different complex *idea*. This made them perceive that the main of their diſpute was about the ſignification of that term, and that they differed very little in their opinions concerning ſome fluid and ſubtile matter, paſſing through the conduits of the nerves, though it was not ſo eaſy to agree whether it was to be called *liquor* or no, a thing which, when conſidered, they thought it not worth the contending about.

§ 17. *Inſtance—Gold.*

How much this is the caſe, in the greateſt part of diſputes that men are engaged ſo hotly in, I ſhall perhaps have an occaſion in another place to take notice. Let us only here conſider a little more exactly the forementioned inſtance of the word *gold*, and we ſhall ſee how hard it is preciſely to determine its ſignification. I think all agree to make it ſtand for a body of a certain yellow ſhining colour; which being the *idea* to which children have annexed that name, the ſhining yellow part of a peacock's tail is properly to them gold: Others, finding fuſibility joined with that yellow colour in certain parcels of matter, make of that combination a complex *idea*, to which they give the name *gold* to denote a sort of substances, and so exclude from being *gold* all such yellow shining bodies as by fire will be reduced to ashes, and admit to be of that species, or to be comprehended under that name *gold*, only such substances as having that shining yellow colour will by fire be reduced to fusion, and not to ashes: Another, by the same reason, adds the weight, which, being a quality as straitly joined with that colour as its fusibility, he thinks has the same reason to be joined in its *idea*, and to be signified by its name, and therefore the other made up of body, of such a colour and fusibility, to be imperfect; and so on of all the rest: wherein no one can show a reason why some of the inseparable qualities, that are always united in nature, should be put into the nominal essence, and others left out; or why the word *gold*, signifying that sort of body the ring on his finger is made of, should determine that sort rather by its colour, weight, and fusibility, than by its colour, weight, and solubility in *aqua regia;* since the dissolving it by that liquor is as inseparable from it as the fusion by fire, and they are both of them nothing but the relation which that substance has to two other bodies, which have a power to operate differently upon it. For by what right is it that fusibility comes to be a part of the essence signified by the word *gold*, and solubility but a property of it? or why is its colour part of the essence, and its malleableness but a property? That which I mean is this, that these being all but properties depending on its real constitution, and nothing but powers, either active or passive, in reference to other bodies, no one has authority to determine the signification of the word *gold* (as referred to such a body existing in nature) more to one collection of *ideas* to be found in that body than to another; whereby the signification of that name must unavoidably be very uncertain, since, as has been said, several people observe several properties in the same substance, and, I think, I may say no body all; and therefore have but very imperfect descriptions of things, and words have very uncertain significations.

§ 18. *The Names of simple* Ideas *the least Doubtful.* FROM what has been said, it is easy to observe what has been before remarked, *viz.* That the *names of simple* ideas *are*, of all others, the *least liable to mistakes*, and that for these reasons: *First*, Because the *ideas* they stand for, being each but one single perception, are much easier got, and more clearly retained, than the more complex ones, and therefore are not liable to the uncertainty which usually attends those compounded ones of *substances and mixed modes*, in which the precise number of simple *ideas* that make them up are not easily agreed, and so readily kept in the mind; and, *Secondly*, Because they are never referred to any other essence, but barely that perception they immediately signify: which reference is that which renders the signification of the names of substances naturally so perplexed, and gives occasion to so many disputes. Men, that do not perversely use these words, or on purpose set themselves to cavil, seldom mistake, in any language which they are acquainted with, the use and signification of the names of simple *ideas*; *white* and *sweet*, *yellow* and *bitter*, carry a very obvious meaning with them, which every one precisely comprehends, or easily perceives he is ignorant of, and seeks to be informed; but what precise collection of simple *ideas*, *modesty* or *frugality* stand for in another's use, is not so certainly known. And, however we are apt to think we well enough know what is meant by *gold* or *iron*, yet the precise complex *idea* others make them the signs of, is not so certain; and I believe it is very seldom that in speaker and hearer they stand for exactly the same collection; which must needs produce mistakes and disputes, when they are made use of in discourses, wherein men have to do with universal propositions, and would settle in their minds universal truths, and consider the consequences that follow from them.

§ 21. *And next to them Simple Modes.*
BY the same rule, the *names of simple modes are*, *next to those of simple ideas*, *least liable to doubt and uncertainty*, espe-

cially thoſe of figure and number, of which men have ſo clear and diſtinct *ideas*. Who ever, that had a mind to underſtand them, miſtook the ordinary meaning of *ſeven* or a *triangle?* And in general the leaſt compounded *ideas* in every kind have the leaſt dubious names.

§ 20. *The moſt doubtful are the Names of very compounded Mixed Modes and Subſtances.*

MIXED modes therefore, that are made up but of a few and obvious ſimple *ideas*, have uſually names of no very uncertain ſignification. But the names of mixed modes, which comprehend a great number of ſimple *ideas*, are commonly of a very doubtful and undetermined meaning, as has been ſhown. The names of ſubſtances, being annexed to *ideas* that are neither the real eſſences nor exact repreſentations of the patterns they are referred to, are liable yet to greater imperfection and uncertainty, eſpecially when we come to a philoſophical uſe of them.

§ 21. *Why this imperfection charged upon Words.*

THE great diſorder that happens in our names of ſubſtances, proceeding for the moſt part from our want of knowledge, and inability to penetrate into their real conſtitutions, it may probably be wondered, *why I charge this as an imperfection* rather *upon our words* than underſtandings. This exception has ſo much appearance of juſtice, that I think myſelf obliged to give a reaſon why I have followed this method. I muſt confeſs then, that when I firſt began this diſcourſe of the underſtanding, and a good while after, I had not the leaſt thought that any conſideration of words were at all neceſſary to it; but when, having paſſed over the original and compoſition of our *ideas*, I began to examine the extent and certainty of our knowledge, I found it had ſo near a connection with words, that unleſs their force and manner of ſignification were firſt well obſerved, there could be very little ſaid clearly and pertinently concerning knowledge, which being converſant about truth, had conſtantly to do with propoſitions; and though it terminated in things, yet it was for the moſt part ſo much by the intervention of words, that they ſeemed ſcarce ſeparable from our general knowledge; at leaſt they interpoſe themſelves ſo much between our underſtandings and truth, which it would contemplate and apprehend, that like the *medium* through which viſible objects paſs, their obſcurity and diſorder does not ſeldom caſt a miſt before our eyes, and impoſe upon our underſtandings. If we conſider, in the fallacies men put upon themſelves as well as others, and the miſtakes in mens diſputes and notions, how great a part is owing to words, and their uncertain or miſtaken ſignifications, we ſhall have reaſon to think this no ſmall obſtacle in the way to knowledge; which, I conclude, we are the more carefully to be warned of, becauſe it has been ſo far from being taken notice of as an inconvenience, that the arts of improving it have been made the buſineſs of mens ſtudy, and obtained the reputation of learning and ſubtilty, as we ſhall ſee in the following chapter. But I am apt to imagine, that were the imperfections of language, as the inſtrument of knowledge, more thoroughly weighed, a great many of the controverſies that make ſuch a noiſe in the world, would of themſelves ceaſe, and the way to knowledge, and perhaps peace too, lie a great deal opener than it does.

§ 22. *This ſhould teach us Moderation, in impoſing our own ſenſe of old Authors.*

SURE I am, that the ſignification of words in all languages, depending very much on the thoughts, notions, and *ideas* of him that uſes them, muſt unavoidably be of great uncertainty to men of the ſame language and country. This is ſo evident in the *Greek* authors, that he that ſhall peruſe their writings will find in almoſt every one of them a diſtinct language, though the ſame words. But when to this natural difficulty in every country, there ſhall be added different countries and remote ages, wherein the ſpeakers and writers had very different notions, tempers, cuſtoms, ornaments, and figures of ſpeech, *&c.* every one of which influenced the ſignification of their words then, though to us now they are loſt and unknown, *it would become us to be charitable one to another in our interpretations or miſunderſtanding of* thoſe *ancient writings;* which though of great concernment to be underſtood, are liable to the unavoidable difficulties of ſpeech, which (if we except the name of ſimple *ideas*, and ſome very obvious things) is not capable, without a conſtant defining the terms, of conveying the ſenſe and intention of the ſpeaker, without any manner of doubt and uncertainty, to the hearer. And in diſcourſes of religion, law, and morality as they are matters of the higheſt concernment, ſo there will be the greateſt difficulty.

§ 23.

THE volumes of interpreters and commentators on the Old and New Teſtament, are but too manifeſt proofs of this. Though every thing ſaid in the text be infallibly true, yet the reader may be, nay, cannot chooſe but be very fallible in the underſtanding of it. Nor is it to be wondered, that the will of GOD, when clothed in words should be liable to that doubt and uncertainty which unavoidably attends that ſort of conveyance, when even his Son, whilſt clothed in fleſh, was ſubject to all the frailties and inconveniences of human nature, ſin excepted. And we ought to magnify his goodneſs, that he hath ſpread before all the world ſuch legible characters of his works and providence, and given all mankind ſo ſufficient a light of reaſon, that they to whom this written word never came, could not (whenever they ſet themſelves to ſearch) either doubt of the being of a GOD or of the obedience due to him. Since, then, the precepts of natural religion are plain, and very intelligible to all mankind, and ſeldom come to be controverted and other revealed truths, which are conveyed to us by books and languages, are liable to the common and natural obſcurities and difficulties incident to words; methinks it would become us to be more careful and diligent in obſerving the former, and leſs magiſterial, poſitive, and imperious, in impoſing our own ſenſe and interpretations of the latter.

CHAP. X.

OF THE ABUSE OF WORDS.

§ 1. *Abuse of Words.*

BESIDES the imperfection that is naturally in language, and the obscurity and confusion that is so hard to be avoided in the use of words, there are several *wilful faults and neglects* which men are guilty of in this way of communication, whereby they render these signs less clear and distinct in their signification, than naturally they need to be.

§ 2. *First, Words without any, or without clear* Ideas. *FIRST*, In this kind, the first and most palpable abuse is, the using of words without clear and distinct *ideas*; or, which is worse, signs without any thing signified. Of these there are two sorts:

I. One may observe, in all languages, certain words, that if they be examined, will be found, in their first original and their appropriated use, not to stand for any clear and distinct *ideas*. These, for the most part, the several *sects* of philosophy and religion have introduced; for their authors, or promoters, either affecting something singular and out of the way of common apprehensions, or to support some strange opinions, or cover some weakness of their hypothesis, seldom fail to *coin* new words, and such as when they come to be examined may justly be called *insignificant terms*; for having either had no determinate collection of *ideas* annexed to them, when they were first invented, or at least such as, if well examined, will be found inconsistent, it is no wonder if afterwards, in the vulgar use of the same party, they remain empty sounds, with little or no signification, amongst those who think it enough to have them often in their mouths as the distinguishing characters of their church, or school, without much troubling their heads to examine what are the precise *ideas* they stand for. I shall not need here to heap up instances; every one's reading and conversation will sufficiently furnish him, or if he wants to be better stored, the great mint-mafters of these kind of terms, I mean the schoolmen and metaphysicians (under which, I think, the disputing natural and moral philosophers of these latter ages may be comprehended), have wherewithal abundantly to content him.

§ 3.

II. Others there be, who extend this abuse yet farther, who take so little care to lay by words, which in their primary notation have scarce any clear and distinct *ideas* which they are annexed to, that by an unpardonable negligence they familiarly *use words*, which the propriety of language has affixed to very important *ideas*, *without any distinct meaning* at all. *Wisdom, glory, grace*, &c. are words frequent enough in every man's mouth; but if a great many of those who use them, should be asked what they mean by them, they would be at a stand, and not know what to answer; a plain proof, that though they have learned those sounds, and have them ready at their tongue's end, yet there are no determined *ideas* laid up in their minds, which are to be expressed to others by them.

§ 4. *Occasioned by learning Names before the* Ideas *they belong to.*

Men having been *accustomed* from their cradles *to learn words*, which are easily got and retained, *before they knew*, or had framed *the complex ideas* to which they were annexed, or which were to be found in the things *they* were thought to *stand* for, they *usually continue to do so* all their lives; and without taking the pains necessary to settle in their minds determined *ideas*, they use their words for such unsteady and confused notions as they have, contenting themselves with the same words other people use, as if their very sound necessarily carried with it constantly the same meaning. This, though men make a shift with, in the ordinary occurrences of life, where they find it necessary to be understood, and therefore they make signs till they are so, yet this insignificancy in their words, when they come to reason concerning either their tenets or interest, manifestly fills their discourse with abundance of empty unintelligible noiſe and jargon, eſpecially in moral matters, where the words for the moſt part ſtanding for arbitrary and numerous collections of *ideas*, not regularly and permanently united in nature, their bare ſounds are often only thought on, or at leaſt very obſcure and uncertain notions annexed to them. Men take the words they find in uſe amongſt their neighbours, and that they may not ſeem ignorant what they ſtand for, uſe them confidently, without much troubling their heads about a certain fixed meaning; whereby, beſides the eaſe of it, they obtain this advantage, that as in ſuch diſcourſes they ſeldom are in the right, ſo they are as ſeldom to be convinced that they are in the wrong; it being all one to go about to draw thoſe men out of their miſtakes, who have no ſettled notions, as to diſpoſſeſs a vagrant of his habitation, who has no ſettled abode: This I gueſs to be ſo; and every one may obſerve in himſelf and others, whether it be or no.

§ 5. 2. *Unſteady Application of them.*

SECONDLY, Another great abuſe of words is, *inconſtancy* in the uſe of them. It is hard to find a diſcourſe written of any ſubject, eſpecially of controverſy, wherein one ſhall not obſerve, if he read with attention, the ſame words (and thoſe commonly the moſt material in the diſcourſe, and upon which the argument turns) uſed ſometimes for one collection of ſimple *ideas*, and ſometimes for another; which is a perfect abuſe of language. Words being intended for ſigns of my *ideas*, to make them known to others, not by any natural ſignification, but by a voluntary impoſition, it is plain cheat and abuſe, when I make them ſtand ſometimes for one thing, and ſometimes for another; the wilful doing whereof, can be imputed to nothing but great folly, or greater diſhoneſty. And a man, in his accounts with another, may, with as much fairneſs, make the characters of numbers ſtand ſometimes for one, and ſometimes for another collection of units, (*v. g.* this character 3 ſtand ſometimes for three, ſometimes for four, and ſometimes for eight) as in his diſcourſe, or reaſoning, make the ſame words ſtand for different collections of ſimple *ideas*. If men ſhould do ſo in their reckonings, I wonder who would have to do with them? One who would ſpeak thus, in the affairs and buſineſs of the world, and call eight ſometimes ſeven, and ſometimes nine, as beſt ſerved his advantage, would preſently have clapped upon him one of the two names men conſtantly are diſguſted with. And yet in arguings and learned conteſts, the ſame ſort of proceeding paſſes commonly for wit and learning; but to me it appears a greater diſhoneſty than the miſplacing of counters in the caſting up a debt, and the cheat the greater, by how much truth is of greater concernment and value than money.

§ 6. 3. *Affected Obſcurity by wrong Application.* *THIRDLY*, Another abuſe of language is, an *affected obſcurity*, by either applying old words to new and unuſual ſignifications, or introducing new and ambiguous terms, without defining either; or elſe putting them ſo together, as may confound their ordinary meaning. Though the peripatetic philoſophy has been moſt eminent in this way, yet other ſects have not been wholly clear of it. There is ſcarce any of them that are not cumbered with ſome difficulties (ſuch is the imperfection of human knowledge), which they have been fain to cover with obſcurity of terms, and to confound the ſignification of words, which, like a miſt before people's eyes, might hinder their weak parts from being diſcovered. That *body* and *extenſion*, in common uſe, ſtand for two diſtinct *ideas*, is plain to any one that will but reflect a little; for were their ſignification preciſely the ſame, it would be proper, and as intelligible to ſay, the *body of an extenſion*, as *the extenſion of a body*; and yet there are thoſe who find it neceſſary to confound their ſignification. To this abuſe, and the miſchiefs of confounding the ſignification of words, logic and the liberal ſciences, as they have been handled in the ſchools, have given reputation; and the admired art of diſputing hath added much to the natural imperfection of languages, whilſt it has been made uſe of and fitted to perplex the ſignification of words, more than to diſcover the knowledge and truth of things; and he that will look into that ſort of learned writings, will find the words there much more obscure, uncertain and undetermined in their meaning, than they are in ordinary converſation.

§ 7. *Logic and Diſpute has much contributed to this.* THIS is unavoidably to be ſo, where mens parts and learning are eſtimated by their ſkill in *diſputing*: And if reputation and reward ſhall attend theſe conqueſts, which depend moſtly on the fineneſs and niceties of words, it is no wonder if the wit of men ſo employed, ſhould perplex, involve and ſubtilize the ſignification of ſounds, ſo as never to want ſomething to ſay, in oppoſing or defending any queſtion; the victory being adjudged not to him who had truth on his ſide, but the laſt word in the diſpute.

§ 8: *Calling it Subtilty.*

THIS, though a very uſeleſs ſkill, and that which I think the direct oppoſite to the ways of knowledge, hath yet paſſed hitherto under the laudable and eſteemed names of *ſubtilty* and *acuteneſs*, and has had the applauſe of the ſchools, and encouragement of one part of the learned men of the world; and no wonder, ſince the philoſophers of old (the diſputing and wrangling philoſophers I mean, ſuch as Lucian wittily and with reaſon taxes), and the ſchoolmen ſince, aiming at glory and eſteem for their great and univerſal knowledge, eaſier a great deal to be pretended to than really acquired, found this a good expedient to cover their ignorance, with a curious and inexplicable web of perplexed words, and procure to themſelves the admiration of others by unintelligible terms, the apter to produce wonder, becauſe they could not be underſtood; whilſt it appears in all hiſtory, that theſe profound doctors were no wiſer, nor more uſeful than their neighbours, and brought but ſmall advantage to human life, or the ſocieties wherein they lived, unleſs the coining of new words, where they produced no new things to apply them to, or the perplexing or obſcuring the ſignification of old ones, and ſo bringing all things into queſtion and diſpute, were a thing profitable to the life of man, or worthy commendation and reward.

§ 9. *This Learning very little benefits Society.*

For notwithſtanding theſe learned diſputants, theſe all-knowing doctors, it was to the unſcholaſtic ſtateſman that the governments of the world owed their peace, defence, and liberties; and from the illiterate and contemned mechanic (a name of diſgrace) that they received the improvements of uſeful arts. Neverthele ſs, this artificial ignorance, and *learned gibberiſh*, prevailed mightily in theſe laſt ages, by the intereſt and artifice of thoſe, who found no eaſier way to that pitch of authority and dominion they have attained, than by amuſing the men of buſineſs and ignorant with hard words, or employing the ingenious and idle intricate diſputes about unintelligible terms, and holding them perpetually entangled in that endleſs labyrinth. Beſides, there is no ſuch way to gain admittance, or give defence to ſtrange and abſurd doctrines, as to guard them round about with legions of obſcure, doubtful and undefined words, which yet make theſe retreats more like the dens of robbers, or holes of foxes, than the fortreſſes of fair warriors, which if it be hard to get them out of, it is not for the ſtrength that is in them, but the briars and thorns, and the obſcurity of the thickets they are beſet with. For untruth being unacceptable to the mind of man, there is no other defence left for abſurdity, but obſcurity.

§ 10. *But deſtroys the Inſtruments of Knowledge and Communication.*

Thus learned ignorance, and this art of keeping, even inquiſitive men, from true knowledge, hath been propagated in the world, and hath much perplexed, whilſt it pretended to inform the underſtanding: For we ſee that other well-meaning and wiſe men, whoſe education and parts had not acquired that *acuteneſs*, could intelligibly expreſs themſelves to one another, and in its plain uſe make a benefit of language: But though unlearned men well enough underſtood the words *white* and *black*, &c. and had conſtant notions of the *ideas* ſignified by thoſe words, yet there were philoſophers found, who had learning and *ſubtility* enough to prove that *ſnow was black*; i. e. to prove that *white* was *black*;

whereby they had the advantage to deſtroy the inſtruments and means of diſcourſe, converſation, inſtruction and ſociety, whilſt with great art and *ſubtility* they did no more but perplex and confound the ſignification of words, and thereby render language leſs uſeful than the real defects of it had made it; a gift which the illiterate had not attained to.

§ 11. *As uſeful as to confound the Sound of the Letters.* THESE learned men did equally inſtruct mens underſtandings, and profit their lives, as he who ſhould alter the ſignification of known characters, and, by a ſubtle device of learning, far ſurpaſſing the capacity of the illiterate, dull and vulgar, ſhould, in his writing, ſhow that he could put *A* for *B*, and *D* for *E*, &c. to the no ſmall admiration and benefit of his reader; it being as ſenſeleſs to put *black*, which is a word agreed on to ſtand for one ſenſible *idea*, to put it I ſay, for another or the contrary *idea*, *i. e.* to call *ſnow black*, as to put this mark *A*, which is a character agreed on to ſtand for one modification of ſound, made by a certain motion of the organs of ſpeech, for *B*, which is agreed on to ſtand for another modification of ſound, made by another certain motion of the organs of ſpeech.

§ 12. *This Art has perplexed Religion and Juſtice.* NOR hath this miſchief ſtopped in logical niceties, or curious empty ſpeculations; it hath invaded the great concernments of human life and ſociety, obſcured and perplexed the material truths of law and divinity, brought confuſion, diſorder and uncertainty into the affairs of mankind, and if not deſtroyed, yet in great meaſure rendered uſeleſs thoſe two great rules, religion and juſtice. What have the greateſt part of the comments and diſputes upon the laws of GOD and man ſerved for, but to make the meaning more doubtful, and perplex the ſenſe? What have been the effect of thoſe multiplied curious diſtinctions and acute niceties, but obſcurity and uncertainty, leaving the words more unintelligible, and the reader more at a loſs? How elſe comes it to paſs that princes, ſpeaking or writing to their ſervants, in their ordinary commands, are eaſily underſtood; ſpeaking to their people, in their laws, are not ſo? And, as I remarked before, doth it not often happen, that a man of an ordinary capacity very well underſtands a text or a law that he reads, till he conſults an expoſitor, or goes to counſel, who by that time he hath done explaining them, makes the words ſignify either nothing at all, or what he pleaſes?

§ 13. *And ought not to paſs for Learning.*

WHETHER any by-intereſts of theſe profeſſions have occaſioned this, I will not here examine; but I leave it to be conſidered, whether it would not be well for mankind, whoſe concernment it is to know things as they are, and to do what they ought, and not to ſpend their lives in talking about them, or toſſing words to and fro; whether it would not be well, I ſay, that the uſe of words were made plain and direct, and that language, which was given us for the improvement of knowledge and bond of ſociety, ſhould not be employed to darken truth, and unſettle people's rights, to raiſe miſts, and render unintelligible both morality and religion; or that at leaſt, if this will happen, it ſhould not be thought learning or knowledge to do ſo.

§ 14. 4. *Taking them for Things.*

FOURTHLY, Another great *abuſe of words is, the taking them for things.* This though it in ſome degree concerns all names in general, yet more particularly affects thoſe of ſubſtances. To this abuſe thoſe men are moſt ſubject, who confine their thoughts to any one ſyſtem, and give themſelves up into a firm belief of the perfection of any received hypotheſis, whereby they come to be perſuaded, that the terms of that ſect are ſo ſuited to the nature of things, that they perfectly correſpond with their real exiſtence. Who is there, that has been bred up in the peripatetic philoſophy, who does not think the ten names, under which are ranked the ten predicaments, to be exactly conformable to the nature of things? Who is there of that ſchool, that is not perſuaded, that *ſubſtantial forms, vegetative ſouls, abhorrence of a vacuum, intentional ſpecies*, &c. are ſomething real? Theſe words men have learned from their very entrance upon knowledge, and have found their maſters and ſyſtems lay great ſtreſs upon them; and therefore they cannot quit the opinion, that they are conformable to nature, and are the repreſentations of ſomething that really exiſts. The *Platoniſts* have their *ſoul of the world*, and the *Epicureans their endeavour towards motion* in their atoms, when at reſt. There is ſcarce any ſect in philoſophy has not a diſtinct ſet of terms, that others underſtand not; but yet this gibberiſh, which, in the weakneſs of human underſtanding, ſerves ſo well to palliate mens ignorance, and cover their errors, comes by familiar uſe among thoſe of the ſame tribe, to ſeem the moſt important part of language, and of all other the terms the moſt ſignificant. And ſhould *aereal* and *ethereal vehicles* come once, by the prevalency of that doctrine, to be generally received any where, no doubt thoſe terms would make impreſſions on mens minds, ſo as to eſtabliſh them in the perſuaſion of the reality of ſuch things, as much as *peripatetic forms* and *intentional ſpecies* have heretofore done.

§ 15. *Inſtance in Matter.*

How much *names taken for things* are apt to *miſlead the underſtanding*, the attentive reading of philoſophical writers would abundantly diſcover, and that, perhaps, in words little ſuſpected of any ſuch miſuſe. I ſhall inſtance in one only, and that a very familiar one: How many intricate diſputes have there been about *matter*, as if there were ſome ſuch thing really in nature, diſtinct from *body?* as it is evident the word *matter* ſtands for an *idea* diſtinct from the *idea* of body: For if the *ideas* theſe two terms ſtood for were preciſely the ſame, they might indifferently in all places be put one for another; but we ſee that though it be proper to ſay, there is *one matter of all bodies*, one cannot ſay, there is *one body of all matters;* we familiarly ſay, one *body* is bigger than another; but it ſounds harſh (and I think is never uſed) to ſay, one *matter* is bigger than another. Whence comes this then? *viz.* from hence, that though *matter* and *body* be not really diſtinct, but wherever there is the one, there is the other; yet *matter* and *body* ſtands for two different conceptions, whereof the one is incomplete, and but a part of the other. For *body* ſtands for a ſolid extended figured ſubſtance, whereof *matter* is but a partial and more confuſed conception, it ſeeming to me to be uſed for the ſubſtance and ſolidity of body, without taking in its extenſion and figure; and therefore it is that ſpeaking of *matter*, we ſpeak of it always as one, becauſe in truth it expreſsly contains nothing but the *idea* of a ſolid ſubſtance, which is every where the ſame, every where uniform. This being our *idea* of *matter*, we no more conceive or ſpeak of different *matters* in the world, than we do of different ſolidities; though we both conceive and ſpeak of different bodies, becauſe extenſion and figure are capable of variation. But ſince ſolidity cannot exiſt without extenſion and figure, the taking *matter* to be the name of ſomething really exiſting under that preciſion, has no doubt produced thoſe obſcure and unintelligible diſcourſes and diſputes, which have filled the heads and books of philoſophers concerning *materia prima;* which imperfection or abuſe, how far it may concern a great many other general terms, I leave to be conſidered. This, I think I may at leaſt ſay, that we ſhould have a great many fewer diſputes in the world, if words were taken for what they are, the ſigns of our *ideas* only, and not for things themſelves; for when we argue about *matter*, or any the like term, we truly argue only about the *idea* we expreſs by that ſound, whether that preciſe *idea* agree to any thing really exiſting in nature or no. And if men would tell what *ideas* they make their words ſtand for, there could not be half that obſcurity or wrangling, in the ſearch or ſupport of truth, that there is.

§ 16. *This makes Errors laſting.*

BUT whatever inconvenience follows from this miſtake of words, this I am ſure, that by conſtant and familiar uſe, they charm men into notions far remote from the truth of things. It would be a hard matter to perſuade any one, that the words which his father or ſchoolmaſter, the parſon of the pariſh, or ſuch a reverend doctor uſed, ſignified nothing that really exiſted in nature: which, perhaps, is *none of the leaſt cauſes, that men are ſo hardly drawn to quit their miſtakes*, even in opinions purely philoſophical, and where they have no other intereſt but truth: For the words they have a long time been uſed to, remaining firm in their minds, it is no wonder that the wrong notions annexed to them ſhould not be removed.

§ 17. 5. *Setting them for what they cannot ſignify.* *FIFTHLY*, Another *abuſe of words, is the ſetting them in the place of things which they do or can by no means ſignify.* We may obſerve, that in the general names of ſubſtances, whereof the nominal eſſences are only known to us, when we put them into propoſitions, and affirm or deny any thing about them, we do moſt commonly tacitly ſuppoſe, or intend they ſhould ſtand for the real eſſence of a certain ſort of ſubſtances. For when a man ſays *gold is malleable*, he means and would inſinuate ſomething more than this, that *what I call gold is malleable* (though truly it amounts to no more), but would have this underſtood, *viz.* that *gold*, i. e. *what has the real eſſence of gold, is malleable;* which amounts to thus much, that *malleableneſs depends on, and is inſeparable from the real eſſence of gold.* But a man not knowing wherein that real eſſence conſiſts, the connection in his mind of malleableneſs, is not truly with an eſſence he knows not, but only with the ſound gold he puts for it. Thus when we ſay, that *animal rationale* is, and *animal implume bipes latis unguibus* is not a good definition of a man, it is plain, we ſuppoſe the name *man* in this caſe to ſtand for the real eſſence of a ſpecies, and would ſignify, that a *rational animal* better deſcribed that real eſſence, than *a two legged animal with broad nails, and without feathers.* For elſe why might not *Plato* as properly make the word ἄνθρωπος or *man* ſtand for his complex *idea*, made up of the *ideas* of a body, diſtinguiſhed from others by a certain ſhape and other outward appearances, as *Ariſtotle*, make the complex *idea*, to which he gave the name ἄνθρωπος or *man*, of body and the faculty of reaſoning joined together; unleſs the name ἄνθρωπος or *man* were ſuppoſed to ſtand for ſomething elſe than what it ſignifies, and to be put in the place of ſome other thing than the *idea* a man profeſſes he would expreſs by it?

§ 18. v. g. *Putting them for the real Essences of Substances.*

It is true, the names of substances would be much more useful, and propositions made in them much more certain, were the real essences of substances the *ideas* in our minds which those words signified; and it is for want of those real essences that our words convey so little knowledge or certainty in our discourses about them; and therefore the mind, to remove that imperfection as much as it can, makes them, by a secret supposition, to stand for a thing having that real essence, as if thereby it made some nearer approaches to it: For though the word *man* or *gold* signify nothing truly but a complex *idea* of properties united together in one sort of substances, yet there is scarce any body in the use of these words, but often supposes each of those names to stand for a thing having the real essence on which those properties depend; which is so far from diminishing the imperfection of our words, that by a plain abuse it adds to it, when we would make them stand for something which not being in our complex *idea*, the name we use can no ways be the sign of.

§ 19. *Hence we think every change of our* Idea *in Substances, not to change the Species.*

This shows us the reason why in *mixed modes* any of the *ideas* that make the composition of the complex one, being left out or changed, it is allowed to be another thing, *i. e.* to be of another species, as is plain in *chance-medley, manslaughter, murder, parricide*, &c.; the reason whereof is, because the complex *idea* signified by that name is the real as well as nominal essence, and there is no secret reference of that name to any other essence but that. But in *substances* it is not so; for though in that called *gold* one puts into his complex *idea* what another leaves out, and *vice versa*, yet men do not usually think that therefore the species is changed, because they secretly in their minds refer that name, and suppose it annexed to a real immutable essence of a thing existing, on which those properties depend. He that adds to his complex *idea* of *gold* that of fixedness or solubility in *aq. regia*, which he put not in it before, is not thought to have changed the ſpecies, but only to have a more perfect *idea*, by adding another ſimple *idea*, which is always in fact joined with thoſe other of which his former complex *idea* conſiſted. But this reference of the name to a thing, whereof we have not the *idea*, is ſo far from helping at all, that it only ſerves the more to involve us in difficulties; for by this tacit reference to the real eſſence of that ſpecies of bodies, the word *gold* (which by ſtanding for a more or leſs perfect collection of ſimple *ideas*, ſerves to deſign that ſort of body well enough in civil diſcourſe) comes to have no ſignification at all, being put for ſomewhat whereof we have no *idea* at all, and ſo can ſignify nothing at all, when the body itſelf is away; for however it may be thought all one, yet, if well conſidered, it will be found a quite different thing to argue about *gold* in name, and about a parcel of the body itſelf, *v. g.* a piece of *leaf-gold* laid before us; though in diſcourſe we are fain to ſubſtitute the name for the thing.

§ 20. *The Cauſe of the Abuſe, a Suppoſition of Nature's working always regularly.*

THAT which I think very much diſpoſes men to ſubſtitute their names for the real eſſences of *ſpecies*, is the ſuppoſition before-mentioned, that nature works regularly in the production of things, and ſets the boundaries to each of thoſe *ſpecies*, by giving exactly the ſame real internal conſtitution to each individual, which we rank under one general name; whereas any one who obſerves their different qualities, can hardly doubt, that many of the individuals, called by the ſame name, are, in their internal conſtitution, as different one from another as ſeveral of thoſe which are ranked under different ſpecific names. *This ſuppoſition*, however, *that the ſame preciſe internal conſtitution goes always with the ſame ſpecific name, makes men forward to take* thoſe *names for the repreſentatives* of thoſe real *eſſences*, though indeed they ſignify nothing but the complex *ideas* they have in their minds when they uſe them; ſo that, if I may ſo ſay, ſignifying one thing, and being ſuppoſed for, or put in the place of another, they cannot but in ſuch a kind of uſe cauſe a great deal of uncertainty in mens diſcourſes; eſpecially in thoſe who have thoroughly imbibed the doctrine of *ſubſtantial forms*, whereby they firmly imagine the ſeveral ſpecies of things to be determined and diſtinguiſhed.

§ 21. *This Abuſe contains two falſe ſuppoſitions.* But however prepoſterous and abſurd it be to make our names ſtand for *ideas* we have not, or (which is all one) eſſences that we know not, it being in effect to make our words the ſigns of nothing, yet it is evident to any one, who ever ſo little reflects on the uſe men make of their words, that there is nothing more familiar. When a man aſks whether this or that thing he ſees, let it be a drill or a monſtrous *fœtus*, be a *man* or no, it is evident the queſtion is not, whether that particular thing agree to his complex *idea* expreſſed by the name *man*; but whether it has in it the real eſſence of a ſpecies of things, which he ſuppoſes his name *man* to ſtand for. In which way of uſing the names of ſubſtances, there are theſe falſe ſuppoſitions contained:

Firſt, That there are certain preciſe eſſences, according to which nature makes all particular things, and by which they are diſtinguiſhed into *ſpecies*. That every thing has a real conſtitution, whereby it is what it is, and on which its ſenſible qualities depend, is paſt doubt: But I think it has been proved that this makes not the diſtinction of *ſpecies*, as we rank them, nor the boundaries of their names.

Secondly, This tacitly alſo inſinuates, as if we had *ideas* of theſe propoſed eſſences; for to what purpoſe elſe is it to inquire whether this or that thing have the real eſſence of the ſpecies *man*, if we did not ſuppoſe that there were ſuch a ſpecific eſſence known? which yet is utterly falſe; and therefore ſuch application of names, as would make them ſtand for *ideas* which we have not, muſt needs cauſe great diſorder in diſcourſes and reaſonings about them, and be a great inconvenience in our communication by words.

§ 22. 6. *A Suppoſition that Words have a certain and evident Signification.*

SIXTHLY, There remains yet another more general, though perhaps leſs obſerved *abuſe of words;* and that is, that men having by a long and familiar uſe annexed to them certain *ideas*, they are apt *to imagine ſo near and neceſſary a connection between the names and the ſignification* they uſe them in, that they forwardly ſuppoſe one cannot but underſtand what their meaning is; and therefore one ought to acquieſce in the words delivered, as if it were paſt doubt, that in the uſe of thoſe common received ſounds, the ſpeaker and hearer had neceſſarily the ſame preciſe *ideas:* Whence preſuming, that when they have in diſcourſe uſed any term, they have thereby, as it were, ſet before others the very thing they talk of. And ſo likewiſe taking the words of others, as naturally ſtanding for juſt what they themſelves have been accuſtomed to apply them to, they never trouble themſelves to explain their own, or underſtand clearly others meaning. From whence commonly proceeds noiſe and wrangling, without improvement or information; whilſt men take words to be the conſtant regular marks of agreed notions, which in truth are no more but the voluntary and unſteady ſigns of their own *ideas;* and yet men think it ſtrange, if, in diſcourſe, or (where it is often abſolutely neceſſary) in diſpute, one ſometimes aſks the meaning of their terms; though the arguings one may every day obſerve in converſation, make it evident, that there are few names of complex *ideas* which any two men uſe for the ſame juſt preciſe collection. It is hard to name a word which will not be a clear inſtance of this. *Life* is a term none more familiar. Any one almoſt would take it for an affront to be aſked what he meant by it; and yet, if it comes in queſtion whether a plant that lies ready formed in the ſeed, have life; whether the embryo in an egg before incubation, or a man in a ſwoon without ſenſe or motion, be alive or no; it is eaſy to perceive that a clear diſtinct ſettled *idea* does not always accompany the uſe of ſo known a word as that of *life* is. Some groſs and confused conceptions men indeed ordinarily have, to which they apply the common words of their language: and such a loose use of their words serves them well enough in their ordinary discourses or affairs: But this is not sufficient for philosophical inquiries. Knowledge and reasoning require precise determinate *ideas*; and though men will not be so importunately dull as not to understand what others say, without demanding an explication of their terms, nor so troublesomely critical, as to correct others in the use of the words they receive from them; yet where truth and knowledge are concerned in the case, I know not what fault it can be to desire the explication of words, whose sense seems dubious; or why a man should be ashamed to own his ignorance, in what sense another man uses his words, since he has no other way of certainly knowing it, but by being informed. This abuse of taking words upon trust, has no where spread so far, nor with so ill effects, as amongst men of letters. The multiplication and obstinacy of disputes, which has so laid waste the intellectual world, is owing to nothing more than to this ill use of words; for though it be generally believed that there is great diversity of opinions in the volumes and variety of controversies the world is distracted with, yet the most I can find that the contending learned men of different parties do, in their arguings one with another, is, that they speak different languages; for I am apt to imagine, that when any of them quitting terms, think upon things, and know what they think, they think all the same, though perhaps what they would have be different.

§ 23. *The Ends of Language.* 1. *To convey our* Ideas. To conclude this consideration of the imperfection and abuse of language; the *ends of language in our discourse with others,* being chiefly these three; *First, To make known* one man's thoughts or *ideas* to another; *Secondly,* To do it *with* as much ease and *quickness* as is possible; and *Thirdly,* Thereby to *convey* the *knowledge* of things. Language is either abused or deficient, when it fails of any of these three.

First, Words fail in the first of these ends, and lay not open one man's *ideas* to another's view; 1. When men have names in their mouths without any determined *ideas* in their minds, whereof they are the signs; or, 2. When they apply the common received names of any language to *ideas*, to which the common use of that language does not apply them; or, 3. When they apply them very unsteadily, making them stand now for one, and by and by for another *idea*.

§ 24. 2. *To do it with quickness.*

SECONDLY, Men fail of conveying their thoughts with all the quickness and ease that may be, when they have complex *ideas* without having distinct names for them. This is sometimes the fault of the language itself, which has not in it a sound yet applied to such a signification, and sometimes the fault of the man, who has not yet learned the name for that *idea* he would show another.

§ 25. 3. *Therewith to convey the Knowledge of things.*

THIRDLY, There is no knowledge of things conveyed by mens words, when their *ideas* agree not to the reality of things. Though it be a defect that has its original in our *ideas*, which are not so conformable to the nature of things, as attention, study, and application might make them; yet it fails not to extend itself to our words too, when we use them as signs of real beings, which yet never had any reality of existence.

§ 26. *How Mens Words fail in all these.*

FIRST, He that hath words of any language, without distinct *ideas* in his mind to which he applies them, does, so far as he uses them in discourse, only make a noise without any sense or signification; and how learned soever he may seem by the use of hard words or learned terms, is not much more advanced thereby in knowledge, than he would be in learning who had nothing in his study but the bare titles of books, without possessing the contents of them. For all such words, however put into discourse, according to the right construction of grammatical rules, or the harmony of well-turned periods, do yet amount to nothing but bare sounds, and nothing else.

§ 27.

SECONDLY, He that has complex *ideas* without particular names for them, would be in no better a caſe than a bookſeller, who had in his warehouſe volumes that lay there unbound, and without titles; which he could therefore make known to others, only by ſhowing the looſe ſheets, and communicate them only by tale. This man is hindered in his diſcourſe, for want of words to communicate his complex *ideas*, which he is therefore forced to make known by an enumeration of the ſimple ones that compoſe them, and ſo is fain often to uſe twenty words to expreſs what another man ſignifies in one.

§ 28.

THIRDLY, He that puts not conſtantly the ſame ſign for the ſame *idea*, but uſes the ſame words ſometimes in one, and ſometimes in another ſignification, ought to paſs in the ſchools and converſation for as fair a man, as he does in the market and exchange who ſells ſeveral things under the ſame name.

§ 29.

FOURTHLY, He that applies the words of any language to *ideas* different from thoſe to which the common uſe of that country applies them, however his own underſtanding may be filled with truth and light, will not by ſuch words be able to convey much of it to others, without defining his terms; for however the ſounds are ſuch as are familiarly known, and eaſily enter the ears of thoſe who are accuſtomed to them, yet ſtanding for other *ideas* than thoſe they uſually are annexed to, and are wont to excite in the mind of the hearers, they cannot make known the thoughts of him who thus uſes them.

§ 30.

FIFTHLY, He that hath imagined to himſelf ſubſtances ſuch as never have been, and filled his head with *ideas* which have not any correſpondence with the real nature of things, to which yet he gives ſettled and defined names, may fill his diſcourſe, and perhaps another man's head, with the fantaſtical imaginations of his own brain, but will be very far from advancing thereby one jot in real and true knowledge.

§ 31.

He that hath names without *ideas*, wants meaning in his words, and ſpeaks only empty ſounds. He that hath complex *ideas*, without names for them, wants liberty and diſpatch in his expreſſions, and is neceſſitated to uſe periphraſes. He that uſes his words looſely and unſteadily, will either be not minded, or not underſtood. He that applies his names to *ideas* different from their common uſe, wants propriety in his language, and ſpeaks gibberiſh. And he that hath *ideas* of ſubſtances diſagreeing with the real exiſtence of things, ſo far wants the materials of true knowledge in his underſtanding, and hath inſtead thereof *chimeras*.

§ 32. *How in Subſtances.*

In our notions concerning ſubſtances, we are liable to all the former inconveniencies; *v. g.* He that uſes the word *tarantula*, without having any imagination or *idea* of what it ſtands for, pronounces a good word; but ſo long means nothing at all by it. 2. He that in a new-diſcovered country ſhall ſee ſeveral ſorts of animals and vegetables unknown to him before, may have as true *ideas* of them as of a horſe or a ſtag, but can ſpeak of them only by a deſcription, till he ſhall either take the names the natives call them by, or give them names himſelf. 3. He that uſes the word *body* ſometimes for pure extenſion, and ſometimes for extenſion and ſolidity together, will talk very fallaciouſly. 4. He that gives the name *horſe* to that *idea* which common uſage calls *mule*, talks improperly, and will not be underſtood. 5. He that thinks the name *centaur* ſtands for ſome real being, impoſes on himſelf, and miſtakes words for things.

§ 33. *How in Modes and Relations.*

In modes and relations generally we are liable only to the four firſt of theſe inconveniencies; *viz.* 1. I may have in my memory the names of modes, as *gratitude*, or *charity*, and yet not have any preciſe *ideas* annexed in my thoughts to thoſe names. 2. I may have *ideas* and not know the names that belong to them; *v. g.* I may have the *idea* of a man's drinking, till his colour and humour be altered, till his tongue trips, and his eyes look red, and his feet fail him, and yet not know that it is to be called *drunkenneſs*. 3. I may have the *ideas* of virtues or vices, and names alſo, but apply them amiſs; *v. g.* when I apply the name *frugality* to that *idea* which others call and ſignify by this ſound, *covetouſneſs*. 4. I may uſe any of thoſe names with inconſtancy. 5. But in modes and relations, I cannot have *ideas* diſagreeing to the exiſtence of things; for modes being complex *ideas* made by the mind at pleaſure, and relation being but my way of conſidering or comparing two things together, and ſo alſo an *idea* of my own making; theſe *ideas* can ſcarce be found to diſagree with any thing exiſting, ſince they are not in the mind as the copies of things regularly made by nature, nor as properties inſeparably flowing from the internal conſtitution or eſſence of any ſubſtance, but as it were patterns lodged in my memory, with names annexed to them, to denominate actions and relations by, as they come to exiſt. But the miſtake is commonly in my giving a wrong name to my conceptions; and ſo, uſing words in a different ſenſe from other people, I am not underſtood, but am thought to have wrong *ideas* of them, when I give wrong names to them; only if I put, in my *ideas* of mixed modes or relations, any inconſiſtent *ideas* together, I fill my head alſo with *chimeras*, ſince ſuch *ideas*, if well examined, cannot ſo much as exiſt in the mind, much leſs any real being be ever denominated from them.

§ 34. 7. *Figurative Speech alſo an Abuſe of Language.* SINCE wit and fancy finds eaſier entertainment in the world, than dry truth and real knowledge, *figurative ſpeeches* and alluſion in language will hardly be admitted as an imperfection or *abuſe* of it. I confeſs, in diſcourſes where we ſeek rather pleaſure and delight than information and improvement, ſuch ornaments as are borrowed from them can ſcarce paſs for faults; but yet if we would ſpeak of things as they are, we muſt allow that all the art of rhetoric, beſides order and clearneſs, all the artificial and figurative application of words eloquence hath invented, are for nothing else but to insinuate wrong *ideas*, move the passions, and thereby mislead the judgment, and so indeed are perfect cheat; and, therefore, however laudable or allowable oratory may render them in harangues and popular addresses, they are certainly, in all discourses that pretend to inform or instruct, wholly to be avoided; and where truth and knowledge are concerned, cannot but be thought a great fault, either of the language or person that makes use of them. What and how various they are, will be superfluous here to take notice; the books of rhetoric which abound in the world, will instruct those who want to be informed; only I cannot but observe, how little the preservation and improvement of truth and knowledge is the care and concern of mankind, since the arts of fallacy are endowed and preferred. It is evident how much men love to deceive and be deceived, since rhetoric, that powerful instrument of error and deceit, has its established professors, is publicly taught, and has always been had in great reputation: and, I doubt not but it will be thought great boldness, if not brutality in me, to have said thus much against it. *Eloquence*, like the fair sex, has too prevailing beauties in it, to suffer itself ever to be spoken against. And it is in vain to find fault with those arts of deceiving, wherein men find pleasure to be deceived.

CHAP. XI.

OF THE REMEDIES OF THE FOREGOING IMPERFECTIONS AND ABUSES.

§ 1. *They are worth seeking.*

THE natural and improved imperfections of languages, we have seen above at large; and speech being the great bond that holds society together, and the common conduit whereby the improvements of knowledge are conveyed from one man and one generation to another, it would well deserve our most serious thoughts, to consider what *remedies* are to be found *for these inconveniences* above-mentioned.

§ 2. *Are not easy.*

I AM not so vain to think, that any one can pretend to attempt the perfect *reforming* the *languages* of the world, no not so much as of his own country, without rendering himself ridiculous. To require that men should use their words constantly in the same sense, and for none but determined and uniform *ideas*, would be to think that all men should have the same notions, and should talk of nothing but what they have clear and distinct *ideas* of; which is not to be expected by any one, who hath not vanity enough to imagine he can prevail with men to be very knowing or very silent. And he must be very little skilled in the world, who thinks that a voluble tongue shall accompany only a good understanding, or that mens talking much or little, shall hold proportion only to their knowledge.

§ 3. *But yet necessary to Philosophy.*

BUT though the market and exchange must be left to their own ways of talking, and gossipings not to be robbed of their ancient privilege; though the schools and men of argument would perhaps take it amiss to have any thing offered to abate the length, or lessen the number of their disputes; yet methinks those who pretend *seriously* to *search after* or maintain *truth*, should think themselves obliged to study how they might deliver themselves without obscurity, doubtfulness, or equivocation, to which mens words are naturally liable, if care be not taken.

§ 4. *Misuse of Words the cause of great Errors.*

FOR he that shall well consider the *errors* and obscurity, the mistakes and confusion, that are *spread in the world by an ill use of words*, will find some reason to doubt whether language, as it has been employed, has contributed more to the improvement or hinderance of knowledge amongst mankind. How many are there, that when they would think on things, fix their thoughts only on words, especially when they would apply their minds to moral matters? And who then can wonder, if the result of such contemplations and reasonings about little more than sounds, whilst the *ideas* they annexed to them are very confused or very unsteady, or perhaps none at all; who can wonder, I say, that such thoughts and reasonings end in nothing but obscurity and mistake, without any clear judgment or knowledge?

§ 5. *Obstinacy.*

THIS inconvenience, in an ill use of words, men suffer in their own private meditations: But much more manifest are the disorders which follow from it, in conversation, discourse, and arguings with others; for language being the great conduit whereby men convey their discoveries, reasonings, and knowledge from one to another, he that makes an ill use of it, though he does not corrupt the fountains of knowledge, which are in things themselves, yet he does, as much as in him lies, break or stop the pipes whereby it is distributed to the public use and advantage of mankind. He that uses words without any clear and steady meaning, what does he but lead himself and others into errors? And he that designedly does it, ought to be looked on as an enemy to truth and knowledge. And yet who can wonder, that all the sciences and parts of knowledge have been so overcharged with obscure and equivocal terms, and insignificant and doubtful expressions, capable to make the most attentive or quick-sighted very little or not at all the more knowing or orthodox, since subtilty, in those who make profession to teach or defend truth, hath passed so much for a virtue; a virtue, indeed, which consisting for the most part in nothing but the fallacious and illusory use of *obscure* or *deceitful terms*, is only fit to *make men* more *conceited* in their ignorance, and *obstinate* in their errors.

§ 6. *And Wrangling.*

LET us look into the books of controversy of any kind; there we shall see, that the effect of obscure, unsteady or equivocal terms, is nothing but noise and wrangling about sounds, without convincing or bettering a man's understanding; for if the *idea* be not agreed on betwixt the speaker and hearer for which the words stand, the argument is not about things, but names. As often as such a word whose signification is not ascertained betwixt them, comes in uſe, their underſtandings have no other object wherein they agree, but barely the ſound; the things that they think on at that time, as expreſſed by that word, being quite different.

§ 7. *Inſtance—Bat and Bird.*

WHETHER a *bat* be a *bird* or no, is not a queſtion; whether a *bat* be another thing than indeed it is, or have other qualities then indeed it has, for that would be extremely abſurd to doubt of: but the queſtion is, 1. Either between thoſe that acknowledged themſelves to have but imperfect *ideas* of one or both of thoſe ſorts of things, for which theſe names are ſuppoſed to ſtand; and then it is a real inquiry concerning the nature of a *bird* or a *bat*, to make their yet imperfect *ideas* of it more complete, by examining whether all the ſimple *ideas* to which, combined together, they both give the name *bird*, be all to be found in a *bat*: but this is a queſtion only of inquiries not diſputers, who neither affirm, nor deny, but examine. Or, 2. It is a queſtion between diſputants, whereof the one affirms, and the other denies, that a *bat* is a *bird*; and then the queſtion is barely about the ſignification of one or both of theſe words, in that they not having both the ſame complex *ideas*, to which they give theſe two names, one holds, and the other denies, that theſe two names may be affirmed one of another. Were they agreed in the ſignification of theſe two names, it were impoſſible they ſhould diſpute about them, for they would preſently and clearly ſee (were that adjuſted between them) whether all the ſimple *ideas* of the more general name *bird*, were found in the complex *idea* of a *bat* or no; and ſo there could be no doubt, whether a *bat* were a *bird* or no. And here I deſire it may be conſidered and carefully examined, whether the greateſt part of the diſputes in the world are not merely verbal, and about the ſignification of words; and whether, if the terms they are made in were defined, and reduced in their ſignification (as they muſt be where they ſignify any thing) to determined collections of the ſimple *ideas* they do or ſhould ſtand for, thoſe diſputes would not end of themſelves, and immediately vaniſh. I leave it then to be conſidered, what the learning of diſputation is, and how well they are employed for the advantage of themſelves or others, whoſe buſineſs is only the vain oſtentation of ſounds; *i. e.* thoſe who ſpend their lives in diſputes and controverſies. When I ſhall ſee any of thoſe combatants ſtrip all his terms of ambiguity and obſcurity (which every one may do in the words he uſes himſelf), I ſhall think him a champion for knowledge, truth, and peace, and not the ſlave of vain glory, ambition or a party.

§ 8. 1. *Remedy, to uſe no Word without an* Idea.

TO remedy the defects of ſpeech before-mentioned to ſome degree, and to prevent the inconveniences that follow from them, I imagine the obſervation of theſe following rules may be of uſe, till ſomebody better able ſhall judge it worth his while to think more maturely on this matter, and oblige the world with his thoughts on it.

Firſt, A man ſhould take care *to uſe no word without a ſignification*, no name without an *idea* for which he makes it ſtand. This rule will not ſeem altogether needleſs to any one who ſhall take the pains to recollect how often he has met with ſuch words, as *inſtinct*, *ſympathy*, and *antipathy*, &c. in the diſcourſe of others, ſo made uſe of, as he might eaſily conclude, that thoſe that uſed them had no *ideas* in their minds to which they applied them, but ſpoke them only as ſounds, which uſually ſerved inſtead of reaſons on the like occaſions. Not but that theſe words, and the like, have very proper ſignifications in which they may be uſed; but there being no natural connection between any words and any *ideas*, theſe, and any other, may be learned by rote, and pronounced or writ by men who have no *ideas* in their minds to which they have annexed them, and for which they make them ſtand; which is neceſſary they ſhould, if men would ſpeak intelligibly even to themſelves alone.

§ 9. 2. *To have diſtinct* Ideas *annexed to them in Modes.*

SECONDLY, It is not enough a man *uſes* his *words as ſigns of* ſome *ideas;* thoſe *ideas* he annexes them to, if they be *ſimple*, muſt be clear and diſtinct; if *complex* muſt be de-

terminate, *i. e.* the precife collection of fimple *ideas* fettled in the mind with that found annexed to it, as the fign of that precife determined collection, and no other. This is very neceffary in names of modes, and efpecially moral words, which having no fettled objects in nature from whence their *ideas* are taken, as from their original, are apt to be very confufed. *Juftice* is a word in every man's mouth, but moft commonly with a very undetermined loofe fignification; which will always be fo, unlefs a man has in his mind a diftinct comprehenfion of the component parts that a complex *idea* confifts of; and if it be decompounded, muft be able to refolve it ftill on, till he at laft comes to the fimple *ideas* that make it up; and unlefs this be done, a man makes an ill ufe of the word, let it be *juftice*, for example, or any other. I do not fay, a man needs ftand to recollect and make this analyfis at large, every time the word *juftice* comes in his way; but this at leaft is neceffary, that he have fo examined the fignification of that name, and fettled the *idea* of all its parts in his mind, that he can do it when he pleafes. If one who makes his complex *idea* of *juftice* to be fuch a treatment of the perfon or goods of another as is according to law, hath not a clear and diftinct *idea* what *law* is, which makes a part of his complex *idea* of juftice, it is plain his *idea* of juftice itfelf will be confufed and imperfect. This exactnefs will perhaps be judged very troublefome, and therefore moft men will think they may be excufed from fettling the complex *ideas* of mixed modes fo precifely in their minds; but yet I muft fay, till this be done, it muft not be wondered that they have a great deal of obfcurity and confufion in their own minds, and a great deal of wrangling in their difcourfes with others.

§ 10. *And conformable in Subftances.*

In the names of *fubftances*, for a right ufe of them, fomething more is required than barely *determined ideas*. In thefe *the names muft alfo be conformable to things*, as they exift; but of this I fhall have occafion to fpeak more at large by and by. This exactnefs is abfolutely neceffary in inquiries after philofophical knowledge, and in controverſies about truth; and though it would be well too, if it extended itſelf to common converſation, and the ordinary affairs of life, yet I think that is ſcarce to be expected. Vulgar notions ſuit vulgar diſcourſes; and both, though confuſed enough, yet ſerve pretty wel the market and the wake. Merchants and lovers, cooks and tailors, have words wherewithal to diſpatch their ordinary affairs; and ſo, I think, might philoſophers and diſputants too, if they had a mind to underſtand, and to be clearly underſtood.

§ 11. 3. *Propriety.*

THIRDLY, It is not enough that men have *ideas*, determined *ideas*, for which they make theſe ſigns ſtand; but they *muſt* alſo take care to *apply their words*, as near as may be, *to ſuch* ideas *as common uſe has annexed them to.* For words, eſpecially of languages already framed, being no man's private poſſeſſion, but the common meaſure of commerce and communication, it is not for any one at pleaſure to change the ſtamp they are current in, nor alter the *ideas* they are affixed to; or at leaſt, when there is a neceſſity to do ſo, he is bound to give notice of it. Mens intentions in ſpeaking are, or at leaſt ſhould be, to be underſtood, which cannot be without frequent explanations, demands, and other the like incommodious interruptions, where men do not follow common uſe. Propriety of ſpeech is that which gives our thoughts entrance into other mens minds with the greateſt eaſe and advantage, and therefore deſerves ſome part of our care and ſtudy, eſpecially in the names of moral words. The proper ſignification and uſe of terms is beſt to be learned from thoſe, who in their writings and diſcourſes appear to have had the cleareſt notions, and applied to them their terms with the exacteſt choice and fitneſs. This way of uſing a man's words according to the propriety of the language, though it have not always the good fortune to be underſtood, yet moſt commonly leaves the blame of it on him, who is ſo unſkilful in the language he ſpeaks, as not to underſtand it, when made uſe of as it ought to be.

§ 2. 4. *To make known their meaning.*

FOURTHLY, But becauſe common uſe has not ſo viſibly annexed any ſignification to words, as to make men know always certainly what they precifely ſtand for; and becauſe men, in the improvement of their knowledge, come to have *ideas* different from the ordinary and received ones, for which they muſt either make new words (which men ſeldom venture to do, for fear of being thought guilty of affectation or novelty), or elſe muſt uſe old ones in a new ſignification; therefore, after the obſervation of the foregoing rules, it is ſometimes neceſſary, for the aſcertaining the ſignification of words, to *declare their meaning*, where either common uſe has left it uncertain and looſe (as it has in moſt names of very complex *ideas*), or where the term, being very material in the diſcourſe, and that upon which it chiefly turns, is liable to any doubtfulneſs or miſtake.

§ 13. *And that three ways.*

As the *ideas* mens words ſtand for are of different ſorts, ſo the way of making known the *ideas* they ſtand for, when there is occaſion, is alſo different; for though defining be thought the proper *way to make known the proper ſignification of words*, yet there are ſome words that will not be defined, as there are others whoſe preciſe meaning cannot be made known but by definition; and perhaps a third, which partake ſomewhat of both the other, as we ſhall ſee in the names of ſimple *ideas*, modes and ſubſtances.

§ 14. 1. *In ſimple* Ideas, *by ſynonymous terms, or ſhowing.*

FIRST, When a man makes uſe of the *name* of *any ſimple idea*, which he perceives is not underſtood, or is in danger to be miſtaken, he is obliged by the laws of ingenuity, and the end of ſpeech, to declare his meaning, and make known what idea he makes it ſtand for. This, as has been ſhown, cannot be done by definition; and therefore, when a ſynonymous word fails to do it, there is but one of theſe ways left: *Firſt*, Sometimes the *naming the ſubject, wherein that ſimple* idea *is* to be found, will make its name be underſtood by thoſe who are acquainted with that ſubject, and know it by that name. So, to make a country man underſtand what *fueillemorte* colour ſignifies, it may ſuffice to tell him, it is the colour of withered leaves falling in *autumn.* *Secondly,* But the only ſure way of making known the ſignification of the name of any ſimple *idea,* is *by preſenting to his ſenſes that ſubject which may produce it in his mind,* and make him actually have the *idea* that word ſtands for.

§ 15. 2. *In mixed Modes, by Definition.*

SECONDLY, *Mixed modes,* eſpecially thoſe belonging to morality, being moſt of them ſuch combinations of *ideas* as the mind puts together of its own choice, and whereof there are not always ſtanding patterns to be found exiſting, the ſignification of their names cannot be made known, as thoſe of ſimple *ideas,* by any ſhowing; but in recompence thereof, may be perfectly and exactly *defined.* For they being combinations of ſeveral *ideas,* that the mind of man has arbitrarily put together, without reference to any archetypes, men may, if they pleaſe, exactly know the *ideas* that go to each compoſition, and ſo both uſe theſe words in a certain and undoubted ſignification, and perfectly declare, when there is occaſion, what they ſtand for. This, if well conſidered, would lay great blame on thoſe, who make not their diſcourſes about moral things very clear and diſtinct; for ſince the preciſe ſignification of the names of mixed modes, or, which is all one, the real eſſence of each ſpecies, is to be known, they being not of nature's but man's making, it is a great negligence and perverſeneſs to diſcourſe of moral things with uncertainty and obſcurity; which is more pardonable in treating of natural ſubſtances, where doubtful terms are hardly to be avoided, for a quite contrary reaſon, as we ſhall ſee by and by.

§ 16. *Morality capable of Demonſtration.*

UPON this ground it is, that I am bold to think that *morality is capable of demonſtration,* as well as mathematics, ſince the preciſe real eſſence of the things moral words ſtand for, may be perfectly known, and ſo the congruity or incongruity of the things themſelves be certainly diſcovered, in which conſiſts perfect knowledge. Nor let any one object, that the names of ſubſtances are often to be made uſe of in morality, as well as thoſe of modes, from which will ariſe obſcurity. For as to ſubſtances, when concerned in moral diſcourſes, their divers natures are not ſo much inquired into, as ſuppoſed; *v. g.* when we ſay, that *man is ſubject to law*, we mean nothing by *man*, but a corporeal rational creature; what the real eſſence or other qualities of that creature are, in this caſe, is no way conſidered; and therefore, whether a child or changeling be a *man* in a phyſical ſenſe, may amongſt the naturaliſts be as diſputable as it will, it concerns not at all the *moral man*, as I may call him, which is this immoveable unchangeable *idea*, *a corporeal rational being;* for were there a monkey, or any other creature, to be found, that had the uſe of reaſon to ſuch a degree as to be able to underſtand general ſigns, and to deduce conſequences about general *ideas*, he would no doubt be ſubject to law, and in that ſenſe be a *man*, how much ſoever he differed in ſhape from others of that name. The names of ſubſtances, if they be uſed in them as they ſhould, can no more diſturb moral than they do mathematical diſcourſes; where, if the mathematician ſpeaks of a *cube* or *globe* of *gold*, or any other body, he has his clear ſettled *idea* which varies not, though it may by miſtake be applied to a particular body to which it belongs not.

§ 17. *Definition can make moral Diſcourſes clear.* This I have here mentioned by the by, to ſhow of what conſequence it is for men, in their names of mixed modes, and conſequently in all their moral diſcourſes, to define their words when there is occaſion, ſince thereby moral knowledge may be brought to ſo great clearneſs and certainty. And it muſt be great want of ingenuity (to ſay no worſe of it) to refuſe to do it, ſince a *definition is the only way whereby the preciſe meaning of moral words can be known*, and yet a way whereby their meaning may be known *certainly*, and without leaving any room for any conteſt about it; and therefore the negligence or perverſeneſs of mankind cannot be excuſed, if their diſcourſes in morality be not much more clear than thoſe in natural philoſophy, ſince they are about *ideas* in the mind, which are none of them falſe or diſproportionate, they having no external beings for the *archetypes* which they are referred to, and much correſpond with. It is far eaſier for men to frame in their minds an *idea* which ſhall be the ſtandard to which they will give the name *juſtice*, with which pattern ſo made, all actions that agree ſhall paſs under that denomination, than, having ſeen *Ariſtides*, to frame an *idea* that ſhall in all things be exactly like him, who is as he is, let men make what *idea* they pleaſe of him: For the one, they need but know the combination of *ideas* that are put together within in their own minds; for the other they muſt inquire into the whole nature, and abſtruſe hidden conſtitution, and various qualities of a thing exiſting without them.

§ 18. *And is the only way.*

ANOTHER reaſon that makes the *defining of mixed modes* ſo neceſſary, *eſpecially of moral words*, is what I mentioned a little before, *viz.* That it is *the only way whereby the ſignification of the moſt of* them can be known with certainty: For the *ideas* they ſtand for, being for the moſt part ſuch whoſe component parts no where exiſt together, but ſcattered and mingled with others, it is the mind alone that collects them, and gives them the union of one *idea;* and it is only by words, enumerating the ſeveral ſimple *ideas* which the mind has united, that we can make known to others what their names ſtand for; the aſſiſtance of the ſenſes in this caſe not helping us, by the propoſal of ſenſible objects, to ſhow the *ideas* which our names of this kind ſtand for, as it does often in the names of ſenſible ſimple *ideas*, and alſo to ſome degree in thoſe of ſubſtances.

§ 19. 3. *In Subſtances, by ſhowing and defining.*

THIRDLY, *For the explaining* the ſignification of *the names of ſubſtances*, as they ſtand for the *ideas* we have of their diſtinct ſpecies, both the fore-mentioned ways *viz.* of *ſhowing and defining, are requiſite* in many caſes to be made uſe of; for there being ordinarily in each ſort ſome leading qualities, to which we ſuppoſe the other *ideas*, which make up our complex *idea* of that ſpecies, annexed, we forwardly give the ſpecific name to that thing, wherein that characteriſtical mark is found, which we take to be the moſt diſtinguiſhing *idea* of that ſpecies. Theſe leading or characteriſtical (as I may ſo call them) *ideas*, in the ſorts of animals and vegetables, is (as has been before remarked, Ch. VI. § 29. and Ch. IX. § 15.) moſtly figure, and in inanimate bodies colour, and in ſome both together. Now,

§ 20. Ideas *of the leading qualities of Subſtances are beſt got by ſhowing.*

THESE *leading ſenſible qualities* are thoſe which make *the chief ingredients of our ſpecific* ideas, and conſequently the moſt obſervable and unvariable part in the definitions of our ſpecific names, as attributed to ſorts of *ſubſtances* coming under our knowledge: For though the ſound *man*, in its own nature, be as apt to ſignify a complex *idea* made up of animality and rationality, united in the ſame ſubject, as to ſignify any other combination, yet uſed as a mark to ſtand for a ſort of creatures we count of our own kind, perhaps the outward ſhape is as neceſſary to be taken into our complex *idea*, ſignified by the word *man*, as any other we find in it; and therefore why *Plato's animal implume bipes latis unguibus*, ſhould not be as good a definition of the name *man*, ſtanding for that ſort of creatures, will not be eaſy to ſhow; for it is the ſhape, as the leading quality, that ſeems more to determine that ſpecies, than a faculty of reaſoning, which appears not at firſt, and in ſome never. And if this be not allowed to be ſo, I do not know how they can be excuſed from murder, who kill monſtrous births (as we call them), becauſe of an unordinary ſhape, without knowing whether they have a rational ſoul or no; which can be no more diſcerned in a well-formed, than ill-ſhaped infant, as ſoon as born. And who is it has informed us, that a rational ſoul can inhabit no tenement, unleſs it has juſt ſuch a ſort of frontiſpiece, or can join itſelf to, and inform no ſort of body but one that is juſt of ſuch an outward ſtructure?

§ 21. Ideas *of the leading qualities of Subſtances are beſt got by ſhowing.*

Now *theſe leading qualities are beſt made known by ſhowing*, and can hardly be made known otherwiſe; for the ſhape of an *horſe* or *caſſuary*, will be but rudely and imperfectly imprinted on the mind by words, the ſight of the animals doth it a thouſand times better; and the *idea* of the particular colour of *gold* is not to be got by any deſcription of it, but only by the frequent exerciſe of the eyes about it, as is evident in thoſe who are uſed to this metal, who will frequently diſtinguiſh true from counterfeit, pure from adulterate, by the ſight, where others (who have as good eyes, but yet by uſe have not got the preciſe nice *idea* of that peculiar yellow) ſhall not perceive any difference. The like may be ſaid of thoſe other ſimple *ideas*, peculiar in their kind to any ſubſtance, for which preciſe *ideas* there are no peculiar names. The particular ringing ſound there is in *gold*, diſtinct from the ſound of other bodies, has no particular name annexed to it, no more than the particular yellow that belongs to that metal.

§ 22. *The* Ideas *of their Powers beſt by Definition.*

But becauſe many of the ſimple *ideas* that make up our ſpecific *ideas* of ſubſtances, are powers which lie not obvious to our ſenſes in the things as they ordinarily appear; therefore in the ſignification of our *names of ſubſtances, ſome part of the ſignification will be better made known by enumerating thoſe ſimple* ideas, *than in ſhowing the ſubſtance itſelf;* for he that, to the yellow ſhining colour of *gold* got by ſight, ſhall, from my enumerating them, have the *ideas* of great ductility, fuſibility, fixedneſs, and ſolubility in *aq. regia*, will have a perfecter *idea* of *gold* than he can have by ſeeing a piece of *gold*, and thereby imprinting in his mind only its obvious qualities. But if the formal conſtitution of this ſhining, heavy ductile thing (from whence all theſe its properties flow) lay open to our ſenſes, as the formal conſtitution or eſſence of a triangle does, the ſignification of the word *gold* might as eaſily be aſcertained as that of *triangle.*

§ 23. *A Reflection on the Knowledge of Spirits.*

HENCE we may take notice how much the foundation of all *our knowledge of corporeal things lies in our senses;* for how spirits, separate from bodies (whose knowledge and *ideas* of these things are certainly much more perfect than ours) know them, we have no notion, no *idea* at all; the whole extent of our knowledge or imagination reaches not beyond our own *ideas* limited to our ways of perception; though yet it be not to be doubted that spirits of a higher rank than those immersed in flesh, may have as clear *ideas* of the radical constitution of substances as we have of a triangle, and so perceive how all their properties and operations flow from thence; but the manner how they come by that knowledge exceeds our conceptions.

§ 24. Ideas *also of Substances must be conformable to things.*

BUT though definitions will serve to explain the names of substances as they stand for our *ideas*, yet they leave them not without great imperfection as they stand for things; for our names of substances being not put barely for our *ideas*, but being made use of ultimately to represent things, and so are put in their place, their signification must agree with the truth of things as well as with mens *ideas*. And therefore in substances we are not always to rest in the ordinary complex *idea* commonly received as the signification of that word, but must go a little farther, and inquire into the nature and properties of the things themselves, and thereby perfect as much as we can our *ideas* of their distinct species; or else learn them from such as are used to that sort of things, and are experienced in them; for since it is intended their names should stand for such collections of simple *ideas* as do really exist in things themselves, as well as for the complex *idea* in other mens minds, which in their ordinary acceptation they stand for, therefore *to define their names right, natural history is to be inquired into*, and their properties are, with care and examination, to be found out. For it is not enough, for the avoiding inconveniences in discourses and arguings about natural bodies and ſubſtantial things, to have learned, from the propriety of the language, the common but confuſed or very imperfect *idea* to which each word is applied, and to keep them to that *idea* in our uſe of them; but we muſt, by acquainting ourſelves with the hiſtory of that ſort of things, rectify and ſettle our complex *idea* belonging to each ſpecific name; and in diſcourſe with others (if we find them miſtake us), we ought to tell what the complex *idea* is that we make ſuch a name ſtand for. This is the more neceſſary to be done by all thoſe who ſearch after knowledge and philoſophical verity, in that children being taught words whilſt they have but imperfect notions of things, apply them at random, and without much thinking, and ſeldom frame determined *ideas* to be ſignified by them; which cuſtom (it being eaſy, and ſerving well enough for the ordinary affairs of life and converſation) they are apt to continue when they are men, and ſo begin at the wrong end, learning words firſt and perfectly, but make the notions to which they apply thoſe words afterwards very overtly. By this means it comes to paſs, that men ſpeaking the proper language of their country, *i. e.* according to grammar rules of that language, do yet ſpeak very improperly of things themſelves; and by their arguing one with another, make but ſmall progreſs in the diſcoveries of uſeful truths, and the knowledge of things, as they are to be found in themſelves, and not in our imaginations; and it matters not much, for the improvement of our knowledge, how they are called.

§ 25. *Not eaſy to be made ſo.*

It were therefore to be wiſhed, that men verſed in phyſical inquiries, and acquainted with the ſeveral ſorts of natural bodies, would ſet down thoſe ſimple *ideas*, wherein they obſerve the individuals of each ſort conſtantly to agree. This would remedy a great deal of that confuſion which comes from ſeveral perſons applying the ſame name to a collection of a ſmaller or greater number of ſenſible qualities, proportionably as they have been more or leſs acquainted with, or accurate in examining the qualities of any ſort of things which come under one denomination. But a dictionary of this ſort, containing, as it were, a natural hiſtory, requires too many hands, as well as too much time, coſt, pains, and ſagacity, ever to be hoped for; and till that be done, we muſt content ourſelves with ſuch definitions of the names of ſubſtances, as explain the ſenſe men uſe them in; and it would be well, where there is occaſion, if they would afford us ſo much. This yet is not uſually done; but men talk to one another, and diſpute in words, whoſe meaning is not agreed between them, out of a miſtake that the ſignification of common words are certainly eſtabliſhed, and the preciſe *ideas* they ſtand for perfectly known, and that it is a ſhame to be ignorant of them; both which ſuppoſitions are falſe, no names of complex *ideas* having ſo ſettled determined ſignifications, that they are conſtantly uſed for the ſame preciſe *ideas*. Nor is it a ſhame for a man not to have a certain knowledge of any thing, but by the neceſſary ways of attaining it; and ſo it is no diſcredit not to know what preciſe *idea* any ſound ſtands for in another man's mind, without he declare it to me by ſome other way than barely uſing that ſound, there being no other way, without ſuch a declaration, certainly to know it. Indeed the neceſſity of communication by language brings men to an agreement in the ſignification of common words within ſome tolerable latitude, that may ſerve for ordinary converſation; and ſo a man cannot be ſuppoſed wholly ignorant of the *ideas* which are annexed to words by common uſe, in a language familiar to him. But common uſe, being but a very uncertain rule, which reduces itſelf at laſt to the *ideas* of particular men, proves often but a very variable ſtandard. But though ſuch a dictionary as I have above mentioned, will require too much time, coſt, and pains, to be hoped for in this age, yet methinks it is not unreaſonable to propoſe, that words ſtanding for things, which are known and diſtinguiſhed by their outward ſhapes, ſhould be expreſſed by little draughts and prints made of them. A vocabulary made after this faſhion would perhaps with more eaſe, and in leſs time, teach the true ſignification of many terms, eſpecially in languages of remote countries or ages, and ſettle truer *ideas* in mens minds of ſeveral things, whereof we read the names in ancient authors, than all the large and laborious comments of learned critics. Naturaliſts, that treat of plants and animals, have found the benefit of this way; and he that has had occaſion to conſult them, will have reaſon to confeſs, that he has a clearer *idea* of *apium*, or *ibex*, from a little print of that herb or beaſt, than he could have from a long definition of the names of either of them. And ſo no doubt he would have of *ſtrigil* and *ſiſtrum*, if inſtead of a *curry-comb* and *cymbal*, which are the *Engliſh* names dictionaries render them by, he could ſee ſtamped in the margin ſmall pictures of theſe inſtruments, as they were in uſe amongſt the ancients. *Toga*, *tunica*, *pallium*, are words eaſily tranſlated by *gown*, *coat*, and *cloak*; but we have thereby no more true *ideas* of the faſhion of thoſe habits amongſt the *Romans*, then we have of the faces of the tailors who made them. Such things as theſe, which the eye diſtinguiſhes by their ſhapes, would be beſt let into the mind by draughts made of them, and more determine the ſignification of ſuch words, than any other words ſet for them, or made uſe of to define them. But this only by the by.

§ 26. *By Conſtancy in their Signification.*

FIFTHLY, If men will not be at the pains to declare the meaning of their words, and definitions of their terms are not to be had; yet this is the leaſt that can be expected, that in all diſcourſes, wherein one man pretends to inſtruct or convince another, he ſhould *uſe the ſame word conſtantly in the ſame ſenſe*. If this were done (which nobody can refuſe without great diſingenuity), many of the books extant might be ſpared; many of the controverſies in diſpute would be at an end; ſeveral of thoſe great volumes, ſwoln with ambiguous words, now uſed in one ſenſe, and by and by in another, would ſhrink into a very narrow compaſs; and many of the philoſophers (to mention no other), as well as poets works, might be contained in a nut-ſhell.

2

§ 27. *When the Variation is to be explained.*

But after all, the provifion of words is fo fcanty in fpect of that infinite variety of thoughts, that men, wa ing terms to fuit their precife notions, will, notwi ftanding their utmoft caution, be forced often to ufe fame word in fomewhat different fenfes. And thou in the continuation of a difcourfe, or the purfuit of argument, there be hardly room to digrefs into a pa cular definition, as often as a man varies the fignifi tion of any term, yet the import of the difcourfe w for the moft part, if there be no defigned fallacy, fu ciently lead candid and intelligent readers into the t meaning of it: but where that is not fufficient to gu the reader, there it concerns the writer to explain meaning, and fhow in what fenfe he there ufes t term.

END OF VOLUME SECOND.

Printed by Mundell & Son,
Royal Bank Clofe, Edinburgh.

CPSIA information can be obtained
at www.ICGtesting.com
Printed in the USA
LVHW080957020819
626293LV00004B/56/P

9 780526 315178